DOMESTIC VIOLENCE, CRIME AND VICTIMS ACT 2004 – A PRACTITIONER'S GUIDE

Richard Ward

Professor of Public Law and Head of Department of Law
De Montfort University, Leicester

Roger Bird

Solicitor, formerly District Judge, Bristol County Court and
High Court District Registry

JORDANS

501350938

R 345.4202 BIRD

Published by
Jordan Publishing Limited
21 St Thomas Street
Bristol BS1 6JS

British Library Cataloguing-in-Publication Data

A catalogue record for this book is available from the British Library.

ISBN 0 85308 9531

Typeset by Etica Press Ltd, Malvern
Printed and bound in Great Britain by Antony Rowe Ltd, Chippenham, Wilts

PREFACE

The Domestic Violence, Crime and Victims Bill was originally intended to introduce changes in the law to implement some, though not all, of the policy proposals relating to domestic violence, and victims generally, made by the Government in a series of Consultation and White Papers over the last couple of years. However, the opportunity was taken by the Government to introduce other changes relating to criminal justice matters, the result being an Act which, whilst having a central theme, contains a very mixed bag of provisions.

The purpose of this book is to provide for practitioners and others working in this area a clear, but concise, explanation and analysis of these provisions, the context in which they are introduced and their likely effect. We do not seek to examine directly the merits of the policy choices that underpin the provisions.

Various individuals have made helpful contributions during the writing of this book. Particular thanks are due to Professor Richard Card, at De Montfort University, who helpfully read and commented on an early draft of Chapter 3, whilst Professor Michael Hirst and Professor Ronnie Mackay, again at De Montfort, made useful comments on aspects of the legislation. The responsibility for the text, and any errors, is, though, that of the authors alone. Thanks are also due to Tony Hawitt and the production team at Jordans, who have provided very helpful support

The law is stated as at 20 January 2005

Richard Ward

Roger Bird

CONTENTS

TABLE OF CASES

References at the right-hand side of the column are to Chapter (in bold) and paragraph numbers

ENGLISH CASES

EUROPEAN CASES

TABLE OF STATUTES

References at the right-hand side of the column are to Chapter (in bold) and paragraph numbers

TABLE OF STATUTORY INSTRUMENTS

References at the right-hand side of the column are to Chapter (in bold) and paragraph numbers

TABLE OF CONVENTIONS

References to the right-side of the column are to Chapters and paragraph numbers

ABBREVIATIONS

CJA	Criminal Justice Act 2003
CJCSA	Criminal Justice and Court Services Act 2000
CJPA	Criminal Justice and Police Act 2001
CJPOA	Criminal Justice and Public Order Act 1994
CPIA	Criminal Procedure and Investigations Act 1996
DVCVA	Domestic Violence, Crime and Victims Act 2004
FLA	Family Law Act 1996
MHA	Mental Health Act 1983
PACE	Police and Criminal Evidence Act 1984
PFHA	Protection from Harassment Act 1997
RTOA	Road Traffic Offenders Act 1988

Chapter One

INTRODUCTION

1.1 This book deals with the provisions of the Domestic Violence, Crime and Victims Act 2004, in so far as they apply to England and Wales. Our purpose is to set out, explain and comment on the provisions of the Act, to explain their rationale and to set them in context. References in this book to 'the Act' or to the 'DVCVA 2004' refer to this Act unless the context otherwise indicates. When references are made to other statutory provisions, they are to such provisions as amended by legislation other than by this Act: any amending legislation has not, generally, been referred to.

1.2 The Act received Royal Assent on 5 November 2004.

The Parliamentary Debates on the Bill were as follows.

HOUSE OF LORDS

2nd Reading   15 December 2003, HL Deb vol 655, no 10–11

Grand Committee, 6 sittings 19 January 2004–9 February 2004-12-17

Report , 4 days, 44 March 2004–15 March 2004-12-17

3rd Reading, 25 March 2004, HL Deb vol 659, no 60

HOUSE OF COMMONS

2nd Reading 14 June 2004, HC Deb, vol 422, no 100, cols 536–616

Ways and Means 23 June 2004, vol 422, no 107, cols 1345–1350

Committee: Standing Committee E, 10 sittings 22 June 2004–6 July 2004

Report 27 October 2004

Commencement

1.3   Section 60 provides that the various provisions come into force in accordance with provision made by order by the Home Secretary. The order-making power is conferred by s 61, and subject to the relevant parliamentary procedure required by s 61(3) or (4). Different provision may be made in respect of different parts of the Act, and may include transitional or supplementary provision (s 61(1))

No commencement orders had been made as at the date of going to press. It is expected that the provisions relating to domestic violence will be 'rolled out' after April 2005, and the Code of Practice for Victims in Autumn 2005.[1]

The context

1.4   At the heart of the Act are a series of provisions to address the issues that arise in the context of domestic violence, primarily drawing on proposals contained in a Government Consultation Paper *Safety and Justice*[2] and earlier approaches identified in the White Paper *Justice for All*.[3]   The Consultation Paper noted the stark fact that each year some 150 people (120 women and 30 men) are killed by a current or former partner, with domestic violence affecting the lives of thousands more.[4] One in four women and one in six men will suffer domestic violence at some point in their lives. 'Domestic violence' is, for these purposes, defined by the Home Office as:

> 'Any violence between current and former partners in an intimate relationship, wherever and whenever the violence occurs. The violence may include physical, sexual, emotional and financial abuse.'

Some other agencies or organisations use [5] different definitions, but, for the purpose of identifying the thrust of Government policy underpinning the Act such differences are unimportant.

1.5   The Consultation Paper recognised that historic attitudes to domestic violence had changed, but considered that the challenge was, now, to ensure that appropriate strategies were in place to mark out domestic violence as unacceptable, to ensure effective prevention, detection and punishment, with appropriate support for the victims of domestic violence. Indeed, the need for proper support for the victims of domestic violence mirrors wider concerns

---

[1]   See www.homeoffice.gov.uk.
[2]   Cm 5847, June 2003 (available at www.homneoffice.gov.uk).
[3]   Cm 5074, July 2002 (available at www.homeoffice.gov.uk).
[4]   Op cit, fn 1 above, p 6.
[5]   See, *Safety and Justice*, p 6, identifying, in particular, the Association of Chief Police Officers (who include family members other than partners) and the Crown Prosecution Service (which includes any criminal offence arising out of physical, sexual, psychological, emotional or financial abuse between current or former partners or family members.

generally about the historic lack of support in the criminal justice process for the victims of crime, another of the major themes of the DVCVA 2004.[6]

Observing the rates of domestic violence, the Consultation Paper reported that domestic violence has the highest rate of repeat victimisation of any crime, and that an incident of domestic violence is reported to the police every three minutes.[7] On average, two women per week are killed by a male partner or former partner, with almost 50% of all female murders being committed by a partner or ex-partner. By contrast some 8% of murders of males are as a result of the act of a female partner or ex-partner. Whether resulting in fatal consequences or not, domestic violence crosses all boundaries in terms of age, gender, or social class, but is predominantly violence by men against women. It is also significantly under-reported, by both the official crime statistics, and the British Crime Survey.[8] *Safety and Justice* concluded (at p 10) that 'a true and accurate assessment of the real levels of domestic violence will not be possible until there is progress in changing attitudes so that all victims of domestic violence feel safe in revealing the violence they have experienced.' To achieve this, the Government proposed a strategy based on three strands: prevention; protection and justice; support. Prevention involves changing public perceptions and attitudes (particularly amongst young people) by education and by tackling the problem by addressing risk factors that lead to domestic violence, or its recurrence, by providing advice on access to legal remedies and support services, and by preventing offenders from re-offending. It is, though, upon protection and justice, and on support, that the DVCVA 2004 focuses.

1.6 The Act is intended to strengthen the protection and support afforded to the victims of crime generally, but that specifically impacts on the victims of domestic violence, by giving new powers to the police and the courts to tackle offenders. Its provisions must be viewed in the context of earlier legislation. Sections 16 to 24 of the Youth Justice and Criminal Evidence Act 1999 introduced provisions giving greater protection to vulnerable witnesses. More recently, significant changes have been made by the Criminal Justice Act 2003 ('CJA 2003').[9] One important change made by the CJA 2003 was the introduction of provisions placing the decision whether to charge, and if so with what, to the Crown Prosecution Service. Significant efforts have been made in recent years to improve the approaches of both the police and Crown Prosecution Services to incidents of domestic violence.[10] The new prosecution arrangements will give the decisions as to whether to proceed, and with what

---

6   See White Paper *A Better Deal for Victims and Witnesses* Home Office (2003), and also Ch 7, *post*.

7   Consultation Paper, op cit, p 9.

8   Ibid, p 10.

9   See, generally, Ward and Davies *Criminal Justice Act 2003 – A Practitioners Guide* (Jordans, 2004).

10 See, generally, Lockton and Ward *Domestic Violence* (Cavendish Publishing, 1997).

evidence, to the CPS: pilot studies have shown that such arrangements can lead to a significant reduction in the number of discontinued cases, and to increased early guilty pleas, results that may encourage victims generally to have confidence in the likely success of prosecution where complaint of an offence is made. The new evidential provisions relating to hearsay and to bad character[11] may also prove important.

1.7   The rationale for the introduction of new specific powers to assist in the achievement of this strategy is dealt with as we examine its detailed provisions. But one important change is made to try to ensure that victims get the support and protection they need. The DVCVA 2004 gives to the Home Secretary the power to make a Code of Practice, which will, for the first time, provide victim's with a range of rights. A copy of the draft Indicative Code is set out as an Appendix to this book, and reflects Government thinking as at the time it was tabled in the House of Lords (January 2004). With this Code, the new range of powers, and the establishment of an independent Commissioner for Victim, the Act is intended to 'put victims at the heart of the criminal justice system.'[12]

1.8   Amongst the detailed provisions of the Act intended to provide greater powers for the police and the courts, and to improve the way in which victims are treated, are the following:

- Common assault is made an arrestable offence.
- New police powers to enable the police to deal with domestic violence include making it an arrestable, criminal, offence to breach a non-molestation order, punishable by up to five years in prison.
- The civil law on domestic violence is strengthened, to ensure cohabiting same-sex couples have the same access to non-molestation and occupation orders as opposite sex couples, and extending the availability of these orders to couples who have never lived together or been married.
- There is stronger legal protection for victims of domestic violence by enabling courts to impose restraining orders when sentencing for any offence. Until now, such orders could only be imposed on offenders convicted of harassment or causing fear of violence.
- The Act enables a court to impose restraining orders on acquittal for any offence (or if a conviction has been overturned on appeal) if they consider it necessary to protect the victim from harassment. This will deal with cases where the conviction has failed but it is still clear from the evidence that the victims need protecting.
- The Act creates a system to review domestic violence homicide incidents, drawing in relevant agencies, to find out what can be done to put the system right and prevent future deaths.

[11]   Criminal Justice Act 2003, ss 84–123.
[12]   Mr David Blunkett, MP, Home Secretary, Press Release (5 November 2004).

- As noted above, the Act provides for a code of practice, binding on all criminal justice agencies, so that victims receive support, protection, information and advice.
- Recourse to the Parliamentary Commissioner is created to deal with complaints by victims if they feel the code has not been adhered to by the criminal justice agencies.
- The Act establishes an independent Commissioner for Victims to give victims a voice at the heart of Government and to safeguard and promote the interests of victims and witnesses, encouraging the spread of good practice and reviewing the statutory code.
- The victims of mentally disordered offenders are given the same rights to information as other victims of serious violent and sexual offences.

It is intended to ensure that more offenders pay towards supporting victims. The Criminal Injuries Compensation Authority will be able to recover money from offenders, and a surcharge will be placed on criminal convictions and fixed penalty notices which will contribute to the Victims Fund. For motoring offenders the surcharge is intended to apply to 'the most serious and persistent offenders.'

1.9 Like virtually all such legislation, the DVCVA 2004 contains a variety of other provisions where change in substantive law, procedure or powers was considered appropriate. The Act also creates a new offence of causing or allowing the death of a child or vulnerable adult. This is intended to ensure that offenders who remain silent or blame each other do not escape justice. It alters the law relating to insanity and unfitness to plead. The Criminal Injuries Compensation Authority is given the right to recover from offenders the money it has paid to their victims in compensation. Powers are introduced to permit a surcharge to be payable on criminal convictions and fixed penalty notices which will contribute to the Victims Fund. For motoring offenders the surcharge will apply to 'serious and persistent offenders'. It makes some detailed changes to sentencing powers. All of these are dealt with at appropriate points of this book.

Chapter Two

DOMESTIC VIOLENCE: NON MOLESTATION ORDERS, HARASSMENT, RESTRAINING ORDERS, OCCUPATION ORDERS

Summary

2.1 The DVCVA 2004 makes substantial changes to the law relating to personal protection from harassment and assault and creates a number of new criminal offences. In particular, it amends Part IV of the Family Law Act 1996 (referred to hereafter as 'Part IV') and the Protection from Harassment Act 1997 (PFHA 1997). At the same time, Parliament has taken the opportunity to amend certain aspects of the criminal law on associated topics.

Some of the changes merely amend the existing law whereas others create new criminal offences and introduce new procedures for monitoring the same.

The changes dealt with in this Chapter are as follows:

(a) amendments to definitions of 'cohabitants' and 'associated persons';
(b) changes to procedure for undertakings;
(c) removal of power of arrest from non-molestation orders; consequent amendments to occupations orders;
(d) creation of new offence for breach of order;
(e) miscellaneous changes to occupation orders.

As noted in Chapter 1, the Act contains a wide range of provisions which relate to the wider treatment of domestic violence, and these are dealt with at the appropriate part of the book

The effect of Part IV of the FLA 1996

2.2 The purpose of this book is not to provide a detailed guide to the whole law relating to domestic violence.[1] Nonetheless, an understanding of those

---

[1]   For this purpose see R Bird 'Domestic Violence Law and Practice' in R.Bird (editor in chief) *Family Law, and Emergency Remedies in the Family Courts* (4th edn) (Family Law).

provisions makes it necessary to summarise briefly the present law as contained in Part IV and the PFHA 1997.

2.3 Part IV was a reforming statute which replaced the Domestic Violence and Matrimonial Proceedings Act 1976, and ss 1 and 9 of the Matrimonial Homes Act 1983. It was based on the recommendations of the Law Commission Report 'Domestic Violence and Occupation of the family home' of 1992[2]. Its effect may be summarised as follows.

Orders which can be made

2.4 The remedies provided by Part IV are non-molestation orders and occupation orders. As their names imply, non-molestation orders are designed to afford personal protection to the victims or potential victims of violence and forbid someone using or threatening violence against the applicant, and/or harassing, pestering or intimidating them.take the form of injunctive relief.

Occupation orders are designed to regulate the occupation of a family home. They allow a person to apply to a court for an order to enforce their entitlement to remain in occupation of the home, make the respondent leave the home, or otherwise regulate the occupation by both parties. That occupation may be because of a legal estate or interest in the home, or be in respect of matrimonial home rights. Such rights may be declared or defined by the court. A spouse who is not entitled to occupy a dwelling house but who is in occupation is protected from eviction and, where not in occupation, he or she may occupy with leave of the court.

Jurisdiction of courts

2.5 Part IV established a unified system of courts in which the powers available under Part IV might be exercised. These consist of the High Court, County Courts and Family Proceedings Courts, all of which operate a unified jurisdiction with similar powers.

Associated persons

2.6 One of the problems of the previous law had been that there were restrictions on the classes of persons entitled to claim relief. Part IV solved this problem by creating the new category of associated persons, containing a very wide series of categories all of whom are entitled to relief. These are summarised at para **2.12**.

Enforcement

2.7 Orders are divided in effect into those which are endorsed with a power of arrest and those which are not so endorsed. Where it is alleged that someone

[2] Law Com No 207.

has disobeyed an order which has been so endorsed with a power of arrest, the complainant can request the police to arrest the alleged wrongdoer, hold him in custody and then bring him before the court at the earliest opportunity. The court is defined as the relevant judicial authority which may dispose of the case or adjourn it and remand on bail or in custody.

Where there is no power of arrest the complainant may apply for a warrant for arrest, with the same results, or issue a notice to show cause why the wrongdoer should not be committed.

The existence of a power of arrest is therefore vital, and Part IV contains a requirement for the court to endorse a power of arrest in certain circumstances.

Guidelines for the courts

2.8   As mentioned above, Part IV requires the court to endorse a power of arrest where it is has made a finding of fact that there has been violence, or a threat of violence, against the applicant, and the evidence indicates that the applicant and the children will not be adequately protected without it. It also prescribes a procedure which a court must follow when deciding whether or not to grant an occupation order. This involves essentially a balance of harm test.

The effect of the Protection from Harassment Act 1997

2.9   Somewhat confusingly, at more or less the same time as Part IV was coming into effect, Parliament enacted the PFHA 1997. It provides remedies which, to some extent overlap with those provided by Part IV. It might at first sight appear unclear why all these remedies were not contained in the same statute. However, it should be borne in mind that the PFHA 1997 is intended to operate in all contexts, and goes beyond harassment in the context of the family or family relationships.

The reason for the passage of the PFHA 1997 seems to have been to provide a remedy against the phenomenon known as 'stalking' whose characteristics are usually the obsessive harassment of a victim, usually but not always, female, by someone who follows her movements, watches her or telephones her. There frequently is no existing relationship between the parties if indeed it ever existed at all. It is therefore not necessary to prove that the applicant and respondent are associated persons.

2.10   In a sense, the PFHA 1997 anticipates the new legislation in that it combines civil and criminal remedies. Section 1 of PFHA 1997 provides that a person must not pursue a course of conduct which:

(a)   amounts to harassment of another, and
(b)   he knows, or ought to know, amounts to harassment of the other.

Section 2(1) then provides that breach of s 1 is an offence. For conduct to amount to a 'course of conduct', it must involve conduct on at least two occasions.

Section 1(3) then prescribes certain defences which need not detain us here.

2.11	The main thrust of the PFHA 1997 is therefore to create a criminal offence. However, it goes on to provide civil remedies, and these are the parts which, to some extent, overlap with Part IV. Section 3 of PFHA 1997 provides that:

(a) an actual or apprehended breach of s 1 may be the subject of a claim in civil proceedings by the person who is or may be the victim of the course of conduct in question;
(b) on such a claim, damages may be awarded for (among other things) any anxiety caused by the harassment and any financial loss resulting from it.

Section 3 therefore provides a cause of action for damages. The right to apply for an injunction to restrain an apprehended breach is not specifically mentioned in the Act but the general law as to interlocutory and final injunction orders applies.[3]

There is no provision for the attachment of a power of arrest to any injunction order. The court may issue a warrant for arrest, or a victim may apply for the committal of the wrongdoer under a notice to show cause.

The new law – changes in entitlement to apply under Part IV Family Law Act 1996

2.12	As was seen at para **2.6**, in order to apply for an order under Part IV an applicant has to show that he or she is within a defined class of persons known as 'associated persons'. The definition of 'associated persons' is contained at s 62(2) of the FLA 1996. That definition in effect provides that the parties must be in a family relationship, or have been married to each other, or be cohabitants or former cohabitants.[4] An 'associated person' also included those who live or have lived in the same household, other than by virtue of being an employee, tenant, lodger or boarder. The definition does not include unmarried partners.

The Government in the White Paper *Safety and Justice*[5] identified several problems with this definition. It did not extend to those who were in a relationship but who had never lived together, and did not extend to same-sex couples. The DVCVA 2004 reflects these concerns, by enlarging the class of associated

---

3	See Civil Procedure Rules, Part 25.
4	Defined as a man and woman living together as man and wife.
5	Op cit, p 32.

persons. It also amends the law with relation to cohabitants applying for occupation orders.[6]

Cohabitants to include same-sex couples

2.13   As noted above, one class of 'associated person' consists of cohabitants. Section 3 of the DVCVA 2004 substitutes for the existing definition of 'cohabitants' in s 62(1)(a) FLA 1996 a new definition, which states:

> 'Cohabitants are two persons who, although not married to each other, are living together as husband and wife or (if of the same sex) in an equivalent relationship'.

No change is therefore made to the existing definition in respect of couples of different sexes but the category is now intended to include homosexual and lesbian couples.

2.14   It will be remembered that the existing definition of 'associated person' includes 'someone who lives, or has lived, in the same household'. Although same-sex couples could not be regarded as cohabitants, because on one view of the language they are not living together as man and wife.[7] It was sometimes assumed that this definition would include (though not be confined to) same-sex couples who lived in the same household. Clearly it is now considered that some further clarification is needed to ensure that homosexual couples are included. This amendment attracted little comment in the parliamentary debates, and it seemed to be assumed that the existing law made no provision for such applicants living in the same household. The explanation may lie in the fact that non-cohabitants living in the same household could only have recourse to an occupation order if they were 'entitled'. Same-sex couples would not have matrimonial home rights

2.15   In practice, there should be little difficulty in implementing this provision. 'Cohabitation' itself is the subject of judicial definition in several cases[8] and the factors given there which have to be applied can easily be applied to same-sex couples. The court would normally look for a sexual relationship but, as with heterosexual couples, this is one of a number of factors to be taken into account and its absence need not be fatal.

Non-cohabiting couples

2.16   The class of 'associated persons' is now extended by s 4 of the DVCVA 2004 so that the relevant part of s 62(3) FLA 1996 reads as follows:

---

[6]   See para **2.13**.

[7]   See *Safety and Justice*, p 32. But note by analogy the broad meaning given to the term spouse, used in Rent Act 1977, in *Ghaidan v Mendoza* [2004] 4 All ER 524, HL.

[8]   See eg *Crake v Supplementary Benefits Commission* [1982] 1 All ER 498; *Re J (Income Support: Cohabitation)* [1995] 1 FLR 660; *G v G (Non-Molestation Order: Jurisdiction)* [2000] 2 FLR 533.

'For the purposes of this Part, a person is associated with another person if …

(ea) they have or have had an intimate personal relationship with each other which is or was of significant duration'.

When explaining the possible meaning of this clause in Standing Committee,[9] the Parliamentary Under-Secretary of State, Paul Goggins, said that it was the Government's intention to close a significant loophole in the protection afforded by the FLA 1996 by including within it non-cohabiting couples. The Act defines the meaning of 'associated person' in the broadest terms and it will be for the court in individual circumstances to determine whether it applies. It was not the Government's intention to include platonic friendships or brief sexual encounters such as one-night stands. Intimacy and duration were the key elements. For short or non-intimate relationships the Protection from Harassment Act powers are available.

2.17   It seems therefore that the intention of the legislation is to include the boyfriend and girlfriend who had not actually lived together. It is easy to see the problems of definition which might be encountered. The court may be faced with significant difficulties in certain cases, both in terms of what amounts to a 'relationship', and what is 'intimate' While it may not have been the Government's intention to include platonic relationships, the word 'intimate' has a variety of meanings and cannot be taken always to import a sexual connotation. The lack of sexual intercourse, or more widely, sexual intimacy falling short of intercourse, is not necessarily determinative of the issue. Again, questions arise as to what is a 'significant duration'? Would one month or one week suffice?

The view stated by the Parliamentary Under-Secretary during debate was clearly that the judges would recognise a suitable candidate for this description when they saw one. This may well be true in the majority of cases but there is certainly room for argument in peripheral cases.

CHANGES TO NON-MOLESTATION ORDERS

2.18   'Molestation' is not defined in the FLA 1996, it being assumed that everyone knows what it means. However, it has been defined elsewhere as:

'some quite deliberate conduct which is aimed at a high degree of harassment of the other party so as to justify the interference of the court….it does not include enforcing an invasion of privacy per se; there has to be some conduct which clearly harasses and affects the applicant to such a degree that the intervention of the court is called for.' [10]

---

[9]   Official Report, HC Standing Committee (22 June 2004), cols 54 and 55. See also *Safety and Justice*, op cit, p 33.

[10]   Sir Stephen Brown P in *C v C (Non-molestation Order:Jurisdiction)* [1998] 1 FLR 554.

Section 42(1) FLA 1996 provides that a non-molestation order means an order containing either or both of the following:

(a) provision prohibiting the respondent from molesting another person who is associated with the respondent;
(b) provision prohibiting the respondent from molesting a relevant child.

The DVCVA 2004 does not amend these definitions. However, it makes important changes in respect of enforcement for breaches of non-molestation orders and it also changes the approach of the court to acceptance of undertakings in lieu of an order.

Powers of arrest

2.19 Section 47(2) FLA 1996 provided that a power of arrest must be attached to one or more provisions of a non-molestation order if it appeared to the court that the respondent had used or threatened violence against the applicant or a relevant child unless the court was satisfied that in all the circumstances of the case the applicant or child would be adequately protected without such a power of arrest. This provision enabled a constable to arrest without warrant a person whom he reasonably suspected had disobeyed the non-molestation order and was regarded as a most important weapon for the protection of victims of domestic violence. The number of orders with a power of arrest attached has generally[11] increased, from 15,600 in 1998 to 17,400 in 2001.

The effect of para 38 of Sch 10 to the DVCVA 2004 is to amend s 47 FLA 996 so that the power to attach a power of arrest to a non-molestation order is removed, while allowing it to remain for occupation orders. The DVCVA 2004 does not, as originally proposed by the Government,[12] alter the arrest powers in respect of occupation orders.

These provisions might seem puzzling at first sight, especially with the growth of the numbers of such powers being attached. However, the reason for it is that breach of a non-molestation order has become a criminal arrestable offence, within the meaning of s 24 Police and Criminal Evidence Act 1984 because the maximum term of imprisonment that may be imposed for the new criminal offence created by the Act[13] is five years. A constable may thus arrest a person on reasonable suspicion that that individual is in breach of a non-molestation order (see para **2.33** below). Alternatively a power of arrest will most likely arise because s 10 of the DVCVA 2004 makes common assault an arrestable offence. The removal of the power to attach a power of arrest goes hand-in-hand with the criminalisation of breach of such orders, and is

---

11   See *Safety and Justice*, op cit, p 33.
12   See *Safety and Justice*, op cit, p 34.
13   See para **2.25**.

discussed further at para **2.21**. It was thought that it would be unduly confusing for police officers to have to decide whether a person arrested by them should be dealt with under the previous procedure of bringing before the family court within 24 hours, or as an arrested person to be subject to the normal processes that flow therefrom, and to be brought before a magistrates court. The result is that the court will no longer be able to attach a power of arrest to a non-molestation order. Methods of enforcement will be considered at para **2.23** et seq below, but the clear objective of the DVCVA 2004 in this context is to criminalise breach of non-molestation orders.

Undertakings

2.20   By section 46(1) FLA 1996, the court has power to accept an undertaking from any party where it has power to make an occupation order or non-molestation order. The only restriction on this power is that referred to in para **2.8** above, namely that the court had to attach a power of arrest where violence had been used, and a power of arrest cannot be attached to an undertaking. Where violence had been used, an order was mandatory.

Because the ability to attach a power of arrest to a non-molestation order has been removed, this position has had to be rethought, and the restriction on the right of the court to accept an undertaking redefined.

2.21   First, s 46(3) is amended by Sch 10, para 37, to the DVCVA 2004 to read as follows:

> 'The court shall not accept an undertaking under subsection (1) instead of making an occupation order in any case where apart from this section a power of arrest would be attached to the order'.

This recognises that a power of arrest may still be attached to an occupation order.

2.22   Secondly, a new s 46(3A) is inserted (by Sch 10, para 37 to the DVCVA 2004) which reads as follows:

> '(3A) The court shall not accept an undertaking under subsection (1) instead of making a non-molestation order in any case where it appears to the court that:
>
> (a)   the respondent has used or threatened violence against the applicant or a relevant child; and
> (b)   for the protection of the applicant or child it is necessary to make a non-molestation order so that any breach may be punishable under section 42A'.

It will be seen that the restrictions on the court's powers and the standard to be applied by the court have not changed in so far as the principal matter is whether the respondent has used or threatened violence. However, the proviso in the old law, contained in s 47(2)(b) and applicable to s 46(3), namely that the court may decline to attach a power of arrest (and therefore feel able to accept an undertaking) if satisfied that the applicant would be adequately protected without a power of arrest, has gone. Now the test is whether the court considers that it is necessary to make a non-molestation order, breach of which is an arrestable offence, for the protection of the applicant. It may be that the end result is very much the same as before, but the wording is different. The question posed in s 46(3A)(c) requires the court to determine whether an order is necessary so that any breach may be punished as a criminal offence.

The change, though, is important for one other reason. The criminalisation of breach of non-molestation orders might lead, without further provision, to an increase in the use of undertakings, with pressure being put on a victim to accept an undertaking rather than to press for an order. The effect of the new s 46(3A) is to remove that potential in many (although not all) cases of actual or threatened violence.

Penalty for breach of as non molestation order – a new criminal offence

2.23 The changes effected by the DVCVA 2004 in respect of the method of enforcing non-molestation orders and punishing breaches thereof are some of the most significant matters contained in the Act. Part IV FLA 1996 laid down a comprehensive code for the enforcement of orders, consisting essentially of a power of arrest and provision for bringing offenders quickly before the relevant judicial authority, normally the court which had made the order. For cases where there was no power of arrest, or that power had not been invoked, the complainant could issue a notice requiring the respondent to show cause why he or she should not be committed.

The Government's view was clearly that that system had been found wanting, though the evidence which led to that conclusion being reached is elusive.[14] The White Paper commented:

> '…given that the power of arrest   is often only attached to specific parts of the order, police officers may be unclear whether they can arrest the respondent or not. Moreover, information on orders and powers of arrest is not recorded centrally, and the arrangements for passing such information between police forces can be inconsistent. If no power of arrest was attached, the victim has to apply to the civil court for an arrest warrant, which can put the victim at risk of further violence until the warrant is issued.'

The result of this is that, as described above, non-molestation orders may no longer bear a power of arrest, and breach of such an order becomes a criminal offence. The definition of 'arrestable offence' contained in s 24 of the Police and Criminal Evidence Act 1984 (by reference to Sch 1A to the 1984 Act) is

---

[14]   See *Safety and Justice*, op cit, pp 33-34.

extended to include common assaults, thus giving a constable a power to arrest where he or she reasonably suspects the breach of a non-molestation order.[15] It might have been thought that this change was unnecessary, given the fact that the DVCVA 2004 creates an offence which is itself arrestable, because of its maximum punishment of five years' imprisonment. The answer lies in the fact that the constable may not know, when called to an incident of domestic violence, whether a non-molestation order is in place.

2.24   Section 1 of the DVCVA 2004 inserts into the FLA 1996 a new s 42A, which creates the offence of breaching a non-molestation order. The reasoning for this was that making a breach an offence would extend the range of sanctions available to the court. Contempt penalties are limited to fine or imprisonment, whereas a criminal court may impose the usual range of community sentences, such as curfew, mental health, drug treatment, voluntary activities etc this would give the court an opportunity to deal with the offending behaviour.[16] The new provision does not remove the power of a court to deal with the breach of the order, but the new s 42A provides that where a person is convicted of the new offence he or she cannot be punished for a contempt of court, or vice versa (FLA 1996, 42A(3), (4)).

2.25   The new s 42A provides as follows:

'(1) A person who without reasonable excuse does anything that he is prohibited from doing by a non-molestation order is guilty of an offence.

(2) In the case of a non-molestation order made by virtue of section 45(1), a person can be guilty of an offence under this section only in respect of conduct engaged in at a time when he was aware of the existence of the order

(3) Where a person is convicted of an offence under this section in respect of any conduct, that conduct is not punishable as a contempt of court.

(4) A person cannot be convicted of an offence under this section in respect of any conduct which has been punished as a contempt of court.'

References in any enactment to proceedings under Part 4 of the Family Law Act 1996 are references to the civil proceedings with which it deals, and do no extend to the criminal proceedings for the offence of breaching a non-molestation order created by the new s 42A (FLA 1996, s 42A(6)).

Section 42A(5) provides that the offence is punishable, on conviction on indictment, to a term of imprisonment not exceeding five years, or a fine, or both; or, if convicted on summary trial, to a term of imprisonment not exceeding 12 months, or a fine not exceeding the statutory maximum, or both.[17] This contrasts with the maximum of two years' imprisonment or a fine in civil contempt proceedings.

---

[15]   See DVCVA 2004, s 10.
[16]   Official Report HL (29 January 2004), cols 237 and 238.
[17]   See Criminal Justice Act 1982, s 37.

2.26 Section 42A(1) therefore contains the ingredients of the offence. The prosecutor must prove (to the normal criminal standard) that the act complained is forbidden by the non-molestation order, and that there is no reasonable excuse for the breach.

It is interesting to note that breach of anything forbidden by the order potentially constitutes a criminal offence, and so renders the offender liable to arrest and prosecution. Under the pre-existing law, in the making of an order, care has always been taken to distinguish between those matters involving violence or the threat of violence, to which a power of arrest could be attached, and other matters not involving violence, to which a power of arrest is not attached. For example, an order not to use or threaten violence would carry a power of arrest; this would not routinely be the case with an order prohibiting harassment, intimidation or pestering. The courts have been anxious to ensure that a person could not be arrested for, say, telephoning the applicant when he was enjoined not to.

There is no such distinction in the DVCVA 2004. This is deliberate. Speaking in the Grand Committee debate during the passage of the Act through the House of Lords, the Home Office Minister of State, Baroness Scotland, said:

> ' The police may be unclear to which part of the order any power of arrest may be attached....Our aim is to ensure the immediate safety of the applicant and any children, and we want to underline the seriousness of any breach. That is why [section] 1 makes a breach of the order a criminal offence.'[18]

The position is therefore that breach of any provision of the order, however comparatively insignificant, will constitute an offence. The seriousness of any breach will be reflected, if at all, in the decision as to whether to prosecute and, on conviction, by sentence.

This might affect the decision whether to make a non molestation order. In *Chechi v Bashier*[19] the court declined to make a non-molestation order despite the fact that violence had been proved, on the ground that it was mandatory to attach a power of arrest and that, in the particular circumstances of the case, arrest was a weapon which the parties should not have available to them. It will be interesting to see whether such reasoning is used in future when the issue of whether to make an order or accept an undertaking is being decided.

2.27 Section 42A(2) refers to orders made under s 45(1) FLA 1996, namely without notice orders. A person can only be guilty of the criminal offence contained in the new s 42A(1) if he or she is aware of the s 45 order. He or she will normally have been made aware by means of personal service of the order. However, the subsection merely says that he must be aware of the existence of the order and it is arguable that if, for example, he had learnt of

[18] Official Report HL (19 January 2004), col GC238.
[19] [1999] 2 FLR 489 CA, per Dame Elizabeth Butler-Sloss P.

the order in some other way, such as a telephone conversation with someone, he would be liable. The prosecutor will need to adduce evidence as to the state of knowledge of the defendant. Section 42A(2) does not specify any knowledge of the detailed terms of the order as opposed to its existence, but that, arguably, is immaterial, because the issue can be put in a different way, but with the same result. If the prosecution cannot show that the defendant was aware of the existence and terms of the order, then clearly the prosecution have failed to show the lack of reasonable excuse. Clearly a defendant who is unaware of the terms of an order has a reasonable excuse for acting in the way that he had (irrespective of whether the acts are, in a wider sense, reasonable).

Relationship between the new offence and contempt proceedings

2.28   Subsections (3) and (4) of s 42A deal with the overlapping of criminal proceedings and contempt proceedings. The position with relation to this was clearly set out by the Government, during the parliamentary debates, as follows:

> 'I was asked what action could be taken in relation to the breach with regard to the person who is protected by the order. Broadly speaking, there are two options. First, the police could be called and, because of the maximum five year imprisonment on conviction, the police will have automatically have the power of arrest for any breach of the terms of a non-molestation order....The decision on whether to prosecute for the breach will be for the police[20] and the Crown Prosecution Service- always of course in consultation with the victim herself[21]. If the decision is not to prosecute for a criminal offence, the victim can still pursue an action through the civil court and breach remains contempt with the same penalties available as now. The second option is to pursue the civil route. The victim may decide that he or she does not want to involve the police at all. in those circumstances the victim will still be able to apply to the civil court for a warrant of arrest if the molestation [sic] order is breached, and to have the perpetrator arrested and brought back to the civil court for the judge to decide what should happen.'[22]

Even though the power of arrest has been removed, therefore, there is no reason why a complainant should not seek to punish breach of an order by means of the issue of a warrant of arrest under FLA 1996, s 47(10) or by the issue and service of a notice to show good reason why the respondent should not be committed to prison (Form N78 in the county court, Form FL418 in magistrates courts). The Act imposes no restrictions or time limits on either a prosecutor[23] or a complainant wishing to enforce by a contempt application.

[20]   Note should be taken of the fact that the Criminal Justice Act 2003 now places the decision as to whether to charge, and with what, in the hands of the Crown Prosecution Service.

[21]   For the position of victims in the criminal justice process, see Ch 6, post.

[22]   Mr Paul Goggins. MP, Parliamentary Under-Secretary of State, Home Office, Official Report HC Standing Committee E (22 June 2004), col 45.

[23]   Subject to the normal rules concerning time-limits for the commencement of criminal proceedings, and for the potential for a stay where delay has amounted to an abuse of process.

Mr Goggins referred above to the warrant of arrest procedure only, but it has to be said that this procedure has been little used and it is most likely that the notice to show good reason procedure would be more widely used.

2.29 As already noted, s 42A(3) and (4) provide, in effect, that a person who has been punished for contempt in the family proceedings may not be convicted of an offence and vice versa. This is obviously fair and sensible as far as it goes but it still leaves an unfortunate lacuna. There is nothing on the face of the section to prevent a complainant beginning contempt proceedings where the respondent has been arrested, and there is nothing to prevent prosecution of an alleged offender where contempt proceedings are pending. It may be that rules of court will deal with this but it has to be said that, at present, there is room for confusion. No obligation is placed on either complainant, or on the police or CPS, to establish what the other proposed to do (if anything), although the new arrangements relating to 'victims' may assist in improving dialogue. Arguably, the basic principle that civil proceedings should defer to criminal proceedings should apply, with courts in any application to commit for contempt routinely requiring whether a charge under s 42A has been laid, or proposed.

However, the position is potentially even worse than that. There is nothing to prevent a complainant who is dissatisfied by the acquittal of a respondent, or the dismissal of contempt proceedings against him, making a second attempt to punish him in the other court, perhaps armed with better evidence. The Act only prohibits duplicate proceedings in the event of a favourable outcome for the applicant; it does not contemplate the result of unsuccessful proceedings.

It cannot be said that the position is anything other than unsatisfactory.

Relationship between new offence and other offences

2.30 The offence under s 42A may overlap with other criminal offences. For example, the breach of the non-molestation order may involve an assault or wounding, or a breach of an order made under PFHA 1997. This overlap is not necessarily crucial, provided that the individual is not being punished twice for the same conduct. Commission of the new offence will require the prosecutor simply to prove the making of the order, its terms and its breach, which may in some circumstances be an easier task than proving the particular facts of an individual assault or other alleged incidents (such as, for example, a public order offence). The burden of proof on the prosecution is the normal criminal standard: the court will have to be satisfied beyond reasonable doubt

Reasonable excuse

2.31 No offence is committed if the act complained of as amounting to a breach of the non-molestation order was done with reasonable excuse. These are, of course, criminal proceedings and Art 6 of the European Convention on Human Rights (the 'fair trial' provision) applies. Section 42A does not expressly allocate a burden of proof in respect of 'reasonable excuse', and the issue arises as to whether s 42A imposes any legal burden of proof upon the defendant, pursuant to s 101 of the Magistrates' Court Act 1980, or under *Hunt*.[24]

The balance of case law suggests that the legal burden of proof remains on the prosecution, with an evidential burden only on the defendant.[25] There is no inevitability about this conclusion, and in the end the question turns on the particular application of the principles set out in *A-Gs Reference (No 1 of 2004), Edwards*.[26] Clearly, an evidential burden lies on the defendant. The prosecution will not (usually) know the circumstances that led to the breach of the non-molestation order. It will be the defendant who will have to explain what he or she did, and why, for otherwise there is no factual issue before the court. An argument exists for imposing a legal burden (on that issue only) on the defendant. If a legal burden was held to exist on the issue of reasonable excuse, the defendant would need to satisfy the court that reasonable excuse existed, on the balance of probabilities. Against that, Parliament has not attempted in s 42A specifically to allocate the burden of proof of establishing

---

24   [1987] AC 1, HL, applicable to trials on indictment.
25   See the significant caselaw now dealing with 'reverse onus' provisions: *Lambert* [2001] 3 All ER 537, HL; *A-G's Reference (No 1 of 2004), Edwards* [2004] All ER(D) 318, CA; *L v DPP* [2002] 1 Cr App R 420, DC; *Johnstone* [2003] 1 WLR 1736.
26   [2004] All ER(D) 318, CA. These are stated as follows: (1) the common law (the golden thread) and Art 6(2) have the same effect, and both permit legal reverse-onus provisions in appropriate circumstances; (2) reverse-onus provisions are probably justified if the overall burden of proof is on the prosecution (ie the prosecution have to prove the essential elements of the offence) but only where there is a significant reason why it is fair and reasonable to deny the defendant the normal general protection given by the presumption of innocence; (3) where the exception goes no further than necessary to achieve its objective (ie it is proportionate) it is sufficient if the exception is reasonably necessary in all the circumstances. The assumption should be that Parliament would not have made an exception without good reason. The role of the judge [or magistrate] is to review Parliament's approach; (4) if only an evidential burden is imposed, there is no risk of infringement of Art 6(2); (5) When deciding whether an exception is justified the courts must establish what will be the realistic effect of the reverse onus, concerning itself with substance rather than form. If the proper interpretation is that the statutory provision creates an offence plus an exception that will be in itself a strong indication that there is no infringement of Art 6(2); (6) the easier it is for the defendant to discharge the burden, the more likely it is that the reverse burden is justified. The court should consider whether the facts are in the knowledge of the accused, and how difficult it would be for the prosecution to establish the facts; (7) the ultimate question is whether the exception prevents a fair trial. If it does, it must be read down or declared incompatible with Art 6; (8) caution should be exercised when considering the seriousness of the offence and the power of punishment. The need for a reverse burden is not necessarily reflected by the gravity of the offence, although the more serious the offence the more important it is that there is no interference with the presumption of innocence.

reasonable excuse on the defendant, unlike in *L v DPP*.[27] If the conclusion is that the legal burden remains on the prosecution, it will have to show, to the normal criminal standard, that there was no reasonable excuse for what the defendant did.

What is a 'reasonable excuse' will be a matter of fact for the court of trial to determine. It should never be found to exist simply because no harm was caused to the original applicant, or was likely to do so. The reasonable excuse must relate to the reasons why the non-molestation order was breached, not the effect of that breach. Nor should the court accept arguments based on the human right of the defendant, despite the terms of s 6 of the Human Rights Act 1998. Issues such as the likely effect of a non-molestation order on the convention rights of the defendant (for example, possible infringement of Art 8 rights in respect of private and family life, or Protocol 1 rights to property) were relevant consideration in determination whether a non-molestation order should be made, and its terms. The prosecution is not concerned with that, to which arguably separate challenge should be made, but with the separate question of whether there has been a breach of the order. The criminal court arguably is not concerned with the question of whether an order should have been made in the first place.

RESTRAINING ORDERS

2.32   The DVCVA 2004 significantly amends powers to make restraining orders, under the PFHA 1997. The PFHA 1997 permits a court, when sentencing for an offence under that Act,[28] to make a restraining order. This may be used to prohibit the offender from conduct specified in the order, with the purpose of protecting the victim or others from further conduct that amounts to harassment or which may cause the fear of violence.

2.33   There is currently no provision that requires the victim to be automatically informed if an application is made to amend or end such an order. That is remedied by the DVCVA 2004. Section 12 of the DVCVA 2004 amends s 5 of the PFHA 1997, by conferring on any person named in the order (ie the victim) the right to be heard on an application under s 5(4) of the PFHA 1997 to amend or end an order This changes the pervasive theme to give a greater say to victims.

2.34   The DVCVA 2004 also increases the powers of a court to make a restraining order following criminal proceedings. This is dealt with at Chapter 5.

---

[27]   [2002] 1 Cr App R 420, DC, where a reverse onus provision was imposed (expressly) by Criminal Justice Act 1988, s 139.

[28]   See para **5.5**.

CHANGES TO OCCUPATION ORDERS

2.35   The changes which the DVCVA makes to occupation orders are limited in comparison with those made to non-molestation orders. However, they are significant and must be noted. They may be summarised as follows:

(a)   considerations when parties cohabitants;

(b)   minor amendments to s 36 FLA 1996;

(c)   non-molestation orders on grant of occupation order;

(d)   power of arrest.

These will be considered in turn.

Additional considerations when parties cohabitants

2.36   Sections 33 to 37 FLA 1996 set out the powers of the court when dealing with applications for occupation orders, and the matters which the court must take into account vary according to whether the parties are or were married, are or were cohabitants, and their legal interest in the property in question. Section 41 FLA provided that where the parties were cohabitants or former cohabitants, in considering the nature of the parties' relationship the court 'is to have regard to the fact that they have not given each other the commitment involved in marriage.' This always was a meaningless provision and it will come as no surprise to learn that this was not part of the Government's original draft Bill   but was accepted as a backbencher's amendment when the progress of the Bill was in difficulty.

Section 2(1) DVCVA repeals s 41 FLA so this is no longer an issue to trouble the court.

Amendments to s 36 FLA

2.37   Section 36 FLA governs the position where the parties are cohabitants or former cohabitants and one party has a right to occupy but the other does not. Subsection (6) sets out the matters to which the court must have regard, and sub-s (6)(e) requires the court to have regard to 'the nature of the parties relationship'.

Section 2(2) DVCVA amends sub-s (6)(e) so that it now reads 'the nature of the parties relationship and in particular the level of commitment attached to it'.

This does not make a material difference to the existing law and in fact makes explicit what was previously implicit.

Certain minor amendments to sub-s (1)(c) are made which change 'lived together as husband and wife' to 'cohabited'.

NON-MOLESTATION ORDERS ON APPLICATION FOR OCCUPATION ORDER

2.38   Section 42(2)(b) FLA provides that the court may make a non-molestation order in any family proceedings to which a respondent is party even though no application has been made if the court considers that such an order should be made for the benefit of any other party or any relevant child. Paragraph 36 of Sch 10 DVCVA amends s 42 FLA by adding two further subsections. Subsection (4A) directs the court, when considering whether to make an occupation order, to consider whether to exercise the power conferred by sub-s (2)(b); in other words it reminds the court of the power it might exercise.

The new sub-s (4B) provides that, in Part IV FLA, the term 'the applicant' includes a person for whose benefit an order is made under sub-s (2)(b), in other words 'any other party or a relevant child'.

Power of arrest and enforcement

2.39   As noted earlier, breach of a non-molestation order is now to be a criminal offence and the power to attach a power of arrest to such an order has been removed. To that end, s 46 FLA has been amended.

It should be made clear however that the court retains the power to attach a power of arrest to an occupation order, so that the procedure for arrest and bringing a contemnor before the county court remains the same. The only difficulty this might bring is where the court chose to make both a non-molestation order and an occupation order. In the event of a breach, a person could be arrested under the power of arrest for breach of the occupation order but not the non-molestation order. It will be interesting to see how the police deal with this difficulty. A further difficulty might be where the court had made an occupation order with a radius clause, eg not to attempt to enter the former home nor to come within 100 metres of it. Breach of such an order might well involve violence but, in the absence of a non-molestation order, would be dealt with under the power of arrest which is normally attached to such a provision. The interesting issue of whether such a radius clause should be classed as an occupation order or a non-molestation order may also become more relevant.

Chapter Three

THE NEW CRIMINAL OFFENCE AND RELATED MATTERS: CAUSING OR ALLOWING THE DEATH OF A CHILD OR VULNERABLE ADULT

Summary

3.1   Section 5 of the DVCVA 2004 creates a new criminal offence of causing or allowing the death of a child or vulnerable adult. The new offence is a significant innovation.[1] It will be committed where a child or vulnerable adult dies as a result of an unlawful act of a person who was a member of the same household as the deceased, and who had frequent contact with him. In order for a defendant to be convicted of the offence, he or she must either have caused the death, or should have been aware that the deceased was at significant risk of serious physical harm and failed to take reasonable steps to prevent that harm.

Consequential evidential changes relating to s 5 also impact on prosecutions for murder or manslaughter on the same facts, modifying the rules relating to inferences from a failure to testify, contained in s 35 of the Criminal Justice and Public Order Act 1994.

This new offence has been introduced to address the problem that arises where it cannot be shown which member of a household caused the death. At present, they may all be acquitted of murder or manslaughter, because of the lack of evidence on this crucial issue. All members of the household (subject to restrictions relating to age or mental incapacity) will be liable in respect of the new offence if the relevant criteria are satisfied.

The maximum punishment for the new offence is 14 years' imprisonment, or an unlimited fine, or both. The offence is indictable only.

---

[1]   Baroness Scotland, Minister of State, Home Office, HL 2nd Reading (15 December 2003), vol 655, col 987.

BACKGROUND

3.2   Each week three infants suffer serious injury or death when in the care of adults who should be protecting them.[2] In many of these cases there is no problem in proving the non-accidental causes of the death or injury, but, rather, the difficulty is in proving who caused that death or harm. On-going concerns at the capacity of the law to get at the truth in such circumstances led to several studies examining how this problem could be overcome whilst maintaining the principle that defendant must only be convicted on a proper evidential basis. In 2003, a NSPCC multi-disciplinary working party published a paper, *Which of you did it?*. It made a series of recommendations designed to improve the flow of information during the investigation.[3] The commencement of that study was the inspiration for a study of the relevant law by the Law Commission, which published its final report in 2003.[4] Section 5 of the DVCVA 2004 draws on, but does not replicate in every respect, the recommendations of the Law Commission.

3.3   Under pre-existing law, if there is no direct evidence showing who caused the non-accidental injury or death, then the defendant, or defendants, must be acquitted, unless the prosecution can establish that the defendants were acting in concert. As Lord Goddard CJ put it in *Abbott*[5]:

> '[there was] a case in which two sisters were indicted for murder, and there was evidence that they had both been in the room at the time when the murder was committed; but the prosecution could not show that either sister A or sister B had committed the offence. Probably one or other must have committed it, but there was not evidence which, and though it is unfortunate that guilty party cannot be brought to justice, it is far more important that there should not be a miscarriage of justice and that the law maintained that the prosecution should prove its case.'

If the evidence shows that one defendant, and one defendant alone, was present when fatal injuries were caused, no evidential problems in this context arise: there is a case to answer against that defendant. By contrast, if there is no evidence adduced by the prosecution to show who was present when fatal injuries were caused, a prosecution will usually fail, irrespective of whether it is for murder, manslaughter or an offence of child cruelty.[6] In *Lane and Lane*[7] a manslaughter conviction of two parents was quashed. There was no evidence

---

[2]   Report from NSPCC Working Group *Which of you did it?* (2003), p 11.

[3]   See n 2 above. The recommendations are at pp 9–10 of the Report.

[4]   *Children: Their Non-Accidental Death Or Serious Injury (Criminal Trials)* Law Com No 282, available on-line at .lawcom.org.uk. For a wider discussion of the issues and possible solutions, see *Law Commission Consultative Paper*, Law Com 279.

[5]   [1955] 2 QB 497, CA. See also *Bellman* [1989] AC 836, HL.

[6]   Under Children and Young Persons Act 1933, s 1, which carries a maximum term of 10 years' imprisonment.

[7]   (1986) 82 Cr App R 5, CA.

to show who was present when the blow was struck that killed the 22-month-old child. Again, in *Aston and Martin*[8], convictions for murder of a 16-month-old child, killed by throwing or battering her against a hard surface, were quashed because of the lack of evidence as to who was present when the fatal injury was inflicted. Nor in that case was there any evidence from which a jury could properly conclude that the defendants were acting in concert.

Of course, if it can be shown that the defendants were acting in concert then different considerations apply. The mere fact that it is not clear which of two or more people was the perpetrator of the alleged offence does not prevent the conviction of all (or any) of them if it can be proved that each must have been either the perpetrator or an accomplice.[9] Occasionally, joint enterprise can be inferred. In *Marsh and Marsh v Hodgson*[10] convictions for causing non-accidental injuries were upheld, because there evidence showed that both defendants had been in joint charge of the child during the period when the injuries probably occurred. In effect, both parents were there all the time.[11] A similar conclusion was reached in *Gibson and Gibson,*[12] where convictions for manslaughter were upheld. There was no evidence to show which parent was responsible for grievous bodily harm suffered by the deceased child, but an inference could properly be drawn that they were jointly responsible. The court distinguished *Abbott* on the basis that, in that case, the deceased was not within the joint custody or control of the defendants. Such conclusions are, though, fraught with difficulty. *Gibson and Gibson* was itself distinguished in *Lane and Lane*[13] where the court concluded that, on the facts, there was no justification for inferring the presence of both defendants or active participation of both parents. On what basis are such inferences to be drawn? A defendant may specifically deny involvement, a denial which in many factual circumstances will make an inference of joint enterprise improper. There may be a failure to offer an explanation for the child's injuries, but it may be that a defendant does not know the true explanation nor has no means of knowing the facts which require explanation.[14] Lack of an explanation can only have evidential value if it happens in circumstances that point to guilt. The evidential provisions of the Criminal Justice and Public Order Act 1994 often will not assist. Although inferences from a failure to mention facts later relied on as part of a defence may attract inferences under s 34 that will in no way assist

---

8   (1991) 94 Cr App R, 180, CA. See also *Strudwick* (1994) 99 Cr App R 326, CA; *S and C* [1996] Crim LR 346, CA, to like effect.
9   Card, Cross and Jones *Criminal Law* (16th ed, Butterworths), para 20.37.
10   [1974] Crim LR 35, DC.
11   The explanation of this case given by Croom-Johnson LJ in *Lane and Lane*, n 6 above.
12   (1985) 80 Cr App R 25, CA. For criticism of this case, see Glanville Williams *Which of you did it?* (1989) 52 MLR 179; Griew *It must have been one of them* [1989] Crim LR 129.
13   See n 6, above.
14   Per Croom-Johnson LJ in *Lane and Lane*, n 6, above.

if the prosecution cannot establish a prima facie case; so, too, with a failure to testify, and the power to draw an inference under s 35.

3.4   These problems may be less acute in cases where child cruelty is charged. Section 1 of the Children and Young Persons Act 1933 makes it an offence for a person having responsibility for a child or young person to wilfully assault, ill-treat, neglect, abandon or expose that child or young person in a manner likely to cause unnecessary suffering or injury to health. There must be an awareness of the risk to the child if the charge is one based on neglect.[15] In such a case there may be evidence of neglect for the jury to consider, because of a failure to seek medical help where it can be shown that a defendant knew that medical help was required.[16] There may well be evidence to sustain a conviction for cruelty because of other conduct, over a period of time.[17]

3.5   A variety of responses to these issues was considered by both the NSPCC and the Law Commission, ranging from more practical inter-agency co-operation, to more fundamental changes in evidence and substantive criminal law. The Royal Commission on Criminal Justice recognised the difficulties in such cases but rejected the possibility of allowing adverse inferences to be drawn from a parent's failure to provide an explanation for a child's injuries.[18] Unsurprisingly, this view was not shared either by the NSPCC or by the Law Commission, and the DVCVA 2004 does permit, by s 6, inferences to be drawn in certain specified circumstances. The Law Commission's approach was, however, much wider than that taken by the new provisions. The Law Commission rejected approaches which would have imposed burdens of proof on defendants,[19] or which would impose requirements (on pain of penalty) to give an account of the child's death or injury.[20] It rejected the use of pre-trial incriminating statements, although that rejection now has to be viewed in the context of changes to the law relating to hearsay statements.[21] The Commission recommended the creation of new offences of cruelty contributing to death, and of failure to protect a child from serious hard resulting from ill-treatment (an offence not confined to serious harm resulting in death).[22] The new law reflects, in part though certainly not in its totality, the approach recommended

---

[15]   *Sheppard* [1981] AC 394, [1980] 3 All ER 899, HL.

[16]   See *S and M* [1995] Crim LR 486, CA.

[17]   See *Lane and Lane* (1987) 82 Cr App R 5, CA; *Strudwick and Merry* (1994) 99 Cr App R 326, CA.

[18]   (1993) Cm 2263, Ch4, para 25. The Royal Commission of course rejected changes in inferences from silence generally, a position rejected by Criminal Justice and Public Order Act 1994.

[19]   Law Commission Report, paras 3.2–3.4.

[20]   Law Commission Report, paras 3.5–3.6.

[21]   Law Commission Report, paras 3 7–3.10. For hearsay changes see para **3.6**, below, and, more generally, Ward and Davies *Criminal Justice Act 2003 – A Practitioners Guide* (Jordans, 2004), Ch 6.

[22]   Law Commission Report, Ch 4.

by the Law Commission, but goes wider in some respects, in particular by extending the new offence to 'vulnerable' persons although on occasion in a somewhat different form. In other respects it draws the law more narrowly, by not extending the new offence to 'serious injury'.

3.6 The recommendations of the Law Commission did not, of course, have regard to the effect, if any, of the changes to the rules relating to evidence of past conduct and hearsay made by the Criminal Justice Act 2003. The provisions relating to character came into force on 15 December 2004.[23]

The effect of these will be, firstly, that evidence of previous abuse of a child by one or more defendants may be admissible in determining which defendant caused the death or injury. Section 101(1)(d) of the Criminal Justice Act 2003 makes a defendant's bad character admissible where it is relevant to an important matter in issue between the defendant and prosecution.[24] Secondly, s 101(1)(e) of the CJA 2003 makes evidence of bad character admissible where it has substantive probative value in relation to an important matter in issue between defendant and co-defendant, which may be important should a trial result in a dispute between defendant and non-defendant as to who caused death or injury. Thirdly, s 114(1)(d) allows hearsay evidence to be admitted if the court is satisfied that it is in the interests of justice for it to be admissible. One can conceive of circumstances where, despite the conclusion of the Law Commission that pre-trial statements by defendants should not be admissible against a co-defendant, a court might conclude that it was appropriate for the court to admit such a statement to assist in determining who caused harm to a child

We return to each of these matters as appropriate during discussion of the new law.

THE NEW OFFENCE

Scope of offence

3.7 The offence created by s 5 is one of *Causing or allowing the death of a child or vulnerable adult.* Two key points are readily apparent. The first is that the new offence does not extend to prosecutions in respect of serious assaults or woundings, or cruelty, which do not result in death. In such cases, the evidential problems described above remain, although, as already noted, a case of cruelty may be easier to establish (because of the duty to seek medical

---

[23] See Ward and Davies *Criminal Justice Act 2003 – A Practitioners Guide* (Jordans, 2004), Chs 5 and 6. The provisions came into force on 15 December 2004.

[24] What is 'an important matter in issue' is defined by CJA 2003, s 103. See, further, para **3.38**.

help)[25] and the provisions of the Criminal Justice Act 2003 may assist. The reasons for such a limitation reflect the Government's caution in the context of an offence that effectively criminalises a breach of duty.

3.8   As noted earlier, the NSPCC Report's concerns were not confined to situations involving fatalities, and, arguably, the problems are no different simply because of the unlawful acts do not, in the event, lead to fatality. [26] The first of the two new offences that had been proposed by the Law Commission (cruelty contributing to death) was indeed confined to conduct resulting in death, but the other changes relating to the offence of failure to protect a child, and the evidential and procedural changes proposed, extended to cases involving serious harm. Whilst it is true that the problems have been illustrated most starkly by cases of homicide, and that they may be less acute in cases where the victim survives, the failure to extend the provisions beyond cases which result in death reflects a cautious approach by Government, perhaps showing an awareness of the difficult balance to be struck between securing convictions and the rights of defendants.

The scope of changes in the law was one issue of some controversy during the passage of the Act through Parliament, and caused the Government 'considerable concern'.[27] The line between death and serious injury is a fine one and depends sometimes on factors which bear no relation to questions of culpability. Baroness Scotland observed:[28]

> 'Why have we confined ourselves to death? The purposes of the new offence are two-fold. First, it is a serious offence in its own right. Secondly, we want it to function in a way that allows us to find, the prime offender, so to speak, in 'which of you did it?' cases.'

The offence of child cruelty under s 1 of the Children and Young Persons Act 1933 will catch cases of serious injury falling short of death, and in such cases the problems are often less acute. The victim will usually be available and able (sometimes) to give information to the police or to testify. Of course, in may of these cases, the victim is too young to give any, or any meaningful, information, and it remains a matter of debate as to whether the Government has been too cautious in preferring an incremental approach to law reform rather than taking on board the wider approach favoured by the NSPCC and Law Commission.

3.9   The second key point is that, unlike the Law Commission's proposals, s 5 extends to both children and to vulnerable adults (hereafter referred to as

---

[25]   See para 3.34 above.
[26]   See the argument of the Criminal Bar Association, cited at Law Com Rep 4.6, but there rejected.
[27]   Baroness Scotland, Minister of State, Home Office, HL Standing Committe (21 January 2004), vol 656, para 340.
[28]   Ibid, col 342.

'V' or 'the victim[s]'). A 'child' is, for this purpose, a person aged under 16 (s 5(6)). The vast majority of victims who will fall within the provisions of s 5 are likely to be significantly younger than 16, and the age of 16 was chosen to ensure consistency with the terms of s 1(1) of the Children and Young Persons Act 1933.[29]

The term 'vulnerable adult' is defined by s 5(6) and applies to a person aged 16 or over, whose ability to protect himself from violence, abuse or neglect is significantly impaired through physical or mental disability or illness, through old age or otherwise. The charge is intended to deal with cases where a vulnerable adult has died in domestic circumstances, where one of the close family members must have been responsible, but the prosecution are unable to say which. As already noted, the inclusion of vulnerable adults goes beyond the proposals of the NSPCC or Law Commission. This is intended to amount to 'a significant change in how we view the responsibility of those in positions of care for vulnerable people, who, quite often, either through age, disability – whether it is mental or physical – are dependant on others for their succour and well being ...'.[30]

3.10 'Physical or mental disability or illness' are not defined. Whether a person's ability to defend himself is 'significantly impaired' will be a matter of fact on which evidence should be adduced and, if disputed, arguably is a matter for the jury to decide. The words 'or otherwise' perhaps serve to confirm that the reasons giving rise to vulnerability are less important than the fact of vulnerability of the victim, but should be construed in the context of the preceding words.[31] That said, the terms of s 5(6) are not as clear as might be: an 85-year-old fail woman, living in sheltered accommodation, would not normally attract the label 'disability' but is surely 'vulnerable' within the meaning of s 5(6). Section 5 is, though, not intended to address issues where the victim is in institutional accommodation, or where V is healthy and well able to care for him or herself, or able to summon relevant help.[32]

3.11 Nothing in the DVCVA 2004 prevents a s 5 offence being combined on the same indictment with a charge of murder, manslaughter, or indeed any other charge arising as a result of the death of a person aged under 16 or of a vulnerable person. The relationship between manslaughter and the new s 5 offence is discussed at para **3.17**. Clearly, however, if a s 5 offence is charged alongside a more serious charge of murder or manslaughter of which a defendant is convicted, a jury will not need to enter a verdict in respect of the

---

[29] Law Com Rep, para 4.1. The argument that 18 should be the chosen age, given the terms of Children Act 1989, s 2, and the UN Convention on the Rights of the Child, was rejected.

[30] Baroness Scotland, Minister of State, Home Office, HL Standing Committee (21 January 2004), vol 656, col 333.

[31] Baroness Scotland, ibid, col 334.

[32] Baroness Scotland, ibid, col 334.

s 5 offence. Given the difficulty which s 5 is intended to overcome, it might be thought that this possibility is small. However, the evidential changes in s 6[33] apply to charges of murder or manslaughter and may have the effect of increasing the potential for conviction on the more serious charge.

The offence

3.12   Section 5 defines the offence as follows:

'(1) A person ("D") is guilty of an offence if –

(a)   a child or vulnerable adult ("V") dies as a result of an unlawful act of a person who:

(i)   was a member of the same household as V; and

(ii)   had frequent contact with him,

(b)   D was such a person at the time of that act;

(c)   at that time was a significant risk of serious physical harm being caused to V by the unlawful act of such a person,

and

(d)   either D was the person whose act caused V's death, or :

(i)   D was, or ought to have been, aware of the significant risk mentioned in para (c)

(ii)   D failed to take such steps as he could reasonably have been expected to take to protect V from the risk; *and*

(iii)   the unlawful act occurred in circumstances of the kind that D foresaw or ought to have foreseen.'

The offence is triable only on indictment, and attracts a maximum term of imprisonment of 14 years, or an unlimited fine, or both (s 5(7))

Who can commit the offence?

3.13   The offence cannot be committed by a person aged under 16 at the date of the act that caused V's death, unless the defendant was the mother or father of V (s 5(3)(a)). That raises questions as to what is the date of such an 'act'. No problem arises in cases where there is a positive series of acts of violence which cause death, although issues of causation may arise. More difficulty arises where the death is due to a series of omissions, for example a pattern of on-going neglect. As noted below, omissions or courses of conduct constitute 'acts' for the purposes of s 5.[34] Difficult issues of causation arise if the date of death occurs after the age of 16 is attained, though one suspects such cases will be few in number.

3.14   There are also limitations contained in s 5(3)(b) which have the effect of limiting criminal liability under s 5 (because of failure) to take such steps as might be reasonably expected to those over 16 years, unless the defendant is the mother or father of V. Thus, where a member of the same household as V

---

[33]   See para **3.33**.

[34]   See para **3.18**.

is the 15-year-old brother of V, there can be no question under s 5 of criminal liability of that 15 year-old, irrespective of what he knew, or might or might not have done. Of course, if that 15-year-old actually caused the death, other offences will have been committed. The evidential changes made by the DVCVA 2004 may overcome problems of proof.[35] Nonetheless, some concerns may arise about a 16- year-old or 17-year-old member of a family being put at risk of prosecution for the new offence,[36] concerns that are not wholly addressed by pointing out that what it is reasonable to expect a 16- or 17-year-old to do to address risks of other family members may well differ from what would be expected of an adult. Such concerns could have been avoided had the Government followed the Law Commission's proposal that criminal liability should attach to those 'responsible' for a child.

What has to be proved?

3.15   The various constituent elements of the offence are discussed below. However, at the outset we should note that the prosecution do not have to prove exactly the basis on which D's criminal liability arises. The offence can be committed either by D having caused the death, or by having failed to take reasonable steps to protect V from the risk of serious physical harm. The prosecution does not have to prove which of these alternatives applies (s 5(2)).

This provision does not appear to infringe the principle against duplicity. A count in an indictment, or charge in information to be tried summarily, which charges or alleges more than one offence infringes that principle. The analogous situation, which may more accurately be described as uncertainty, is where a statutory provision contains one offence, which may be committed by a variety of means, or by virtue of different states of mind. Whether a count may charge simply by reference to the statutory provision, or must allege specific ingredients in more than one count if necessary, is a question of the construction of the relevant statute.[37] In *Courtie* Lord Diplock (with whom the other Law Lords concurred) held that where one provision involved the imposition of different penalties depending on whether the prosecution established particular factual ingredients then Parliament had created two separate offences, and these should be the subject of separate informations. Applying this principle a Divisional Court in *DPP v Corcoran*[38] held that an information charging a failure, without reasonable excuse, to provide a specimen of breath, blood or urine contrary to s 7(6) of the Road Traffic Act 1988, was bad for duplicity, because the maximum punishment for the offence depended on the purpose for which the specimen was being sought. However, a short time later a

---

[35]   See para **3.33** et seq.
[36]   See, eg, Lord Borrie, HL Standing Committee (21 January 2004), vol 655, col 995.
[37]   *Courtie* [1984] AC 463, [1984] 1 All ER 740, HL.
[38]   [1993] 1 All ER 912, DC.

differently constituted court, in dismissing appeals in several cases, overruled *Corcoran* and distinguished *Courtie*. On a construction of the statutory provisions this was one offence: the question of punishment was relevant only to sentence.

The s 5 offence is, arguably, to be regarded as one offence, albeit with two, alternative, means of commission, and probably does not infringe the principle of duplicity if indicted in one count.[39] There is one maximum punishment, and Parliament clearly intends that this one offence can be committed in one of two ways, the prosecution being under no obligation to prove which. Often the prosecution will not know, at the time of charge and arraignment, which route to go down – that is, after all, why the offence has been created. Nonetheless, the appropriate punishment if the defendant is convicted will vary considerably depending on whether D caused the death or, alternatively, failed to take reasonable steps to prevent it. To indict separately, in separate and alternative counts, would avoid arguments of duplicity, and assist a judge in knowing the basis of the jury's verdict should they choose to convict of a s 5 offence. In addition, the concept of a fair trial surely includes the basic right to know what the prosecution case is. A prosecutor who wishes to allege that D caused the death should specifically say so on the indictment, although that may be implicit from charges of murder or manslaughter on the same indictment.

'Unlawful act'

3.16   This is defined by s 5(5). It includes any act that amounts to an offence, or which would be an offence but for the fact that it was the act of a person under the age of 10 (and thus beyond the age of criminal responsibility) or an act of a person entitled to rely on a defence of insanity. In this context one should bear in mind that whether an act is lawful or unlawful usually depends not simply on the nature of the act itself, but also on the circumstances in which it occurs, and the mental state of the person who does the act. The fact that a blow is struck may constitute an assault but might, in certain circumstances, for example a boxing match, not do so.[40] The new s 5 offence requires the act to be unlawful, and thus the whole context of that act have to be considered.

The cryptic last line of s 5(5) ('Paragraph (b) does not extend to an act of D') is intended to ensure, and has the effect of ensuring, that a person aged under 10, or who is insane, is not made criminally liable under s 5(1). However, such a person may be the person who commits the 'unlawful act', and it may be that another person who is aged 10 or over and of sound mind (such as a parent

---

[39]   There is a suggestion from Lord Donaldson that the prosecution must charge separately, referring back to an earlier speech of Baroness Scotland, Minister of State. A perusal of that speech does not indicate any Government intention to require this offence to be indicted separately: see HL Standing Committee (28 January 2004), vol 657, col 162.

[40]   See Card, Cross and Jones, *op cit*, at para 7.53.

or elder sibling) is criminally liable under s 5(1) for that unlawful act commit by the person aged under 10, or who is insane.

3.17 The DVCVA 2004 does not in any way limit the type or nature of the conduct or offence that may constitute the 'unlawful act' for the purposes of s 5. Clearly, the mischief being addressed by s 5 means that murder and the wide range of offences against the person (grievous bodily harm, assaults, sexual offences) obviously fall within the scope of s 5. It might be thought that the scope of s 5 is wide. Arguably, the act itself (if performed in the appropriate circumstances) must be unlawful: by analogy with constructive manslaughter, the negligent performance of a lawful act will not generally suffice.[41]: The 14-year-old boy who is killed by the careless driving of his parent would not (on this view) be killed by an 'unlawful act' for these purposes, although interesting arguments might arise if the parent was driving under the influence of drink or drugs. The Law Commission, in formulating its proposed offence of failure to protect a child, chose to identify the relevant offences by way of a schedule of offences. Section 5 does not follow that approach. What it does do is potentially limit the operation of s 5 by reference to the concept of 'serious harm'. Even if a minor offence causes death, there must be a significant risk of serious physical harm, defined by s 5(6) by reference to 'grievous bodily harm for the purpose of the Offences Against the Person Act 1861. Nonetheless, even relatively minor offences have the potential to cause harm that reaches that threshold.

'Grievous bodily harm' means 'really serious harm'.[42] The level of harm is to be judged objectively.[43] Although it can include serious psychiatric injury,[44] the use of the term 'physical harm' might point to this being outside the scope of s 5. In any event it is unlikely that psychiatric harm will of itself cause death. It is, though, certainly within the bounds of possibility that psychiatric harm might form part of a course of mistreatment, physical or mental, that leads to death, and is not something which a court should be constrained from considering.

3.18 Section 5 speaks of an unlawful 'act'. This term is defined by the *Concise Oxford English Dictionary* as including 'something done, a deed, the process of doing something' and in its normal sense suggests a positive act. But s 5(6) imposes a special meaning, by stating that the term 'act' includes a course of conduct and also includes omission. Thus a systematic series of assaults which cumulatively cause death will be within s 5, as will a failure to

[41] See *Andrews* [1937] AC 576, HL The position may differ in cerain exceptional and extreme circumstances.
[42] *DPP v Smith* [1961] AC 290, [1960] 3 All ER 161, HL.. For discussion of the precise meaning of 'really' see *Saunders* [1985] Crim LR 230, CA; *Janjua & Coudgury* [1999] 1 Cr App R 91, CA.
[43] *Brown & Stratton* [1998] Crim LR 485, CA.
[44] *Ireland; Burstow* [1998] AC 147, [1997] 4 All ER 225.

feed, clothe or seek medical treatment. Omissions can, of course, constitute the offence of cruelty under s 1 of the Children and Young Persons Act 1933, and may constitute manslaughter, by virtue of gross negligence or because of an unlawful act. The relationship between these offences is discussed further, below,[45] but clearly omissions which constitute manslaughter or cruelty are unlawful 'acts' for this purpose.

'Member of the same household'

3.19   The offence applies in the context of the domestic, family, environment, and is not intended to apply to cases where the victim was in public institutional care. The defendant must be a 'member of the same household' at the time of the unlawful act which caused V's death, and have had frequent contact with V (s 5(1) (a), (b)). The concept of 'living in the same household' is used by Part IV of the Family Law Act 1996 to define an 'associated person', and, indeed, is amended by the DVCVA 2004 to include non-cohabiting couples.[46] That is addressed in this context by s 5(4)(a), which provides that a person is to be regarded as a 'member' of a particular household even if he does not live in that household, if he visits it so often and for such periods of time that it is reasonable to regard him as a member of it. No further definition or guidance is given or offered by the Act as to how this is to be applied, and findings of fact will have to be made. No doubt issues such as the number of visits, the length of visits, the extent to which D eats or sleeps with the household, and any financial arrangements will be relevant. The child who spends half the week in the household, and then the other half with an estranged spouse or partner would no doubt be held to be 'living in the same household'. It will be the conclusion of the court that matters, not the state of mind of D, although that will, no doubt, be a relevant consideration in deciding whether in fact it is reasonable to so regard the defendant.

3.20   In deciding who falls within the concept of 'same household', the purpose of the s 5 offence should be borne in mind, that is to punish those who are guilty of, or complicit in, violence within the domestic context.[47] It means those who are living together as a family group in the same house, subject to the broadening out of the concept of 'household' discussed above.[48] The FLA 1996 excludes from its ambit a person in the same household by virtue of being another person's employee (eg live in domestic help), tenant, lodger or border. No such limitation is contained in the DVCVA 2004, which suggests that we should not seek to limit s 5 in this way. Some support for this can be found in

---

[45]   See para **3.33** et seq.
[46]   The DVCVA 2004, s 4. See para **2.14**.
[47]   An adaptation of the Law Com formulation, at para 6.14.
[48]   Baroness Scotland, Minister of State, Home Office, HL Standing Committee (21 January 2004), op cit, col 334.

the Law Commission Report,[49] which concluded that a similar restriction was unnecessary in the context of the new offences it proposed, because their formulation in any event restricted criminal liability to those who had responsibility for the child. Of course, real differences exist between the Law Commission proposals and s 5. The latter is not confined to child victims, and no such limitation as described above in the context of the FLA 1996 is incorporated into s 5. Thus there is probably no problem in categorising the au pair, or live-in staff, lodger or housemaster as part of the same 'household', for the purposes of s 5. By contrast, child carers, babysitters, teachers, social workers working (but not living) in sheltered accommodation are outside the scope of s 5

3.21 It is possible that V lived in different 'households' at different times. Section 5(4)(b) provides that in such circumstances 'the same household as V' refers to the household in which V was living at the time of the act that caused V's death. Given the potential for a course of conduct over a period of time to constitute an 'act', that raises not dissimilar issues of causation and time to those identified at para **3.13.** It must be shown that D's action (ie course of conduct, including omissions), *caused* the death. Where V has been, intermittently, a member of more than one household, a court will have to determine that it was D's actions that were the substantive cause of death. Of course, any failure of the prosecution to satisfy the court to the criminal standard of proof that this is so will mean that the charge is not made out.

3.22 The prosecution must show 'frequent contact' between V and the individual who caused the death of V. That is a question of fact. A person may be part of the same household, but have infrequent contact. The student who has a 'gap-year' travelling the world may be part of the same household but nonetheless has limited contact; so, too, with the student away at university, or the husband working away, perhaps overseas. Difficulties will arise if, on their return, the death of a child or vulnerable adult occurs. Further, even if a decision is made on the facts that D *is* a member of the same household, the level of presence will be relevant to the separate question about what actions it would be reasonable to expect D to have taken.

'Significant risk of serious physical harm'

3.23 The prosecution must show that there was a significant risk of serious physical harm being caused to V by the unlawful act of 'such a person'. The meaning of this last phrase is not entirely clear. Obviously it refers to a person who falls within s 5(1)(a) (member of the same household, etc), but it is less clear that the anticipated risk must be in a risk in respect of the person who causes the death, as opposed to any member of that household. Arguably, it is

---

[49]   Law Com Rep, para 6.16.

the former: the purpose of the s 5 offence is to criminalise a failure to protect against known risks. In any event the point is theoretical rather than real, because if the anticipated risk is not from the person who actually causes the death, it can hardly be said that D 'has failed to take reasonable steps' to protect V from the risk, within the meaning of s 5(1)(d).

3.24 The level of risk is important, so as not to criminalise those who are careless with the safety of the child or vulnerable person, who then is killed by an unlawful act.[50] 'Risk' relates to the probability that a harmful event or behaviour will occur.[51] The risk must be 'significant', a term that certainly distinguishes those risks that are trivial or remote. The Law Commission formulation used the term 'real', pointing out that in *Re H and Others (Minors)(Sexual Abuse: Standard of Proof)*[52] Lord Nicholls had equated 'likely' with 'real', describing a real risk as one 'that ought not to be ignored'. The choice of 'significant' rather than 'real' might, on the other hand, suggest a higher standard, and reflecting the fact that s 5 is criminalising failures to take action in response to those risks.

It will, arguably, be for the judge to decide what the level of risk is. If the prosecution were to fail to establish, in the mind of the trial judge, that there was evidence showing a significant risk, a submission of no case to answer by the defence would inevitably succeed, although that statement must be viewed in the context of the evidential changes made by s 6.[53] If the judge takes the view there is evidence supporting a conclusion of 'significant risk', it will then be for the jury to conclude as to what level that risk was and the level of steps the defendant could have been expected to take in the light of that level of risk.

The risk is one of which the defendant was aware, or ought to have been aware (s 5(1)(d)(i)). The wording of that provision ('…of the risk mentioned in paragraph (c)…') confirms that the defendant must be aware that the risk is a significant risk, and is one of serious physical harm. Whether the risk is one of which the defendant 'ought to have been aware' introduces an objective element, and is not to be determined in purely subjective terms, because the defendant cannot escape criminal liability by being so careless of the safety of the victim that they did not think there was any risk when they ought to have done so.[54] On the other hand the standard is not that of the reasonable person but, rather, whether that particular individual ought to have been aware of the significant risk of serious physical harm. That will turn on the whole picture: the characteristics of the defendant, and the circumstances of the relationship

---

50   Law Com Rep, para 6.20.
51   See Kemshall *Reviewing Risk* (Home Office, 1997) and the sources therein cited.
52   [1996] AC 563, HL.
53   See para **3.28** et seq.
54   Law Com Rep, para 6.23.

of the defendant with others, including the victim. The Law Commission, in its formulation, made specific provision for the disregard of voluntary intoxication.[55] The DVCVA 2004 does not, but arguably that is unimportant. Clearly the state of sobriety of the defendant is one of the many factors to which a court will have regard, but there is no reason why, as is usual in the criminal law, the position of the law in this context should be any different from that in others. Voluntary intoxication does not remove the obligation to have regard to the risks appertaining to those in the same household. It may provide an explanation as to why the mind of the defendant did not address the issue, but that is not the issue: it is whether the defendant ought to have addressed the issue.

3.25 The significant risk that the prosecution must show is one of serious physical harm caused to V by the *unlawful* act of a person who is a member of the same household, etc. The term 'unlawful' is intended to ensure that what is criminalised is criminal, and not accidental, harm resulting in death. That said, if of course the neglect is such as to amount to manslaughter then the threshold for a s 5 offence will be reached. The Law Commission's equivalent offence was framed by reference to a real risk of the commission of specified offences. By contrast, s 5 requires the significant risk to be one of 'serious physical harm'. This term is not defined and, as already noted,[56] some doubt must exist as to the extent (if at all) mental trauma may fall within the terms of s 5. The 'serious physical harm' must naturally flow from the unlawful act, but it does not inevitably follow from that that the offence must *of itself* be one that involves serious physical harm. Thus the driver of a car who has an accident whilst driving with excess alcohol has, by his or her unlawful act, caused the fatality, and yet it can hardly be said that the relevant offence of itself causes serious physical harm. Alternatively, it may be that s 5 should be limited in its effect to incidents, or risks, of deliberately inflicted harm. That would fit well with the rationale underpinning the introduction of the offence and, arguably, is the better view.

Death caused by D, or D's failure to take steps

3.26 Clearly, if the prosecution can prove the above, to the appropriate standards and V dies as a result, the offence is made out. Given that the purpose of the offence is to deal with the 'who did it?' type of cases, it may well be that this will be achieved only in a minority of cases.

As an alternative it suffices if the prosecution show that D failed to take such steps as he could reasonably have been expected to take to protect V from the risk. It is possible to envisage a situation where, indeed, there was a failure

---

[55]   Op cit, para 6.32.
[56]   See para **3.17**.

to take steps to protect V from the risk of serious physical harm, but where the death followed an unlawful act of a member of the household that was not within the anticipated risk. In that situation there is no s 5 offence. The Act in this context links together the risk, the death and failure to take reasonable steps. That is clear from the purpose of the legislation, and, more specifically, from the wording of s 5(1) (d) (iii) ('that [the death] occurred in circumstances of the kind that D foresaw or ought to have foreseen')[57]

3.27 What amount to the steps that D could have reasonably be expected to take will be a matter of fact, to be determined by the jury. The concept is partly objective. It will not be enough for the matter to be judged on what *this* defendant thought it was appropriate to do. The matter is one which is part of the prosecution case, however the case is presented to the jury, and thus the prosecution will have to adduce evidence that shows that D failed to take reasonable steps, because otherwise it will have failed to establish a prima facie case and a submission of no case to answer would be bound to succeed.[58] Evidence that shows opportunity to report or intervene, whether to the police, social services, voluntary agencies or to responsible adults (whether in outside the family), or evidence that D could have taken other actions to prevent opportunities arising where V was at significant risk will all be relevant. So, too, may appropriate evidence from neighbours, friends, health visitors and other professionals aware of the family situation. The judge, and ultimately the jury (if the case gets that far), will then have to make a judgment about what was reasonable for this defendant to do. That *does* involve a subjective element, looking at the intelligence and personal qualities of the defendant, the circumstances of the household and the defendant's position in it, his or her age and any other relevant factors. Thus the steps reasonably expected of a 16-year-old suffering from learning difficulties will, and probably should, be very different from those expected from an adult who has responsibilities for the victim. Perhaps the nature and relationship with the victim is relevant. The court will need to look at all relevant matters, drawing such inferences from them as the evidence supports.

Proof

3.28 Nothing in s 5 places the burden of proof on the defendant. It is for the prosecution to establish the component elements. This includes whether the defendant knew, or ought to have known, of the significant risk, and whether he or she failed to take such steps as he or she could reasonably be expected to take. This may be a difficult matter for the prosecution to establish, and could, perhaps, reduce the utility of the new s 5 offence. The Law Commission observed:[59]

---

[57]   For discussion of this concept, see para **3.24**.
[58]   See also para **3.24**.
[59]   Law Com Rep, op cit, para 6.29.

'It may be a difficult task for the prosecution, but a balance has to be struck. It must be remembered that such a prosecution will be brought only when, the jury will know , the child[60] will have suffered harm. It is easy to judge with hindsight and we think that the risk of a jury doing so (against which a judge would no doubt warn them) would be enhanced if an evidential burden were placed on the defendant. A defendant ought to be convicted only where the jury is sure that any reasonable person in the defendant's position would have taken action and that should be for the prosecution to prove. Whilst we can see that it might not always be straightforward for the prosecution, we believe that for the most part in the commonplace situation in which offences against children occur it will be a matter of obvious common sense to identify what it was reasonable to expect the responsible person to do.'

That view was, though, taken in the context of a variety of evidential changes that would have assisted in the proof of the case.[61] Those changes are not, in most respects, implemented by the DVCVA 2004, and this may in some instances result in the prosecution facing real challenges. As already noted, the s 5 case will no doubt be proved through evidence of a variety of types: evidence of the conduct and injuries that led to the death of the victim; evidence of domestic relationships in the household, evidence as to the whereabouts of the defendant at critical times, statements of fact and admissions to the police, the evidence of neighbours, friends and other members of the family, the evidential value of evidence of bad character, or of lies. Evidence of bad character could be of various types. It may be evidence of acts of physical violence against the victim, which might well be admissible under s 101(1)(d) of the Criminal Justice Act 2003.[62] It could be evidence of a general propensity to neglect, or indifference to the welfare of the victim. In a case based upon a failure to act (bearing in mind that the prosecution does not have to prove whether it was the defendant who actually killed, or merely failed to prevent the death) the court will be asked to draw the inference that any reasonable person in the defendant's position would have taken steps to prevent whatever happened from occurring. What will not be possible is to adduce expert evidence as to what a reasonable person would do, because that would be the very matter in issue, and the ultimate issue for the jury.[63]

3.29 The prosecution will not have the help of any testimony in court (or lack of it) of the defendant, at any rate until a case to answer has been established. It may well have statements made by the defendant during investigation. In this context, care will need to be exercised by those investigating the case. In some cases it will be only too clear that V was unlawfully killed, and that it could only have been, say, one of the two parents

---

[60] The Law Commission proposal, unlike s 5, was only addressing the issue of child victims.

[61] See para **3.5**.

[62] In this context, see CJA 2003, s 103, and Criminal Justice Act 2003 (Categories of Offences) Order 2004, SI 2004 No 3346.

[63] *Turner* [1975] QB 834, CA; *cf Davies* [1962] 3 All ER 97, CA; *DPP v A &BC Chewing Gum Ltd* [1968] 1 QB 159, DC.

(the classic 'who did it?' situation). It may be fairly easy, therefore, to identify those parents as suspects and deal with them accordingly. PACE Code C in particular deals with the rights of a suspect in respect of caution, legal advice and interview. But in the context of a s 5 charge based on a failure to take reasonable steps, the facts may not be so clear cut. Statements later used by the prosecution to establish a failure to take reasonable steps will amount in law to confessions.[64] At a difficult time involving a family death, judgments will have to be made as to when the investigation shows that there are grounds to suspect that D has committed a s 5 offence, and thus should be cautioned under para 10.1 of Code C.[65] A failure to get that right will imperil the admissibility of answers given when D should have been cautioned.

3.30   It will not, though, always be possible to draw inferences from silence. Section 34 of the Criminal Justice and Public Order Act 1994 permits a court to draw such inference as is proper from a failure when being questioned under caution to mention a fact later relied on as part of his defence. Whilst facts relating to the reasons why the defendant did not act to prevent serious harm to the victim would be facts 'relied on as part of [the defence]', at the stage when the prosecution has to discharge its duty to establish a case to answer those matters will not be before the court. Although matters can be raised as part of one's defence by being put to prosecution witnesses,[66] that will not invariably occur, and, indeed, it could be argued that one is entitled to put the prosecution to proof of integral parts of its case without bringing s 34 into play.[67]

Nor will s 35 of the CJPOA 1994 assist. The prosecution will have to demonstrate the existence of a case to an answer, and the burden of providing an evidential basis to make a case under s 5(1)(d) arises before the defendant has to testify. For these reasons, the failure of the DVCVA 2004 to implement some of the evidential changes proposed by the Law Commission is curious.

3.31   Of course, once the prosecution has established that there is a case to answer, the situation changes dramatically. A failure to adduce evidence at

---

[64]   A confession is a statement wholly or partly adverse to the maker: PACE, s 76(8). Anything used to support failure to take reasonable steps which comes from statements made by D is thus a confession

[65]   The relevant part of Code C states: 'A person whom there are grounds to suspect of an offence must be cautioned before any questions about an offence, or further questions if the answers provide the grounds for suspicion, are put to them if either the suspect's answers or silence (ie failure or refusal to answer or answer satisfactorily) may be given in evidence to a court in a prosecution'. Certain limited exceptions to that are specified in para 10.1.

[66]   *B (MT)* [2000] Crim LR 181, CA; *Webber* [2004] 1 All ER 770, HL. For further discussion of relevant principles relating to s 34 see *Beckles* [2004] All ER (D) 226, HL.

[67]   For the same reason, the enhanced defence statement provisions in Criminal Procedure and Investigations Act 1996, inserted therein by CJA 2003 (when in force) will not always assist. See, generally, Ward & Davies, op cit, ch 3.

all will leave the prosecution in a strong position, with conviction highly likely. Reliance on facts by way of explanation as to what happened to cause death, or who caused it, or to establish that reasonable steps were taken to prevent serious injury to V will be judged in the light of s 34 of the CJPOA1994, and any inference that the court chooses to draw will strengthen a prosecution case that has already crossed the threshold of sufficiency of evidence. In such circumstances it will also be difficult for the defendant to avoid testifying. The s 5 offence will thus have achieved another of its aims, of flushing out the defendant from his or her stance of silence, forcing the defendant to give an explanation as to what really happened. As it was put in the House of Lords[68]:

> 'We should be aiming for something clear, simple and well-focussed initially to add to the statute book ... this is strengthened if we look at the second purpose of the offence: to use to aid identification of the prime offender. For this to work the maximum penalty needs to be set under the level of the prime offence. So our proposal ... set the maximum penalty at 14 years, given that the maximum penalty for murder and manslaughter is life. This provides the incentive for the lesser offender to break ranks and give evidence ...'

It is this aspect that has been one of the concerns during the passage of the Act: that effectively s 5 forces the defendant to testify, and de facto removes his right of silence. Coupled with the evidential change, discussed at para **3.33** et seq, some have concerns that human right issues are engaged.

3.32   The Government believe s 5 to be convention-compliant. That is not the view of the Joint Committee on Human Rights, which concluded that s 5 did not pose a significant threat of a violation of a Convention right.[69] The prosecution have to prove the case in the normal way, and establish a prima facie case. Thus by the time the defendant decides whether or not to testify the prosecution will have established a set of facts which merit explanation. The real Human Rights difficulties come from the combination of s 5 and the changes to rules of evidence in cases of murder or manslaughter, which will often be combined with a s 5 charge. These are discussed below.

Amendments to the evidential rules in cases of murder or manslaughter

3.33   Inherent in the Law Commission's scheme were changes to evidential and procedural rules. It proposed that a person who had responsibility for the welfare of a child should be subject to a statutory responsibility, to give such account as they can for the death or injury. In some circumstances the judge would not rule as to whether a case to answer existed in respect of the new

---

[68]   Baroness Scotland, Minister of State, Home Office, HL Standing Committee (21 January 2004), vol 656, col 341.
[69]   Joint Cmtte, 2003/2004, 3rd Report, para 2.7, to be found at http:// www.publications.parliament.uk/pa/jt.200304/

offence until the close of the defence case, and that amendments be made to s 35 of the Criminal Justice and Public Order Act 1994 to allow silence at trial to be used to assist in convicting the defendant even if he or she could not properly be committed solely on the other evidence in the case. This last change would have, in this type of case, overturned the *now* well-established principle in *Cowan*.[70] The Commission thought that each of these changes was necessary if the problems that occurred in cases like *Lane and Lane*, and which are the very problems the legislation is addressing, were to be overcome.

3.34   None of these changes are made by the DVCVA 2004 in that form. As already noted,[71] whether a defendant is guilty of the new s 5 offence is to be determined under the existing rules of evidence. although consequential changes are made to the rules of evidence applicable in charges of murder or manslaughter tried with a s 5 offence. The Act does not contain the proposed 'Statutory Responsibility', which was an integral part of the scheme proposed by the Law Commission, the Government preferring to implement a different offence than that proposed by the Commission.[72]

The prosecution, on a s 5 prosecution must demonstrate a sufficient case and the defence can make the appropriate submission of no case to answer. For the reasons explained at para **3.27** the inference provisions in s 34 of the Criminal Justice and Public Order Act 1994 will not always apply, and the s 35 provisions will not, by definition, apply at the stage when the prosecution has to demonstrate a case to answer. The reasons why this cautious approach was taken reflect the combination of a new type of offence that, effectively, imposes a 'duty of care' on an individual, and concerns about the compatibility with Art 6 of the European Convention on Human Rights of wider evidential changes in the context of s 5. It may also reflect a belief that in most cases, including the cases of complete silence where are the typical cases being addressed by this provision, it may be relatively straightforward to demonstrate a case to answer. That would certainly be true if s 5 were to be construed as imposing an evidential burden on the defendant to explain his or her failure to act. It does not do that, at least not until the prosecution has demonstrated the existence of a prima facie case. The Government also hope that the structure of s 5, and the evidential change described below, will encourage defendants to testify.

3.35   It is intended that, where appropriate, charges based on s 5 will be accompanied by charges for the more serious offences of murder or manslaughter, and the effect of s 6 is in reality to give the prosecutor an incentive to do so. The DVCVA 2004 changes the evidential position in such cases where

---

[70]   [1996] QB 373, CA.

[71]   See para **3.28**.

[72]   Baroness Scotland, Minister of State, Home Office, HL Standing Committee (21 January 2004), vol 656, col 371.

murder and/or manslaughter are charged in the same proceedings as a s 5 offence

Section 6 applies where a defendant is charged *in the same proceedings* with an offence of murder or manslaughter and with an offence under s 5 in respect of the same death. It does not matter on what basis the charge under s 5 is being put. The same proceedings presumably mean on the same indictment, a factor to be borne in mind if there were any application to sever the indictment.

3.36 In respect of the s 5 offence, if the defendant does not testify, or refuses to answer a question, a jury may draw such inference as is proper from that failure or refusal. Although a defendant cannot be convicted solely on an inference (CJPOA 1994, s 38) by that stage the prosecution will have established its case to answer, and s 38 will not operate to limit the jury. Nor will the principle in *Cowan*, which remains unchanged for the purposes of s 5.[73]

Section 6(2) provides that, where a jury is entitled to draw an inference under s 35 in respect of the s 5 offence, the court may also draw such inference as appears proper in determining whether the defendant is guilty (a) of murder or manslaughter, or (b) of any other offence of which he could lawfully be convicted on the charge of murder or manslaughter. It is also supplemented by s 6(4) which provides that the question of whether there is a case to answer on the murder or manslaughter charge is not to be considered until the close of all evidence on the s 5 offence (or until the time when he ceases to be charged with the s 5 offence)

3.37 These are significant changes. Section 6(2) modifies the rule in *Cowan*. Although it remains the case that the defendant cannot be convicted *solely* on an inference (1994 Act, s 38), the rule in *Cowan* required that the prosecution establish a case to answer before an inference could be drawn under s 35. The Law Commission criticised that rule as 'unduly artificial ... that the only legitimate meaning of "a situation which clearly calls for an explanation" is that on the evidence, without any inference being drawn, a jury could convict a particular defendant.'[74] The Government agreed with that analysis. As Baroness Scotland put it:[75]

> 'We do not think the strict requirement in *Cowan* should apply in these cases ... The key question is whether the circumstances where an inference can be drawn are such that they call for an explanation from the defendant ...'.

The change made by s 6(4) postpones decisions as to the case to answer until the conclusion of the evidence on the s 5 offence. By that time, the defendant

---

[73]   [1996] QB 373, CA. Law Commission's proposals would have led to modification of the *Cowan* principle.

[74]   Law Com Rep, op cit, citing the formulation from *Cowan*.

[75]   Minister of State, Home Office, HL Standing Committee (28 January 2004), vol 657, col 157.

will have testified (or not testified, as the case may be) on the s 5 offence. He will therefore have given his version of events in respect of the death with which he is charged, and effectively he has testified in respect of the charge of murder or manslaughter. In short, the combination of the s 5 charge and the s 6 evidential changes flush out the defendant in a 'who did it? type of case, which is the clear intention of the carefully constructed provisions of the Act.

3.38 But are these changes, which were strenuously debated in Parliament, Convention-compliant? The principle against self incrimination and the right of silence are key (though not absolute) parts of the Art 6 fair trial provisions.[76] A conviction based wholly or mainly on an inference potentially infringes *art 6*.[77] In *Murray v United Kingdom* the Court of Human Rights stated:

> '…before inferences can be drawn [under the relevant provision] appropriate warnings must have been given to the accused as to the legal effects of maintaining silence … The question in each case is whether the evidence adduced by the prosecution is sufficiently strong to require an answer. The national court cannot conclude that the accused is guilty merely because he chooses to remain silent. It is only if the evidence against the accused "calls" for an explanation which the accused ought to be able to be in a position to give that a failure to give an explanation "may as a matter of commonsense allow the drawing of an inference that there is no explanation an that the accused is guilty." Conversely if the case presented by the prosecution had so little evidential value that it called for no answer, a failure to provide one could not justify an inference of guilt.'

In these cases, the argument to demonstrate compliance with Art 6 relies on the totality of the proceedings as opposed to the individual charge. They will already have been shown a case to answer on the s 5 charge, without any inference. If no case on s 5 arises, the question of whether there is a case on the murder or manslaughter charge will have then to be determined. The prosecution will already have demonstrated that a death had occurred, that that death was caused by a member of the household, and that the defendant was a member of that household. It will have also produced evidence capable of proving that either the defendant caused the death or was aware of the risk to the deceased and did not take reasonable steps to prevent serious harm. That, it is argued, entitles the law to call for an explanation.[78]

3.39 The Joint Committee on Human Rights, after considerable concerns, concluded[79] that the Government were entitled to conclude that there was no significant risk of s 6 giving rise to incompatibility with Art 6. That said, the provisions do effectively put a defendant in a position where he has little choice

---

[76]   *Murray v United Kingdom* (1996) 22 EHRR 29, ECHR; *Saunders v United Kingdom* (1997) 2 BHRC 358, ECHR; *Beckles v United Kingdom* (2003) 36 EHRR 13, ECHR.

[77]   *Murray v United Kingdom*, above n 72.

[78]   Baroness Scotland, Minister of State, Home Office, HL Standing Committee, op cit, col 156.

[79]   2003/2004, 4th Report, paras 2.12 -2.13.

but to testify. If he does not, he risks an inference in respect of both the s 5 offence and the charge of murder or manslaughter for the decision on the latter will not be taken until the conclusion of the evidence on the s 5 charge. Any inference on the murder or manslaughter can bolster a shaky prosecution case where the evidence does not otherwise establish a prima facie case. It will be open to a defendant to make a submission of no case on the murder or manslaughter charge, at the end of the evidence. If that is accepted that, of course, is the end of the case on that charge; if it is not, it is still open to the defendant to put to the jury that it should not draw an inference or, even with an inference, it should not convict of murder. Given the case that is likely to have been established under s 5 that may be a difficult argument to sustain.

The alternative is that the defendant testifies. The jury will have heard the defendant's version of events, and his or her explanation. It may well have heard about the bad character of the defendant. The legislation has then achieved the objective set by the NSPCC, Law Commission and Government.

Chapter Four

TRIAL WITHOUT JURY FOR MULTIPLE OFFENCES

Summary

4.1 Section 17 of the Domestic Violence, Crime and Victims Act 2004 ('DVCVA') permits the prosecution to apply to the Crown Court to request that the trial of some, but not all, of the counts included in an indictment be conducted without a jury. Any such order will specify the counts to be tried without a jury, and be made at a preparatory hearing. The effect will be that a jury trial will be held in respect of a sample count or counts, with other, multiple, counts being tried by judge alone. Section 18 deals with the effects of such an order.

This innovation is intended to implement some of the recommendations of the Law Commission Report, 'The Effective Prosecution of Multiple Offending',[1] and designed to ensure the more effective prosecution of multiple offending.

THE BACKGROUND

4.2 Cases of fraud raise particular issues in respect of multiple charges. So, too, do offences such as theft, counterfeiting, corruption and internet child pornography,[2] although these issues can arise in a wide variety of settings. At the heart of the issue are questions about the length and nature of indictments and the basis on which a defendant may be sentenced if convicted on sample counts. Until relatively recently a pragmatic approach was taken in such cases, with charges being selected to reflect a wider range of offending. Indeed, the Royal Commission on Criminal Justice[3], whilst considering restrictions on jury trial to be outside its remit, echoed the calls from professional bodies for the number of counts on an indictment to be kept to a minimum. However, the

---

[1] Law Com No 277, October 2002.
[2] Examples specifically identified by the Law Commission, op cit, para 1.1, fn 2.
[3] 1993, Cm 2263, HMSO, Ch 8, para 71.

decision in *Kidd*[4] removed the possibility of maintaining this position, and created the problem that s 14 is designed to cure.

4.3   An indictment may charge only one offence in each count.[5] A 'charge' reflects 'one activity',[6] which can, on occasion, involve more than one act. Two exceptions to this rule exist.

The first exception are cases of 'general deficiency', defined by the Law Commission[7] as cases 'in which the evidence does not disclose the precise dates and amounts of each individual transaction but where it is clear on the evidence that there has been a large amount of property taken.'

The second exception is in respect of cases which constitute a 'continuous offence'. This is where:

> 'the individual transactions are known but where there are many transactions of the same type, frequently individually of small value against the same victim, and it is convenient in order to reflect the overall criminality to put them together in one information, or one count, so that the criminality can be proved, without prejudice to the defendant and having regard to the known defence, then the court will be in a situation to sentence appropriately.'[8]

In *Barton* the accused had stolen a total of £1,338.23 from the till at which she worked, on 94 occasions over a period of a year. The Law Commission accepted that whether acts constitute a single criminal enterprise is a matter of fact and degree, but clearly it had real doubts about the decision, categorising it as 'stretching the concept of what constitutes a single continuous offence capable of being charged in a single count about as far as it can properly be taken.'[9] The difficulties of the approach in *Barton* were highlighted by the Law Commission: how would the sentencing judge In a Crown Court trial (which this was not) know what level of offending had been found to exist by the jury?

4.4   Except in cases that can be brought within one of the two exceptions summarised above, multiple offending must be the subject of separate counts. The defendant is entitled to have each proved, and should only be sentenced in respect of what has been proved. This was the rationale of the decision in *Kidd*.[10] In that case the defendant was convicted on four specimen counts of indecent assault. The judge used them as specimen examples for the purpose of sentencing for the totality of the offending. This approach was said by the

---

4   Otherwise known as *Canavan* [1998] 1 WLR 604, CA.
5   Indictment Rules 1971, r 4(2).
6   *DPP v Merriman* [1973] AC 584 per Lord Diplock.
7   Report, op cit, para 3.4.
8   *Barton* [2001] Cr App R, DC, per Kennedy LJ.
9   Law Commission Report, op cit, para 3.9. The Divisional Court certified a point of law of general public importance arose in that case.
10   [1998] 1 WLR 604, CA, otherwise known as *Canavan*.

Court of Appeal to be wrong, Lord Bingham approving the decision in *Clark*[11]
where it had held that it was not open to a sentencer to sentence on the basis
that the offence of which the defendant had been convicted was aggravated
by unproven, separate and distinct allegations. To view sample counts as
indicative of total offending was wrong, the court disapproving *Mills*,[12] where
the sentencing court took the view that by convicting on the same transaction
(corrupt receipt of payments) the jury had inevitably[13] accepted the totality of
the multiple offending.

In *Kidd,* the actual sentence imposed was held not to be inappropriate for the
offences of which he was actually convicted, pointing to the fact that in a sexual
case the level of seriousness of even a few such offences means that the
problem of multiple counts is not always a crucial one. In fraud cases, cases
of multiple theft and deception, the value of the totality may be crucial to the
sentencer having a clear basis for reflecting the seriousness of the offence.[14]

4.5   Adding multiple counts to an indictment is not necessarily a practical
solution. In *Novac*,[15] the court deprecated long, complicated indictments and
trials. So, too, in *Cohen.*[16] In *Evans*[17] the prosecutor presented a multiple
benefit fraud case in 24 counts. Mantel LJ observed that 'had every cheque
which had been procured been included in this indictment as a separate offence,
there would have been 200 counts or more ... We cannot see any judge
embarking on a trial with a jury in those circumstances with any degree of
enthusiasm and without firmly insisting that the number of counts be substantially
reduced.' The court in *Evans* also pointed out that the defendant who pleads
guilty to multiple offending may be in a worse position than a defendant who
contests but has been convicted of sample counts. As the Law Commission
put it:[18]

> 'Since *Evans* it is clear that in multiple fraud cases of this type, the defendant
> who pleads guilty to all of his or her offending is liable to a heavier sentence
> than one who goes to trial on a limited number of counts. This is contrary to
> basic principles of fairness and cannot be right. It emasculates a principal feature
> of sentencing and court procedure, that, as a starting point, there should be one
> third discount for a timely guilty plea.'

The Commission thus identified the tension between the two fundamentals –
that an offender should not be sentenced for something that it has not been
proved he did, and the need to reflect the totality of the offending. Yet it also

---

[11]   [1996] 2 Cr App R 282, CA.
[12]   (1979) 68 Cr App R 154, CA.
[13]   That was the case found to exist in *Bradshaw* [1997] Crim LR 239, CA.
[14]   See *Adewuyi* [1997] 1 Cr App R (S) 254, CA; *Stewart* (1987) 9 Cr App R (S) 135, CA.
[15]   (1976) 65 Cr App R 107, CA.
[16]   [1992] NLJR 1267, CC.
[17]   [2000] 1 Cr App R (S) 144, CA.
[18]   Law Commission Report, op cit, para 3.14.

recognised that a number of factors limit the likely impact of the principle in *Kidd* in cases involving sexual offences, downloading of indecent images or possession of obscene material or similar offences. Theft and fraud are likely to be the areas in which it causes serious problems.

The Law Commission's proposal

4.6   After extensive consultation, the Law Commission made three separate recommendations which, together, would address the problem caused by *Kidd*.

The first recommends the extension of the ambit of the offence of fraudulent trading, in s 458 of the Companies Act 1985, to the non-corporate trader. This would allow an individual to be prosecuted in a single count for *the activity* of fraudulent trading, though that activity might be made up of a number of otherwise discrete offences.

The second recommendation is that where a defendant is being tried for an offence which might be regarded as a 'continuous offence'[19], special verdicts be permitted.

The third is that where there are allegations of repetitious offending which are not apt to be described as a continuous offence but which, prior to *Kidd*, could have been dealt with by means of specimen counts, there be a two-stage procedure. The first stage would involve trial before judge and jury on an indictment containing specimen counts. In the event of conviction on one or more counts, a second stage might follow, involving trial by judge and judge alone. At that stage the judge would determine issues of guilt in respect of offences linked, at a pre-trial hearing, to a specimen count of which the defendant has been convicted.[20]

4.7   The Law Commission considered that this two-tiered approach preserves jury trial in respect of core examples of the offending, ensures that jury trial is manageable and comprehensible, and ensures that a defendant does not take advantage of the practical limitations of jury trial and as a result go unpunished. It would ensure defendants are sentenced only in respect of offences of which they have been tried and convicted, encourage defendants to plead guilty, yet fully recognise the principles described above.

It is this two-tiered approach that the DVCVA implements. No action is taken, in this Act, to implement the first or second recommendations summarised above.

4.8   It explained its proposal as follows:[21]

---

[19]   As to which, see para **4.3**.
[20]   See Law Commission Report, op cit, Executive Summary, para 6.
[21]   Law Commission Report, op cit, paras 7.2–7.6.

'In essence the scheme borrows elements from two familiar procedures – the trial of a sample count and the *Newton* hearing. It combines them in a process in which the jury trial … is a definitive element. At the ends of the two stage trial the judge can sentence the offender for the full range of criminal activity … the first stage of the procedure would be a conventional jury trial on an indictment containing charges to show samples of the offending. The second stage would take place only in the event of a guilty verdict on one or more counts tried before the jury. The trial judge will have made a ruling at the end of stage one on the further disposal of the case … At stage two, the judge would decide on the guilt or innocence of the defendant in respect only of offences linked to those upon which the jury has convicted. Those linked offences will have been pre-selected and placed in a schedule attached to an indictment. The schedule would reflect the full extent of the alleged offending. The offences will be listed, as appropriate, in groups and each group linked with a specific sample count in the indictment …

After hearing evidence and argument the judge would decide whether or not the defendant is guilty of any, some or all of the scheduled offences. It is of crucial importance to emphasise that the judge at the second stage will not be bound by the convictions of the jury at stage one, but will be free to come to his or her own view of the evidence, even if that conclusion may be thought to be inconsistent with that of the jury with which, on occasions, the judge was undoubtedly find him or herself in disagreement. There will be no presumption of, or necessary expectation of, further findings of guilt. The judge will of course be aware of the conviction and may well be aware of the evidence … This is not a cause for concern because … a case will only be ruled as suitable for this procedure if the evidence on, and conviction of, the specimen and linked offences would be cross-admissible before any tribunal of fact…'.

The detailed points raised by this summary are discussed below.

4.9   The Law Commission did not consider its proposals to raise Human Rights Act 1998 issues. Those might arise if the courts had not, in *Kidd*,[22] limited the right of a court to sentence in respect of the totality of offending not always established by a proper finding of fact, but there is no inalienable right to trial by jury as part of the Art 6 right to a fair trial provisions. Further, jury trial on sample counts is built into this two-stage procedure, and is, it concluded,[23] a proportionate response to the problems of multiple offending.[24]

This confidence was shared by the Joint Committee on Human Rights in its 3rd Report for 2003–2004, when it examined the provisions of what is now the

---

[22]   See para **4.4**.

[23]   Report, op cit, para 7.78.

[24]   Applying the principles stated in *de Freitas v Permanent Secretary of Ministry of Agriculture Fisheries Land and Housing* [1999] 1 AC 69, HL: (i) whether the legislative objective is sufficiently important to justify limiting a fundamental right; (ii) whether the measures designed to meet the legislative objective are rationally connected to it; and (iii) whether the means used to impair the right or freedom are no more than is necessary to accomplish the objective.

DVCVA. It concluded that the judge-only trial provisions in this form, and in these cases, did not engage any convention right.[25]

The wider context in respect of jury trial

4.10   Before moving to the provisions themselves, some comment is called for in respect of the wider context, if only because any limitation on jury trial is seen, by some, as part of a process of erosion of the whole concept of jury trial. Less than 12 months prior to the passage of the DVCVA, the non-jury trial provisions of the Criminal Justice Act 2003 ('CJA') were the most contentious and bitterly fought parts of that piece of legislation. They were seen as a back-door attempt to introduce non-jury trial following the unsuccessful attempts to limit non-jury trial in the two Mode of Trial Bills in 1999 and 2000.

Section 43 of the CJA has not been brought into force, and the Government gave an undertaking that it would not, for the moment, implement it. It will, if implemented, permit a prosecutor to apply for a judge-only trial where the subject matter is likely to be complex, the trial long or both long and complex. The White Paper *Justice for All*[26] identified the great strain on trial in serious and complex fraud cases imposed on ordinary jurors. Such trials may well last for months. During this time a juror is away from work, perhaps with child care problems unable to talk to non-jurors about what is happening in court all day, unable to make future plans or take time off unless the court agrees to adjournments. The subject matter might be dry and technical, perhaps even tedious. Yet the conviction rate of the Serious Fraud Office is now around 86%.[27] Perhaps, in part, that is due to the steps taken to keep the number of counts in indictments within sensible limits.

4.11   When in force, s 43 of the CJA 2003 will permit trial on indictment by a judge sitting alone, without a jury, where, either due to the length of the trial or its complexity or to both length and complexity, being a juror would likely to be so burdensome to jury members that the trial should be by judge only. Section 43 makes it clear that complexity and length are alternative, but not mutually exclusive, grounds. A short trial can nonetheless be complex.

When deciding on the merits of the application s 43(6) obliges the court to look at ways in which the trial could be simplified so that the length or complexity might be reduced Although a judge will be required to consider 'reasonable' steps to simplify matters, a step is not to be regarded as reasonable if it significantly disadvantages the prosecution (CJA 2003, s 43(7)). For example

[25]   Third Report, para 2.12.
[26]   Op cit, paras 4.26–4.31.
[27]   The figure cited during debate of the Criminal Justice Bill 2003. See HL Standing Committee (14 January 2003), col 110.

an attempt by the defence to cut down the size of the indictment may result in the full extent of the criminality not being revealed to the court.

What is not clear from the debates on the DVCVA is the extent to which the new two-tiered approach could, or will, marry with the power to order non-jury trial in s 43 of the CJA 2003. There is no reason why, if s 43 is in fact introduced, it could not be used to deal with the problem of multiple counts in an indictment, which would fall four-square with the complex or burdensome test in s 43

THE NEW PROVISION

4.12   Section 17(1) of the DVCVA states that the prosecution may apply to a Crown Court judge for a trial on indictment to take place on the basis that the trial of some, but not all, of the counts included in the indictment may be conducted without a jury.

Procedure

4.13   Such an application must be determined at a preparatory hearing held under the Criminal Procedure and Investigations Act 1996 ('CPIA ').[28] or Criminal Justice Act 1987.[29] (s 18(1)). Section 18(2) provides that the CPIA 1996 and CJA 1987 are now to have effect so as to ensure that the grounds for the making of an order for a preparatory hearing, and its purposes (see fn 23), include the need for the determination of a s 17 application.

Where a court is determining an application under s 17, at a preparatory hearing, all parties must be given an opportunity to make representations in respect of the s 17 application (s 18(4)). It will therefore be open to a defendant to make representations that non-jury trial is not permitted or appropriate.

It is intended that rules of court regulate the process, and an enabling power is conferred by s 20 for that purpose. No such rules had been made as at the date of going to press. Thus a significant number of important questions relating to time limits, procedure and evidence cannot definitively be answered at this stage.

---

[28]   Section 29(1) of the CPIA 1996 authorises a Crown Court judge to order that a preparatory hearing be held, to be exercised where the indictment reveals a case of such complexity or a case whose trial is likely to be of such length that substantial benefits are likely to accrue from such a hearing. The purpose of a preparatory hearing are set out by s 29(2): (a) defining issues which are likely to be material to the verdict of the jury; (b) assisting their comprehension of any such issues; expediting the proceedings before the jury; (c) assisting the judge's management of the case.

[29]   The powers in respect of the 1987 Act mirror those in the CPIA 1996, in the context of cases of serious or complex fraud.

Appeal from a determination of a Crown Court judge in respect of a s 17 application lies to the Court of Appeal (Criminal Division) (s 18(5)). The effect of the relevant statutory provisions[30] means that any party may appeal a determination made in a preparatory hearing (DVCVA, s 18(5)).

The decision at the preliminary hearing   – the grounds

4.14   The judge must be satisfied that three conditions are satisfied (s 17(2)).

The *first condition* is that the number of counts included in the indictment is likely to mean that trial by jury involving all of those counts would be impracticable (s 17(3)).

The *second condition* is that, if an order were made each count or group of counts which would accordingly be tried by a jury can be regarded as a sample of counts which could accordingly be tried without a jury (s 17(4));

The *third condition* is that it is in the interests of justice for an order to be made (s 17(5)).

4.15   In deciding whether those three conditions are satisfied the judge must have regard to any steps which might reasonably be taken to facilitate a trial by jury (s 17(6)). However, in deciding that question a step is not to be regarded as reasonable if it could lead to the possibility of a defendant receiving a lesser sentence than would be the case if that step were not taken (s17(7)). The scope of this provision might be extremely broad, if it were to be taken literally. It could theoretically be argued that anything that might make the prospect of acquittal greater might fall within the terms of s 17(7), but that is not the intention of s 17(7). Rather, it addresses the issues with which the DVCVA is concerned. A defendant who argued that the number of counts should be reduced, in order to ensure an indictment with which a jury could cope would, because of *Kidd*, be placing himself in a situation where, if he or she were convicted, a lesser sentence would inevitably have to be imposed.[31] Paradoxically, therefore, the effect of the new provision may be to reduce the pressure on prosecutors to accept or propose shorter indictments, thus reversing the trend described above.[32] This is also inherent in the fist condition.

The first condition

4.16   As noted above, the first condition is that the number of counts in the indictment is likely to mean that a trial by jury involving all of those counts would be impracticable.

---

[30]   Criminal Justice Act 1987, s 9(11) and CPIA 1996, s 35(1).
[31]   See para **4.4**.
[32]   See para **4.5**.

Again, this has to be read in the context of the problem being addressed. *Kidd* requires a court only to sentence for the offences of which the defendant has been convicted, or which have been admitted. The initial decision to be made will be, therefore, one for the prosecutor. How many counts are needed to reflect the totality of the offending? How many of the instances fall within the pre-existing exceptions of a 'general deficiency' or 'continuous offence'?[33] Will specimen counts be sufficient to attract an appropriate sentence on conviction? By the time the matter comes before the court these questions will already have been answered by the prosecutor, and, because of s 17(7),[34] it will be virtually impossible for the *defendant* to challenge them successfully on the grounds that the number of charges deprives the defendant of his or her right to trial by jury unless what can be shown is deliberate overcharging intended to deprive a defendant of that right. This is probably unlikely and may be close to arguing that an abuse of process exists. Nonetheless, the new procedure provides no incentive to a prosecutor to reduce the number of charges in an indictment to facilitate jury trial. Of course, the *court* at a preparatory hearing will be alive to this, and no doubt will wish to be satisfied that the number of counts charged is appropriate.

4.17   The role of the court appears, though, to be constrained by the wording of s 17(3) itself. The use of the words 'those counts' possibly points to the fact that it is not for the court to decide whether jury trial would be practicable if there were different, or a different number of, counts. The court must answer the question on the basis of the judgment the prosecutor has made, although the third condition may provide some solution for a court concerned at the approach taken by the prosecutor.[35] In so doing, the court must not consider whether jury trial is *impossible* but, rather, whether it is *impracticable*. Perhaps, in this context the meanings of the two words 'impossible' and 'impracticable' shade into each other; but, arguably, the use of the term 'impracticable' will allow a court to take into account the length of the trial, the nature of the evidence, the number of witnesses and a whole host of other factors, perhaps the factors implicit in the Law Commission's proposed test that a 'manageable jury trial' was not possible.[36]

The second condition

4.18   The second condition is that, if an order is made, each group of counts which would be tried by jury can be regarded as sample counts.

The term 'sample count' is not defined, although s 17(9) makes clear that a count may not be regarded as a sample of other counts unless the defendant

---

[33]   See para **4.3**.
[34]   See para **4.15**.
[35]   See para **4.20**.
[36]   Report, op cit, para 7.7.

in respect of each count is the same person. Section 17(9) is silent as to the position if a defendant is co-accused in counts with different defendants. However, there is nothing in the Law Commission Report, the parliamentary debates or the context of s 17 to rebut the normal presumption that the singular includes the plural.[37] Arguably a count is only a sample of others if it relates to identical defendants.

4.19   The fact that there is no definition of 'sample count' is surely an omission, and was significantly criticised during the passage of the DVCVA.[38] It also leaves unclear the extent to which` the DVCVA is intended to implement the Law Commission's view that the evidence on and/or conviction of each sample count would be admissible on each of the offences in the schedule that are linked to the sample count, and vice versa.[39] Provision to that effect was removed from the Bill during its passage, the Government being content, first, that judges would know what a sample count was, and, second, that the Act contained many safeguards.[40]

The DVCVA could have dealt with matters of such specificity but, arguably, that is unimportant. First, Rule 9 of the Indictment Rules prescribes what can properly be combined in one indictment. Further, nothing in the Act itself changes the basic principle that, whether at first stage or second stage, a trial must be conducted with regard to the rules of evidence. As noted later,[41] the rules relating to bad character and previous convictions contained in the CJA 2003 will apply in the normal way, and cross-admissibility is surely one of the matters to which the court must have regard in determining whether this second condition (and also the third) is met.

The third condition

4.20   Nor does the Act provide any indication as to when the third condition is to be satisfied. It merely requires the court to be satisfied that it is in the interests of justice for an order to be made (s 17(5)). Clearly it is in the interests of justice if the range of charges that may as a result be tried reflects the totality of offending in respect of which the defendant may be sentence if convicted. It will also be a relevant matter for the court to consider questions of cross-admissibility (see above), and also whether the indictment is fairly drawn in terms of the its number and content of counts, and the nature and quantity of evidence in respect of the linked offences that the prosecution will wish, or need, to adduce.

---

[37]   See Interpretation Act 1978.
[38]   See eg HC Report, 27 October 2004, cols 1513 et seq.
[39]   Report, op cit, para 7.7.
[40]   Solicitor-General, Harriett Harman, MP, HC Rep, 27 October 2004, col 1517.
[41]   See para **4.22**.

Some indication of how this third condition might properly be used can be gleaned from the Law Commission Report, which states:[42]

> 'The type of case that we would regard as suited to this procedure is where it would be unthinkable that any judge would order separate trials in relation to the activity covered in the schedule for any reason other than overloading of the indictment, or where it would be inconceivable that a judge might direct a jury that they should disregard the evidence in the sample offence when considering liability in respect of the linked offences in the schedule. The specimen count in the indictment ought to be a true sample of the linked offences. The two-stage process is intended for use in respect of cases of frequently repeated offending of a similar nature, rather than wide-ranging complex and factually differentiated cases. It will thus only be used in those cases where the similarity between the specimen and the linked charges is such that the evidence will be susceptible to being presented in schedule form, or given by a small number of witnesses, or if given by a number of individuals, gone through relatively quickly.'

Of course, those principles are not given statutory force by s 17 or other related provisions, but s 17 is intended to implement the Law Commission recommendation, and so the Report should carry significant weight.

The effect of the order

4.21   Where such an order is made during proceedings, then if a defendant is found guilty by a jury on a count which can be regarded as a sample of other counts to be tried in those proceedings, those other counts may be tried without a jury in those proceedings (s 19(1)). That trial is by a judge, without a jury. Nothing in the Act requires that trial to be by the same judge as that who tried the jury trial of the specimen counts, but that may often in fact be the case.

The jury trial

4.22   This will be conducted in the normal way on the counts identified at the preparatory hearing as sample counts. Arguably the indictment put to the defendant on arraignment at the jury trial will be in respect of the sample counts only, because the jury will not be expected to have any role in determining guilt or innocence on the offences which are linked, and to be dealt with on a non-jury basis.

But that does not mean that the linked offences are irrelevant. It would be tempting to conclude that, since the whole purpose of the procedure is to keep the trial within a practicable, manageable size, the jury should consider the sample counts without regard to the mass of other potential offending. That was not, though, the intention of the Law Commission,[43] and is not the effect

---

[42]   At para 7.8.
[43]   Report, op cit, para 7.9.

of s 17. Nothing in s 17 limits in any way the admissibility of evidence, which must be determined in accordance with the normal rules. At the time the Law Commission reported, the CJA 2003 had not been enacted. Section 101 et seq of that Act, which came into force in December 2004, alters radically the principles that govern the admissibility of evidence of bad character.

By s 101 of the CJA 2003, evidence of bad character[44] is admissible if one of the seven conditions stated therein is satisfied, subject, of course, to any exclusion by a judge exercising a statutory discretion. Patently, the defendant has not been convicted of the scheduled linked-offences – that is, after all, the purpose of stage 2, to determine whether the defendant *should* be convicted on them – and thus there is no question of s 103(2) of the CJA 2003 applying (in respect of the charges in this same indictment).[45] But that is not necessarily crucial. The CJA 2003 – like the similar fact evidence rule before it[46] – does not turn on the fact of conviction. Evidence of bad character is evidence that shows misconduct, or disposition towards misconduct, that has probative force in relation to an important matter in issue between prosecution and defence (CJA 2003, s 101(1)(d)). For the purpose of deciding whether it does so relate, evidence that shows the defendant has a propensity to commit offences of the kind with which he is charged[47] is admissible. That propensity does not have to be proved by previous convictions (as the words in parenthesis in s 103(2) of the CJA 2003 make clear),[48] and if the facts of linked offences have probative force in proving guilt on the sample offence (for example by negating a defence) they may be used to do so, subject to any exclusionary discretion under s 101(3) of the CJA 2003 or s 78 of PACE.

As an alternative basis of admissibility, the bad character inherent, potentially, in the linked counts might on occasion be admissible as 'important explanatory evidence' within the meaning of s 101(1)(c) and s 102 of the CJA 2003.[49] Thus,

---

[44]   Defined by s 98 of the CJA 2003 to mean evidence of misconduct, or a disposition towards it, on the part of the defendant, other than evidence which (a) has to do with the alleged facts of the offence with which the defendant is charged, or (b) is evidence of misconduct in connection with the investigation or prosecution of that offence. 'Misconduct' is defined by s 112(1) of the CJA 2003 as meaning the commission of the offence or other reprehensible behaviour.

[45]   Section 103 of the CJA 2003 allows evidence of bad character where it is relevant to an important matter in issue between the defendant and prosecution. This may be established if the evidence shows propensity. Section 103(2) provides, in effect, that propensity may be proved by showing previous convictions.

[46]   See, eg, *Z* [2000] 3 All ER 385, HL.

[47]   An offence of the same 'kind' is not defined. Section 103(2) deals with this but in terms relating to previous convictions, which (as explained in the text) is not apposite here.

[48]   'without prejudice to any other way of doing so'.

[49]   'important explanatory evidence' is evidence which, without it, the court or jury would find it impossible or difficult properly to understand other evidence in the case, and its value for understanding the case as a whole is substantial. It equates to what fell within

if the case on the sample charge is only comprehensible by reference to a wider pattern of offending, then such evidence is potentially admissible.

4.23   All of the above serves to demonstrate that, at the preparatory hearing stage, the judge will need to carefully consider what evidence the prosecution will want, or need, to adduce at the trial of the sample counts, in order to determine the advantages or otherwise of making a s 17 order.

The outcome of the jury trial

4.24   Clearly, at the end of the jury trial verdicts of either guilty or not guilty will be entered in respect of each of the sample counts, unless the jury fail to agree a verdict on any or all of them. Beyond that, the position is less clear. Nothing in the DVCVA deals with some of the issues that might arise, though some of the possibilities are canvassed by the Law Commission.[50] It is, though, clearly envisaged that the trial judge, at the conclusion of the jury trial, will make appropriate directions as to how (if at all) the remaining stage is to proceed. No doubt the procedure to be followed will be clarified by the proposed rules of court.

4.25   The effect of an acquittal on all or any of the sample counts is one issue. The Act does not require acquittal on the linked charges. The Law Commission commented that a presumption in favour of a directed acquittal on the linked charges should arise. This is a logical conclusion, because the very selection of the sample count was so that jury trial could be determinative of the principle of the offending in like cases. However, that is not inevitable. No question of autrefois acquit arises, because there has been no acquittal on the scheduled linked charges. It may be, for example, that an acquittal on a sample count arose because a key prosecution witness became unavailable.[51] In such circumstances, the Law Commission identified the proper approach as follows:

> 'It should therefore be open to the prosecution in such cases to seek to persuade the judge that in the particular exceptional circumstances, justice requires that the Crown should be free, at some future date, to seek leave to proceed with a new prosecution (not the second stage of a two stage trial) on some or all of the allegations linked to the sample count upon which there has been an acquittal. The trial judge should not, however, be permitted to allow the prosecution to proceed with a new prosecution on linked allegations on the basis that he or she considers that the acquittal by the jury was perverse or erroneous. *Express provision should be made to that effect* [our emphasis]'.

No such express provision is contained in the Act itself. We therefore need to await the rules of court to establish whether such a safeguard is put in place.

---

the test propounded in *Pettman* (2 May 1985, unreported), CA. See, generally, Ward and Davis, op cit, Ch 5.

[50]   Report, op cit, paras 7.10 et seq.

[51]   The example given by the Law Commission at para 7.11.

4.26   In respect of linked counts where acquittals on the sample count, or counts, occurred, the clear choice is between a court-ordered acquittal or allowing charges to lie on file, not to be proceeded with in the absence of the leave of the court. It might be thought, though, that since it was the prosecution who sought a two-stage trial that a defendant is entitled, if he or she wishes, to have a formal verdict on those counts. It is far from clear whether the prosecution or, for that matter, defence, is entitled to go on to stage 2. Arguably, this is a matter for the court. This was the view of the Law Commission, who distinguished existing authority (to the effect that a prosecutor is entitles to proceed with a trial unless the proceedings were oppressive or vexatious) on the basis that the prosecution had already had the chance to put the thrust of the case before a jury.[52]

4.27   The alternative position is that convictions are obtained on one or more of the sample counts. Clearly, in such cases, there is no problem with the case proceeding to second-stage trial (by judge alone), for the basis for dealing with the linked counts has been established. The Law Commission proposed that the defendant be given the opportunity at this stage to change his or her plea.[53] This would, if it occurred, obviate the need for a second-stage trial, save time and expense, and allow the court to proceed quickly to the sentencing stage. In such circumstances there would have been a plea of guilty before trial (of the relevant linked offences) and thus some sentence discount for a plea of guilty would be appropriate though, arguably, less than would otherwise be the case had a plea of guilty been entered prior to the jury trial.[54]

Where convictions on sample counts have been obtained, the trial judge might form the view that his or her powers of sentencing were adequate for the purpose, that there are already sufficient convictions for an adequate sentence to be imposed. Of course that would have to be adequate in the context of the offences in respect of which convictions were obtained (for that was the mischief that *Kidd* addressed, and the problem now being tackled by s 17). One might wonder why, if that was the case, the prosecution chose to proceed with the full range of allegations in the first place. But, whatever the logic, there may be cases that fall within that category and the question remains (as discussed above) as to whether the court can prevent the case proceeding to stage two if the prosecutor (or for that matter, defendant, insists), or whether, ultimately, it is a matter for the prosecution.

4.28   If the court does have the power to prevent the prosecution proceeding to stage two, that is to be regarded as a 'terminating ruling' within the meaning of s 57 of the CJA 2003, with resultant prosecution rights of appeal.[55]

---

[52]   Report, op cit, para 7.22, citing *Attorney-General's Reference (No 2 of 2000)* [2001] 1 Cr App R 503, CA .

[53]   Report, op cit, para 7.14.

[54]   Powers of Criminal Courts (Sentencing) Act 2000, s 152.

[55]   See Ward and Davis, op cit, Ch 7. The CJA 2003 does not ascribe a specific definition to the phrase 'terminating ruling'.

Stage two – trial by judge alone on linked counts

4.29   Section 19(2) provides that where a trial of a count is conducted without a jury because of an order made under s 17(2), the court has all the powers, authorities and jurisdiction which the court would have had if the trial of that count had been conducted with a jury (including power to determine and question and to make any finding which would be required to be made by a jury). Thus the judge retains all powers normally vested in a trial judge (on matters relating to law, evidence and procedure) but has in addition all the powers of the jury. Thus his or her determination will amount to an acquittal or conviction in the normal way rendering the doctrines of autrefois acquit or autrefois convict operative where appropriate in the future.[56]

This is particularly pertinent in the context of rules of evidence. A trial judge will where necessary have to direct him or herself in respect of the admissibility of evidence, disregarding that which it held to be inadmissible. This may be a particular issue in the context of evidence of bad character, potentially admissible under s 101 of the CJA 2003. If the judge is the same trial judge who presided at the jury trial he or she might already have determined an application for the use of evidence of bad character.[57] He will already be aware of the issues of bad character and will, if such evidence was not admitted, have to exclude it from his mind. If, by contrast, the matter arises afresh during the non-jury trial the judge will have to exclude any such evidence from his mind if such evidence is for any reason excluded.

4.30   We discussed earlier some of the issues relating to bad character evidence that might arise at the stage one trial.[58] These are equally important at stage two. Whether the fact of conviction (proved by a certificate of conviction pursuant to s 73 of PACE) is admissible will turn on the application, in the normal way, of s 101 of the CJA 2003. It is, arguably, inconceivable the fact of conviction on a sample count would be inadmissible. The very fact that it is a sample count is because it has probative value in respect of the other offending, and the terms of s 101(1)(d) and s 103 of the CJA 2003 are fully engaged. No problems are likely to be encountered in making both the fact of conviction, and the facts underpinning that conviction, properly admissible evidence.

4.31   Nothing in s 17 requires a judge, sitting alone, to do anything other than take a view of the evidence. The Government explained:

'The second stage takes place only in the event of a guilty verdict on one or more of the counts tried before the jury. The judge alone decides on the guilt or innocence of the defendant in respect only of the offences linked to those on which the jury has convicted. The judge is not bound by the conviction of the

---

[56]   See also the provisions of DVCVA, s 19(3).
[57]   For the grounds of admissibility see Criminal Justice Act 2003, s 101, and, generally, Ward & Davis *Criminal Justice Act 2003 – A Practitioners' Guide*, op cit, Ch 6.
[58]   See para **4.22**.

jury at stage one but is free to come to his or her own view of the evidence. In the event that the jury has acquitted on a sample count, there is a presumption in favour of a directed acquittal on the linked counts.'

Likewise, as noted earlier, acquittal on the sample count does not *automatically* or *inevitably* lead to the termination of the proceedings for the linked offences

4.32   When a court convicts the defendant of a count tried pursuant to an order made under s 17(2), it must, at the time of conviction or as soon as reasonably practicable thereafter (s 19(4)). No such duty arises following an acquittal. The judgment must state the court's reasons for the conviction. The relevant date for notice of appeal or application for leave to appeal, runs from the date of that judgment not (if different) the date of the actual conviction (s 19(4)(b)). Further, the relevant time limits in respect of appeal against the jury convictions do not run until the end of the whole proceedings (ie the date of their judgment in the non-jury trial) (s 19(5)).

Chapter Five

CRIMINAL JUSTICE CHANGES

SUMMARY

5.1 The DVCVA makes a wide range of changes in respect of substantive criminal offences, and in respect of the procedure and powers of the courts. Some, though not all, of these changes are related to the theme of reducing or preventing domestic violence. The two new criminal offences of breach of a non-molestation order, and causing or allowing the death of a child or vulnerable adult, have already been noted and are discussed at chapters 2 and 3 respectively. Changes to powers of arrest are noted at paras **2.19**, **2.20** and **5.2**. Other changes related to the same theme are discussed in this chapter. These include additional powers to make restraining orders under the Protection from Harassment Act 1997 (PFHA)[1] and amendments to the power to use common assault as an alternative verdict.[2]

The Government took the opportunity to include a number of changes that go beyond the specific theme of domestic violence and victims. Trial by jury of sample counts only has been discussed in chapter 4. In this chapter we discuss a range of changes that includes, at the paragraphs indicated:

- minor changes to police powers of arrest (**5.2**);
- the procedure for determining fitness to plead, and appeals against such a finding (**5.24**);
- the powers of the court on a finding of insanity or unfitness to plead (**5.28**);
- powers to impose surcharges on conviction (**5.10**);
- increases in maximum on-the-spot penalties for disorderly behaviour (**5.13**);
- higher fixed penalties for repeat road traffic offences (**5.14**);
- powers relating to warrants (**5.15**);
- amendments to procures on community penalties (**5.19**);
- changes to intermittent custody (**5.20**).

[1] See para **5.3**.
[2] See para **5.23**.

By definition, how victims are treated is one of the major issues and challenges for the criminal justice system and process. The provisions relating to victims are, again, at the heart of this Act, and are discussed separately, at chapter 6

ARREST

Arrestable offences

5.2   As already noted,[3] s 10 of the Act includes common assault as one of the specified offences in Sch 1A to the Police and Criminal Evidence Act 1984. This has the effect of enabling a constable who reasonably suspects the commission of a common assault to arrest, pursuant to s 24(1) of PACE. This will enable a constable to make an arrest in a domestic violence context irrespective of whether a non-molestation order is in place. It removes any uncertainties that might have existed hitherto in respect of the full extent of powers relating to breaches of the peace, or the need for reliance on the general arrest conditions contained in s 25 of PACE.[4]

It is also clear that a power of arrest exists in respect of the new criminal offence of breach of a non-molestation order (see para **2.23**). This is so because the maximum punishment available on conviction of an adult for that offence is five years' imprisonment (PACE, s 24(1))

RESTRAINING ORDERS

5.3   We have already noted[5] that restraining orders made under the PFHA form an integral part of the machinery for the protection of victims of domestic violence, as well, of course, as others. Section 5 of the PFHA provides that when a court is sentencing or otherwise dealing with a person ('the defendant') who is convicted of an offence under s 2[6] or s 4[7] of that Act, then, as well as

---

[3]   See para **2.19**.

[4]   PACE, s 25(3)(d)(i) will permit arrest without warrant where a constable has reasonable grounds for believing that arrest is necessary to prevent the arrested person causing physical injury to himself or any other person. That will not assist where there is no risk of continued assault. A power of arrest also exists under PACE, s 25(3)(e) where a constable has reasonable grounds for believing that arrest is necessary to protect a child or other vulnerable person from the relevant person.

[5]   See para **2.32**.

[6]   A s 2 offence is committed by a person who pursues a course of conduct (a) which amounts to harassment of another, and (b) which he knows or ought to know amounts to harassment of another. A course of conduct does not fall within the above if the defendant shows: (a) that it was pursued for then purpose of preventing or detecting crime, (b) that it was pursued under any enactment or rule of law or to comply with any condition or requirement imposed by any person under any enactment; or (c) that in the particular circumstances the pursuit of the course of conduct was reasonable (see s 1 of the PFHA).

[7]   A s 4 offence is committed by a person whose course of conduct causes another to fear, on at least two occasions, that violence will be used against him, if the defendant knows

sentencing him or dealing with him in any other way, it may make a restraining order under s 5.

The s 5 order may, for the purpose of protecting the victim of the offence or any other person mentioned in the order from further conduct which (a) amounts to harassment[8] or (b) will cause fear or violence, prohibit the defendant from doing anything described in the order. The s 5 order may have effect for a specified period or until further order. A defendant who, without reasonable excuse, does anything which he is prohibited from doing by the s 5 order is guilty of a criminal offence (PFHA, s 5(5)).

5.4 The Government regards the restraining order power as the most innovative feature of the PFHA, particularly useful in domestic violence cases because it provides for the continued safety of the victim.[9] However, a restraining order could only be made in cases where a conviction had been obtained for a s 2 or s 4 offence. The DVCVA changes that by permitting the making of a restraining order following any conviction, or following an acquittal.

Restraining order following conviction

5.5 Section 12 of the DVCVA amends s 5 of the PFHA. It does so by deleting the references in s 5(1) to s 2 or s 4 of the PFHA. Under the pre-existing s 5, a restraining order could only be made following conviction for a s 2 or s 4 offence. The effect of the change is to allow a court to make a restraining order irrespective of the offence for which the defendant is being sentenced. Section 2 offences were only triable summarily, unlike s 4 offences which were either-way. The result therefore is to widen considerably the powers of both magistrates' courts and the Crown Court.

The power to make a restraining order will now exist irrespective of whether the offence of which the defendant has been convicted comprises conduct which is of a type related to harassment. Nonetheless, the DVCVA does not amend s 5(2) of the PFHA, and the restraining order must be 'for the purpose of protecting the victim of the offence'. The court will no doubt be reminded by or on behalf of the Crown Prosecution Service of its power to make a restraining order in appropriate cases – particularly those involving conduct such as criminal damage, burglary and stalking There will need to be an evidential basis to permit the conclusion that the 'victim' of the offence of which the defendant has been convicted needs that protection. Indeed, the making of a s 5 restraining order without a proper evidential basis for its need runs the

---

    or ought to know that his course of conduct will cause the other so to fear on each of those occasions. The exceptions stated in n 6 above (in the context of s 2) apply equally to s 4.

8   'Harassment' is further defined by PFHA, s 7 which states that references to 'harassment' includes alarming the person or causing the person distress. A 'course of conduct' must involve conduct on at least two occasions.

9   *Safety and Justice,* op cit, p 36, para 33.

risk of challenge under the Human Rights Act 1998, for possible breaches of art 8 rights (respect for private and family life, etc).

This evidential basis may have been created by the evidence adduced during the trial (in the case of a not guilty plea) or by the facts accepted by a plea of guilty. On summary trial the magistrates or district judge will have a clear view as to what facts they find established. The problem is more acute in trial on indictment. A judge sentences on his view of the case, subject to not being able to act on a view that is inconsistent with the verdict.[10] In a case of burglary a trial judge is entitled to form a view, for example, as to how much fear the burglar put the householder under.

To supplement this, a new s 5(3A) is inserted into the PFHA by s 12(3) of the DVCVA. This allows the prosecution and defence to lead, as further evidence, any evidence that would be admissible in proceedings for an injunction under s 3 of the PFHA. As noted earlier[11] it is s 3 that provides the power for a civil court to award damages, and to attach a power of arrest to an injunction or issue an injunction Thus a criminal court will be entitled to adduce any evidence admissible in civil, injunctive, proceedings, including hearsay evidence in accordance with the Civil Evidence Act 1996. Criminal practitioners will need to be alive to the need to be au fait with relevant principles of civil evidence (which differ markedly from those in criminal proceedings). What the new s 5(3A) does not do, however, is to negate any rule of criminal evidence. Any relevant rule of evidence, whether criminal or civil, that permit admission of a piece of evidence may be relied on. Thus, even if rules of criminal evidence would prohibit evidence, or permit discretionary exclusion, that will not prevent admission if civil law rules permit.

5.6   Nothing in s 5 of the PFHA affects the incidence of the burden of proof. The amendments to s 5 made by the DVCVA are specific in nature, relate to what may be adduced, but do not deal with the standard of proof. Thus, normal rules might be thought to apply: where there is an issue in dispute between prosecution and defence that has to be resolved by the prosecution satisfying the court beyond reasonable doubt.[12] Any other conclusion would in turn raises interesting issues as to whether the proceedings remain 'criminal' for the purpose of art 6 of the European Convention on Human Rights. Against that, the use of the civil rules of evidence, the nature of the order, and the ability to go to a civil court under s 3 of the PFHA for a remedy might all point in a contrary direction, and support a conclusion that the civil standard of proof ('the balance of probabilities') should be applied. This problem has not arisen before,

---

[10]   See Law Commission No 277 'The Effective Prosecution of Multiple Offending', para 3.15, citing a response to a Consultation Paper made by Buxton LJ.

[11]   See para **2.11**.

[12]   *Ahmed* (1984) 60 Cr App Rep 296, CA.

because the power to make a restraining order was directly related to conviction for a harassment offence, and permitted of no wider evidence. The point may possibly be more academic than real, if the approach taken in *R (On the application of McCann and others) v Crown Court at Manchester*[13] is replicated in this context. In *McCann*, the House of Lords ruled that, because of the nature of proceedings in respect of anti-social behaviour orders (under s 1 Crime and Disorder Act 1998), the criminal standard of proof should be applied despite the fact that the application for an ASBO was, technically, civil in nature. That was because the allegations were of behaviour that was either criminal or 'quasi-criminal'. Much will turn on the nature of the matters that are being adduced and alleged, but, arguably, a court should be following the approach taken in *McCann*.

Restraining order following acquittal

5.7 Section 12(5) of the DVCVA inserts a new s 5A into the PFHA. The new section permits a court to make a restraining order despite the fact that the defendant has been acquitted of an offence. It may make an order if it considers it necessary to do so in order to protect a person from harassment by the defendant. The order may prohibit the defendant from doing anything described in the order.

5.8 The procedure to be followed will be governed by the relevant parts of s 5 (s 5A(2)). An appropriate evidential basis must be established. That basis might be the facts uncontested in the trial. Clearly although a Crown Court is entitled to take its own view of what the jury verdict means, it is not open to a court to rely on matters that have clearly been rejected by the jury.[14]

The problems identified at para **5.6** above are magnified in the case of this new power. The standard of proof, and the evidence that may be adduced, all remain key issues. It will also be necessary to amend court rules to allow the hearing of evidence on acquittal.[15] And, arguably, if a restraining order is based on alleged misconduct by the acquitted person the standard of proof in respect of the allegation should be a high one. In addition, if the process is designed to provide some protection for those in fear or subject to harassment (which it is), there will be a need for the process of consideration of the making of an order, and the reception of new evidence, to occur as quickly as possible after the determination of innocence. Where the defendant has been convicted, there is no problem: bail conditions can if necessary be imposed. No power to grant bail (and therefore to impose conditions) arises after an acquittal.

---

[13] And its companion case *Clingham v Kensington and Chelsea Royal London Borough Council*, both reported at [2002] 4 All ER 593, HL
[14] See para **5.5**.
[15] Christopher Leslie, MP, Parliamentary Under-Secretary of Sate, Department of Constitutional Affairs, HC Standing Committee (29 June 2004), col 160.

Of course, nothing in the DVCVA prevents an immediate civil application being made in the normal way. Some concerns have been aired that these changes are moving the criminal courts into areas that might be more properly be dealt with by the Family Court. That, though, is to overlook the fact that the restraining order procedure, although important in the context of domestic violence and family matters, is in no way confined to that group of cases.

Questions also arise about the funding basis for representation. The criminal proceedings will be at an end, and it is unclear whether funding for representation in those criminal matters will continue.[16] Given that the matter is consequential on the criminal proceedings, arguably it should, as it no doubt would where there is consideration of a restraining order following conviction.

5.9   Where a conviction of a magistrates' court is overturned by the Crown Court, the Crown Court is the court that has acquitted the defendant for the purpose of s 5A (PFHA, s 5A(4)). The same is true when a case is remitted to it by the Court of Appeal (as it may) following the quashing of a conviction by that court. In such a case an appeal would lie to the Court of Appeal (Criminal Division), a court not usually involved in what are clearly civil matters.

SURCHARGES

5.10   Less than 12 months after the Criminal Justice Act 2003 was passed[17] the Government has continued the insatiable quest to add new, or different, sentences and orders. Sections 14-16 of the DVCVA provide new, additional or amended powers in respect of surcharges and fixed penalties. The provisions are part of a strategy stated to be to ensure that funds are contributed by offenders to resource measures designed to support victims. The Government intends to establish a Victims Fund, resourced principally from a surcharge on criminal convictions and penalty notices, and from resources released by changes to the Criminal Injuries Compensation Scheme.[18]

The provisions relating to surcharges follow responses to a consultation paper 'Compensation and Support for Victims of Crime'.[19] The responses to the proposals form, generally, the basis of the proposals in the DVCVA. The Parliamentary Under-Secretary of State described the approach as follows:[20]

> 'Our aim is to make offenders pay a small sum to a fund for the victims of crime. The fund will provide practical and emotional support to a range of victims.'

---

[16]   See comments of Vera Baird QC at HC Standing Committee (29 June 2004), col 175.
[17]   It received Royal Assent on 20 November 2003. Royal Assent for the DVCVA was given on 5 November 2004.
[18]   See, generally, ch 6.
[19]   Home Office, 12 January 2004.
[20]   Paul Goggins, MP, HC Standing Committee, 8th Sitting (1 July 2004), col 293.

Victim and witness support is seen as one of the key elements of the Government's criminal justice strategy.[21] The wider issues are discussed in chapter 6. But one key element is funding. The Home Secretary, on 2nd Reading of the Bill,[22] observed:

> 'We desperately need to add to the £650million pus that goes into broader services for victims. We have the £30 million going into victim support … I think that the start that we are making by establishing a new victims fund in addition to these contributions will be welcomed by everybody. A sum of £4 million from asset recovery will be made available immediately to kick-start the new fund… We expect people who are committed to custody to pay a minimum of £30 in a levy or surcharge, but that depends on whether we can use the Proceeds of Crime Act 2002. We will change the regulations on earnings of people in prison to make that possible. In addition we will levy a contribution from   people who are subject to fines. Substantial fines of more than £1000 will be subject to a £30 surcharge, and fines under £1000 to a £15 surcharge. There would be a £10 surcharge on fixed penalty notices… There is no proposed surcharge for parking offences, which are a civil offence[sic]'.

The proposals draw on experience from overseas.[23] The surcharge provisions of the DVCVA, introduced after the Bill had received its House of Lords' consideration, are intended to provide the legislative framework necessary to make such a scheme work. The establishment of such a fund does not need primary legislation, and thus the DVCVA does not contain direct provision in that regard. Surcharges will be paid into the Consolidated Fund and be 'ring-fenced, by analogy with the recovered assets fund into which were paid the proceeds of crime obtained through confiscation orders.'[24] They will be distinct from compensation orders. It should be noted that s 56 of the DVCVA permits the payment of grants to victims and witnesses.[25]

One general issue should be noted at the outset. The surcharges are to be seen as separate and distinct from the fine or penalty, or from any compensation order made. Nonetheless the sentencer must be alive to the fact that the total sentence should be proportionate to the crime. The Government recognises that, and is proposing to liaise with sentencers and with Sentencing Guidelines Council, though the Government considers it unlikely that the proposed scheme will take sentences into the realms of disproportionality.

[21]   See *Justice for All*, op cit, ch 2.
[22]   David Blunkett, MP, 422 HC Official Report (14 June 2004), no 100, cols 539-540.
[23]   See 'Compensation and Support for Victims of Crime' (Home Office, January 2004), para 39.
[24]   Ibid.
[25]   See para **6.42**.

Court's duty to order the payment of a surcharge

5.11 Section 14 inserts a new s 161A into the Criminal Justice Act 2003 ('CJA'). The new s 161A will, generally speaking,[26] require a court (when dealing with an offender for one or more offences) to order the offender to pay a surcharge. The duty will not apply in respect of cases to which the Home Secretary has prescribed by order (CJA, s 161A). No order had been made as at the date of going to press, but the offences to which it applies may be varied, following experience, if it is shown that certain categories of offender are being unfairly penalised.[27]

The obligation created by the new s 161A is a duty. The court must impose a surcharge, subject to the matters set out in para **5.12** below. The surcharge will be such sum as is specified by order made by the Home Secretary (CJA, s 163B(1)). Again, no such order has yet been made, but 'the intention is that the surcharge should be a relatively small amount: on our current figures, up to £30. so as to maximise payment by the vast majority of offenders to a wide range of victims.'[28] The new s161B(2) provides that an order may provide for the amount of the surcharge to depend on:

(a) the offence or offences committed;
(b) how the defendant is otherwise dealt with i(including, where the offender is fined, the amount of the fine);
(c) the age of the offender.

What we have at the moment is nothing more than a legislative framework. The workings of the scheme will depend very much on the detail. In 'Compensation and Support for Victims of Crime' one possible model was set out, as follows:[29]

Sentence type	Proposed surcharge
Penalty notice up to £80	£5
Penalty notice greater than £80	£10
Fines up to £1000	£15
Fines greater than £1000	£30

5.12 The legislation addresses the relationship between compensation orders, surcharges and fines. Where a court considers that a compensation order is appropriate, but the offender has insufficient means to pay both the surcharge

---

[26] A court is not 'dealing with' an offender for this purpose if it makes an absolute discharge or an order under Mental Health Act 1998.
[27] Paul Goggins, Parliamentary Under-Secretary of State, Home Office, ibid, at col 294.
[28] Ibid, col 294.
[29] Op cit, at para 44.

and appropriate compensation, the court must reduce the surcharge accordingly (if necessary to nil) (s 161A(3)). By contrast the court must not reduce the amount of any fine on account of any surcharge, except to the extent that he has insufficient means to pay both (CJA, s 164(4A) inserted by the DVCVA, s 14(2)). The wording of this latter provision seems to require that in such a case, where the cumulative effect of fine and surcharge are beyond the means of the individual, it is the fine rather than the surcharge that is reduced. For the offender the point is probably academic and unimportant, given that the new provisions generally apply the relevant powers relating to the collection of fines to these surcharges (DVCVA s14(3)–(5)). One suspects that a 'surcharge' is, to an offender – and perhaps to others – just another fine.

Wide powers are conferred on the Home Secretary by s 14(5) to vary relevant legislation relating to fines in so far as surcharges are concerned.

Increases in maximum on-the-spot penalty for disorderly behaviour

5.13   The Criminal Justice and Police Act 2001 ('CJPA') introduced on-the-spot penalties for disorderly behaviour. In accordance with the same philosophy used to justify surcharges for convicted offenders, an increase in fixed penalties is provided for by s 15 of the DVCVA. It amends s 3 of theCJPA to provide for an addition to the relevant fixed penalty by 'half of the relevant surcharge'. The Government intends to make secondary legislation to increase the amount of the fixed penalty payable, so that the surcharge as part of the fixed penalty.

The relevant surcharge is the amount of surcharge a person of the age of the person subject to the fixed penalty would pay, assuming he was fined the maximum possible for the offence (CJPA, s 3(2A), inserted by DVCVA, s 15(3)). Again the lack of any detail on the surcharge provisions prevents an assessment of the likely impact of this change, but surcharges are likely to be small – of the order of £5 on each penalty notice (see the Table at para **5.11**). A victims fund will support victims of anti-social behaviour and disorder.

Higher fixed penalty for repeated road traffic offences

5.14   Dissatisfaction among motorists about speed cameras and the perceived unfairness of the fixed-penalty system is well known and documented. The Government has recognised the force of some of the arguments in this context,[30] and the Department of Transport has engaged in a review of the wider road traffic issues. Suffice to say that in 2002 some 1,606,404 notices were issued for endorsable speeding offences, and 142,389 for non-speeding offences. The

---

[30]   See generally, HC Standing Committee, 8th sitting (1 July 2004). The Road Safety Bill is (as at January 2005) before Parliament and will, inter alia, introduce a system of graduated fixed penalties.

surcharge provisions discussed below are not, as yet, confined to any particular road traffic offences.

Section 16 of the DVCVA amends the Road Traffic Offenders Act 1988 ('RTOA'). The effect of the amendments made to s 53 of the RTOA is to make 'persistent offenders' (the term used by the Government, though not by the Act itself)[31] liable for a surcharge. Considerable – and heated – debate[32] occurred as to who fell within the description of 'persistent offender'. The Home Secretary stated his intention, and purpose, thus:[33]

> '... We accept that it would be wrong for low-level first-time offenders to be subject to a surcharge. Hopefully, the Department of Transport will shortly consult on changes in the points system for fixed penalty notices. The new system will be introduced in 2006, which is when we will consider introducing a levy of £10 on fixed penalty notices for serious repeat offenders, as opposed to general fixed penalty notices. We will link the levy to the higher number of points added to people's licences, so that the system will be fair to everybody...'.

The reality of who is caught by the new scheme is evident on perusal of the amended s 53. Section 53 of the RTOA applies the provisions to any person who, in the period of three years ending with the date of the offence in question, has been disqualified from driving or received penalty points on his licence. Thus any person who commits a second or further speeding offence (or, indeed, any other offence attracting penalty points) during a three-year period will be caught by a higher fixed penalty. The aim is that a small amount will be added to the penalty to contribute to a victims fund, which will provide support to victims of road traffic accidents.

The Act confers powers to make regulations to implement the scheme, including power to issue 'surcharge notices' to those who it becomes apparent are liable for the surcharge.

POWERS IN RESPECT OF WARRANTS

Powers of enforcement officers

5.15   Section 27 and Sch 4 of the DVCVA amend the Magistrates' Courts Act 1980, by inserting therein a new Sch 4A. This new schedule gives civilian enforcement officers and approved enforcement agencies additional powers

---

[31]   See Paul Goggins, HC Standing Committee, 8th sitting (1 July 2004), col 309; David Blunkett MP, Home Secretary, 422 HC Official Report, 2nd Reading, (14 June 2004), no 100, col 640.

[32]   See, in particular, HC Standing Committee (1 July 2004), col 293 et seq.

[33]   David Blunkett, MP, Home Secretary, 422 HC Official Report, 2nd Reading (14 June 2004), no 100, col 540.

needed to help improve the enforcement of fines and community penalty breach warrants.[34]

5.16   The new powers can be summarised as follows:

- power to enter premises to execute warrant of arrest, commitment, detention or distress, where the officer has reasonable suspicion that the offender who is subject to a warrant is present;
- power to search offenders for dangerous article (eg hypodermic needles, knives and items that could facilitate escape);
- power to use reasonable force.

The rationale for the changes flows from the greater role of civilian enforcement officers following recent legislation, such as Criminal Justice Act 2003. At the moment only about 30% of distress warrants and 36% of community penalty breach warrants are executed successfully. The power of entry is designed to deal with those cases where the offender refuses to open his or her door, when it is clear to the authorised officer that they are present – believed to be some 6–7% of cases.[35] Such officers also sometimes escort offenders into custody or take them to court, but no power hitherto has existed to search them for items that may cause harm or may be used to assist escape. These powers are already conferred on police officers by PACE, s 32.

Disclosure orders for the purpose of executing warrants

5.17   Section 28 inserts into the Magistrates' Courts Act 1980 a new s 125CA and a new s 125CB The problem these provisions address is that which arises in cases where the whereabouts of the offender are unknown because, for whatever reason, the offender has not informed a court of changes in name or address. It authorises a magistrates' court to make a disclosure order, the effect of which is to require the person to whom it is directed to supply information relating to the name, date of birth or national insurance number, or address (or addresses or any of them) of an offender where the court is seeking to execute a warrant of arrest, commitment, detention or distress in connection with the enforcement of a fine or other order imposed or made on conviction (s 125CA(2),(3)).

Such an order can be made requiring any body or organisation, including government, and organisations in the private sector, such as financial institutions, to supply the relevant information. There are, on its face, no limits to the power to issue such an order, and nothing, for example, appears to limit the making of an order addressed to a legal representative or tax authority.

---

[34]   Christopher Leslie, Parliamentary Under-Secretary of State, Home Office, HC Standing Committee (6 July 2004), col 359.

[35]   Ibid, col 362.

No doubt issues under art 8 are engaged (respect for private and family life, etc), but the purpose for which the power is given (to facilitate the proper working of the legal process) would appear to clearly satisfy art 8(2). The inability, at present, to access up-to-date data and information is seen as a 'substantial barrier'[36] to an effective enforcement regime.

5.18   Clearly, though, safeguards are needed to ensure that information obtained is not misused. Schedule 1 of the Data Protection Act 1998 sets out the relevant   principles governing disclosure of data. The first and second principles therein allow the disclosure of data where necessary for the administration of justice, and for (or in connection with) legal proceedings. The new s 125CB creates a new criminal offence.

By s 125CB(2) a person who intentionally or recklessly:

'(a)   discloses information supplied under a disclosure order otherwise than as permitted by subsection (1) [which identifies the limited distribution of the information permitted], or

(b)   uses information as supplied otherwise than for the purpose of facilitating the execution of the warrant concerned

commits an offence, triable either on indictment or summarily. In either case the punishment on conviction is a fine, limited in the case of summary conviction to the statutory maximum.'

However, by s 125CB(3), it is not an offence to disclose information in accordance with any enactment, or order of the court, or for the purposes of any proceedings before a court, or to disclose any information which has previously been lawfully disclosed to the public.

BREACH OF COMMUNITY PENALTY

5.19   Section 179 and Sch 8 of the Criminal Justice Act 2003 provided for the powers and procedures in respect of the beach, revocation or amendment of community orders. Paragraph 7(1) of that Schedule gave the power to dealing with breach of such an order to the court supervising that order. Only such a court could issue a warrant to bring the offender before the court.

A similar position exists in respect of detention and training orders, suspended sentence supervision and attendance centre orders under the Powers of Criminal Courts (Sentencing) Act 2000.

This position has, apparently, caused problems in practice. Section 29 and Sch 5 of the DVCVA address this issue. The effect of the detailed changes in Sch 5 is to allow any magistrates court to issue a warrant or summons to secure the attendance of an offender. Reference should be made to the detail of the new Sch 5.

---

36   Ibid, col 366.

INTERMITTENT CUSTODY

5.20 Section 31 and Sch 6 of the DVCVA amend the provisions of the Criminal Justice Act 2003 relating to intermittent custody.

Intermittent custody was introduced by s 183 of the CJA, and permits a court to impose a sentence of at least 28 weeks but not exceeding 51 weeks, to be served during intermittent periods. Consecutive periods must not exceed 65 weeks in total. The order specifies periods during which the offender is to be released temporarily on licence before he has served the appropriate number of days in custody (CJA, s 183(1)).[37] The provisions are being piloted.[38]

The changes made by Sch 6 of the DVCVA reflect experience during the pilot of the intermittent custody provisions. The pilot has revealed certain situations where there are unintentional inconsistencies between the licence provisions applicable to those sentenced to a term of intermittent custody and those serving custody plus.[39] Two basic problems have arisen.[40]

5.21 The first main issue concerns the calculation of 'custodial days' for the purpose of eligibility for home detention curfew under s 246 of the CJA. An offender is not eligible for home detention curfew unless they have served the requisite number of custody days, defined, in the case of intermittent custody, by s 246(8) of the CJA as (in the case of two or more sentences of intermittent custody) the aggregate of the numbers of custodial days specified. This is inconsistent with the rule in respect of custody-plus (see ss 244(3), 181(3)). The change necessary to remove this anomaly was explained by Baroness Scotland as follows:[41]

> '[Schedule 6] provides that, when an offender has been sentenced to concurrent terms of intermittent custody, the required custodial days for home detention curfew purposes is the aggregate of the custodial days less the number of days to be served concurrently.'

The effect therefore is that the position in respect of intermittent custody and custody plus will be identical. It does not affect the normal release date on intermittent custody where there is no early release on home detention curfew.

---

[37] For discussion of the intermittent custody provisions, see Ward and Davies *Criminal Justice Act 2003 – A Practitioners' Guide* (2004, Jordans).

[38] Criminal Justice Act 2003 (Commencement No 1) Order 2003, SI 2003/3282; Criminal Justice (Sentencing)(Licence Conditions) Order 2003, SI 2003/3337.

[39] Custody plus is the new form of sentence in respect of sentences of less than 12 months' imprisonment, introduced by s 181 CJA. It involves a specified custody period followed by a specified licence period. See, in particular, Ward and Davies, op cit, paras 9.2–9.20.

[40] The following explanations draw heavily on those given to the House of Lords by Baroness Scotland, Minister of State, Home Office, 658 HL Official Report, no 52, cols 1422-1423.

[41] 658 HL Official Report, no 52, col 1421.

5.22   The second change is made by a new s 264A of the CJA, which deals with the position of consecutive sentences of intermittent custody. This sets out, more clearly than hitherto, the fact that the offender must serve the aggregate of custodial days under the consecutive orders before being eligible for release on licence, and then be subject to a period of licence for the longest licence period for any one of his sentences.

COMMON ASSAULT AS AN ALTERNATIVE VERDICT

5.23   Section 11 of the DVCVA amends s 6(3) of the Criminal Law Act 1967. Section 6(3) of that Act states:

> 'Where on a person's trial on indictment for any offence except treason or murder, the jury find him not guilty of the offence specifically charged in the indictment, but the allegations in the indictment amount to or include (expressly or by implication) an allegation of another offence falling within the jurisdiction of the court of trial, the jury may find him guilty of that other offence or an offence of which he could be found guilty on an indictment specifically charging that other offence.'

The amendment of s 3 introduces two new subsections, (3A) and (3B). The effect of these is to open up the potential for an alternative verdict of common assault, even if a count charging the offence is not included in the indictment. Prior to this change, the effect of s 40 of the Criminal Justice Act 1988[42] was that an alternative verdict of common assault could not be substituted unless common assault was the subject of a specific count.[43] Clearly, in dealing especially with cases of domestic violence that is not a helpful situation, and the new Act gives the court of trial the scope to return a verdict of common assault where that is what the facts found by the court justify.

UNFITNESS TO PLEAD AND INSANITY

5.24   The DVCVA contains a range of measures dealing with both the procedure to be followed in determining fitness to plead under the Criminal

---

[42]   Section 40 provides: 'A count charging a person with a summary offence to which this section applies may be included in an indictment if the charge (a) is founded on the same facts or evidence as a count charging an indictable offence, or (b) is part of a series of offences of the same or similar character as an indictable offence which is also charged, but only if (in either case) the facts or evidence relating to the offence were disclosed [by material which, in pursuance of regulations made under paragraph 1 of Schedule 3 to the Crime and Disorder Act 1998 (procedure where person sent for trial under s 51 (or s 51A) has been served on the person charged.].' The wording in square brackets reflects the changes to sending for trial made by Criminal Justice Act 2003, and alternative wording reflects cases which may (prior to commencement) may be subject to pre-existing provisions.

[43]   See *Mearns* [1991] 1 QB 82, CA.

Procedure (Insanity) Act 1964 and the powers of the court when a court has determined that the defendant is insane or unfit to plead.

Procedure for determining fitness to plead

5.25 Section 4(5) of the Criminal Procedure (Insanity) Act 1964 provides that the question of fitness to plead shall be determined by a jury. Section 22 of the DVCVA amends s 4(5) by substituting the words 'the court' for 'a jury'. Thus such matters are now to be decided by the judge. A consequential amendment is made to s 4(6) to like effect.

The reasons for the change are essentially based on efficiency, removing the need for a jury determination (and sometimes two juries)[44] where in the vast majority of cases there is no dispute of substance. Research conducted into the question of the trial of issues relating to unfitness to plead[45] showed that in the vast majority of cases the issue of unfitness was of concern to the court before the finding of unfitness. In only three of the surveyed cases was the issue raised during trial. The researchers found that in the vast majority of cases the function of the jury was 'somewhat ritualistic'. In some 78.4% of cases the issue of unfitness was not disputed, with only 8% of cases clearly indicating a dispute. The authors wrote as follows:

> 'In three cases where the issue was disputed by the Crown the finding that the defendant was unfit to plead was the result of a majority verdict, with one of the cases requiring two juries after the first could not reach a decision. Also in one case, returning to the mediaeval roots of fitness to plead, a defendant had a jury enquire whether he was 'mute by malice or visitation of God' before another jury inquired whether he was unfit to plead.'

Fascinating as the examples above are, the clear conclusion of the research was that a genuine need for jury determination of this issue does not exist. The change made should not, therefore, concern us, and should not be regarded another contribution yo a wider agenda of the restriction and limitation of trial by jury.[46] The cogency of the arguments supporting the change was well explained by Baroness Scotland in the House of Lords:[47]

> 'It is not in the interests of vulnerable defendants to have to undergo a lengthy process involving two separate juries with the first having to hear evidence from two medical practitioners. The provision does not detract from the defendant's right to be tried by a jury. In the event that the defendant is found unfit to plead a jury must still consider the facts of the case and acquit if not satisfied that the

---

44 See s 4(5)(b) which states 'where it falls to be determined at any later time, it shall be determined by a separate jury or by the jury by whom the accused is being tried, as the court may direct'.

45 See Mackay and Kearns 'The Trial of the Issue of Unfitness to Plead' [2000] Crim LR 536–537.

46 For wider issues, see para **4.10**.

47 Minister of Sate, Home Office, 659 HL Official Report, 3rd Reading, no 60, col 836.

defendant did the act as charged. … I … suggest that a jury is unlikely to be as well qualified as a judge to interpret the complex evidence of a professional nature. Moreover, under the new regime, if the defendant subsequently wishes to challenge a finding as to whether he is unfit to plead he will have a judge's reasons for the conclusion…'.

5.26   The terms of s 22(2) (and of a further consequential amendment in s 22(3)) are curious. Section 22(2) replaces the words 'a jury' with 'the court'. That clearly amends the opening statement in s 5(5) and the words of s 4(5)(a), but on a literal interpretation does not amend s 4(5)(b).[48] The words used by s 4(5)(b) are 'a separate jury' and 'the jury'. This is presumably a legislative oversight, and not intended to preserve jury trial of the issue where it arises after arraignment. That latter conclusion would be difficult to reconcile with the opening of s 4(5) ('The question of fitness to be tried shall be determined by the court without a jury'). By contrast, the amendment to s 4A (see below) does indeed envisage jury trial of the question of whether the accused did indeed do the act, once a finding of unfitness has been made.

5.27   Section 22(4) and (5) amend s 4A of the Criminal Procedure (Insanity) Act 1964. Section 4A, inserted into the 1964 Act in 1991, deals with the question of what happens if it is determined that the accused is under a disability. Under the existing provision a jury had to determine on evidence already heard and on any further evidence adduced by the prosecution or defence whether they are satisfied, as respect the count or each of the counts on which the accused was to be, or was being, tried, that he did the act or omission charged against him as the offence. There would thus be findings of fact as to whether the accused did, or did not, commit what would be the offence but for the unfitness.

The amendments now give this role to the judge, unless the issue arises after arraignment, in which case it will be determined by the jury by whom the defendant was being tried.

Powers of the court on finding of insanity or unfitness to plead

5.28   Section 24 of the DVCVA replaces s 5 of the Criminal Procedure (Insanity) Act 1964 with substitute provisions, providing a new range of disposals for the court when it has made a finding of unfitness to plead, and that the defendant did the act charged, or where the court has found the defendant not guilty by reason of insanity under the 1964 Act. They allow for the defendant to receive treatment and support if the court thinks that this is appropriate.

---

[48]   For the wording of s 4(5)(b) see n 42, above.

5.29 A new s 5 gives a court[49] three options in such circumstances. It may make a hospital order (with or without a restriction order),[50] supervision order[51] or order the defendant's absolute discharge.

If the court wishes the defendant to be detained, a hospital order will be the appropriate course, and the court will need to be satisfied by appropriate medical evidence that the defendant is mentally disordered and requires specialist medical treatment. A restriction order can be made where the defendant poses a risk to the public. The pre-existing s 5 prescribed a power to make an admission order, without the need for the court to act on medical evidence and allowed a court to specify restrictions (that is now the role of the Secretary of State). Once the court had made an admission order the Secretary of State had two months to issue a warrant for the defendant's admission to hospital. Now, there is no role for the Secretary of State to determine whether or not the defendant should be admitted, and a court must act on medical evidence.

The pre-existing s 5(3) and related provisions[52] required the court to admit the defendant to hospital subject to restrictions when he was charged with murder. That position is preserved, provided that the court has the power to make a hospital order (see the new s 5(3)). If the power to make a hospital order does not exist (because, for example, the evidence does not show *mental* disorder) the court must make a supervision order or absolutely discharge the defendant.[53]

5.30 A new s 5A is inserted into the 1964 Act. It makes provision in respect of these orders. Section 5A(1) and (3) modify the Mental Health Act 1983 to apply the provisions of that Act to hospital orders made where such an order is made under s 5. This is needed because hospital orders can be made following conviction, without regard to insanity or unfitness, but the modifications made by s 5A allow a court to require admission to hospital (that is not otherwise the case).

Powers to remand an accused to a hospital for reports or treatment, and to make an interim hospital order (contained in the 1983 Act), are extended to s

---

[49] For the position where the Court of Appeal substitutes a finding of insanity or unfitness for another finding, see s 24(3). The Court of Appeal will have the same powers, but will no longer have the power to order a person's admission hospital where it substitutes a verdict of acquittal for a verdict of not guilty by reason of insanity, and there is medical evidence that the person is mentally disordered. In such cases civil powers under Mental Health Act 1983 should be used.

[50] Under Mental Health Act 1983, ss 38, 41.

[51] Within the meaning of Part 1 of Sch 1A of the DVCVA.

[52] See Criminal Procedure (Insanity and Unfitness to Plead) Act 1991, Sch 1, para 2(2).

[53] The provisions of Powers of Criminal Courts (Sentencing) Act 2000, s 12, apply to absolute discharges under s 5 of the 1964 Act (Criminal Procedure (Insanity) Act 1964, s 5A(6)).

5 orders (s 5A(2)). Section 5A(4) replicates existing provisions[54], and allows the Secretary of State to remit for trial a person who is found unfit to plead and given a hospital order with a restriction order, and who subsequently recovers.

5.31   A new Sch 1A is introduced into the Criminal Procedure (Insanity) Act 1964 by the new s 5A(5). The new schedule is to be found at Sch 2 to the DVCVA. The effect is that the supervision order replaces the existing supervision and treatment order, available hitherto under Sch 2 to the Criminal Procedure (Insanity and Unfitness to Plead) Act 1991. The new order enables treatment to be given under supervision for physical as well mental disorder. It cannot now include a requirement that the patient receive treatment as an in-patient. It is intended to provide support and treatment which may prevent re-offending. No sanction exists for breach of the order: the new Sch 1A makes no change in that respect.

Powers of appeal courts

5.32   Section 25 of the DVCVA inserts new provisions (ss 16A and 16B) into the Criminal Appeal Act 1968. Rights of appeal will exist against a supervision order or a hospital order made under the new s 5. The Court of Appeal will have the right to quash those orders, and substitute or amend them in any way open to the court that made the order which is being appealed.

PROSECUTION RIGHTS OF APPEAL

5.33   Section 58 of the CJA introduced extended rights of appeal for the prosecution.[55] The right of appeal is in respect of a ruling at 'the applicable time'. The pre-existing s 58(13) defines this as meaning 'any time (whether before or after the commencement of the trial) before the start of the judge's summing-up'. For clarification, s 30 of the DVCVA amends that to '…the time when the judge starts his summing up' thus envisaging that a summing-up may be interrupted.

A further amendment anticipates the bringing into force of Part 7 of the Criminal Justice Act 2003, which in certain circumstances permits trial by judge-only, without a jury. A new s 58(14) is inserted into the CJA to reflect that (DVCVA, s 30(2)). The appropriate time will be the time when the summing-up would have started if there had been a jury.

---

[54]   Criminal Procedure (Insanity and Unfitness to Plead) Act 1991, Sch 1, para 4, which is repealed (DVCVA, s 24(5)).

[55]   See Ward and Davies *Criminal Justice Act 2003 – A Practitioners' Guide* (2004, Jordans), para 7.6 et seq.

Chapter Six

VICTIMS

Summary

6.1   Part 3 of the Domestic Violence, Crime and Victims Act 2004 ('DVCVA') makes provision in respect of victims and witnesses of crime. Section 32 obliges the Home Secretary to issue a Code of Practice as to the services to be provided to victims of criminal conduct, and which will replace the non-statutory standards set out in the current Victim's Charter.

Section 41 empowers the Parliamentary Commissioner for Administration to investigate complaints made by members of the public in relation to breaches of the Code.

Section 42 creates the office of Commissioner for Victims and Witnesses. The Act also provides for a statutory Victims' Advisory Panel, provides for the recovery of criminal injuries compensation from offenders and deals with disclosure of information.

The Act makes other miscellaneous changes, including power to make grants to bodies which help victims and witnesses.

BACKGROUND

6.2   Part 3 of the DVCVA 2004 is part of a strategy to address the needs of victims of crime. It fits within the wider context discussed in chapter 1. *Justice for All*[1] observed:

> 'Justice is not simply about punishment for its own sake. Many victims, when asked, say that they simply want to ensure that none else has to go through the kind of experience they themselves have. And the best way of ensuring that is to catch, convict and rehabilitate offenders and prevent further crime. Victim's own evidence is crucial in bringing offenders to justice. They must be nurtured and not subject to a host of delays, postponements and barriers ... The criminal justice agencies have a particular responsibility to support victims and witnesses.

---

[1]   Op cit, paras 2.11–2.12.

This includes ensuring that they are protected, if vulnerable from intimidation or further crime, and taking into account the impact of the offence on victims when sentencing offenders…'.

Victims of crime generally expect to see the perpetrator brought to justice, but the reality is often different. A large gap exists between the amount of reported crime and the number of offences in respect of which the offender is brought to justice. Government strategy has been to engage with this issue on a variety of fronts, an approach which, Baroness Scotland reported,[2] had seen the number of offenders brought to justice increase by 4.3% between March 2002 and March 2003. A consultation paper 'A Better Deal for Victims and Witnesses'[3] was published in 2003, and reviewed what was, and was not, working. A further consultation paper 'Compensation and Support for the Victims of Crime'[4] was published in January 2004, concentrating particularly on the compensation arrangements for victims.

The needs of victims

6.3   The consultation paper 'Compensation and Support for the Victims of Crime' identified the context quite well.[5] Amongst some key points that provide an important context and explanation for the provisions of the new Act relating to victims are:

- the chances of being a victim of crime are 'the lowest for many years', but nonetheless one in four people are victims;[6]
- 28% of victims wanted some form of help, whilst only 13% got some;[7]
- victim satisfaction has fallen from 68% in 1994 to 58% in 2002;
- one in ten women reported experiencing some form of victimisation since age 16 and one in twenty said they had been raped at least once since age 16.[8] Only 20% of alleged rapes and 18% of alleged sexual victimisation were reported to the police;
- people from minority ethnic groups are more likely to be victims of crime than white people, mainly due to demographic and geographical factors;[9]
- domestic violence has the highest rate of repeat victimisation of any crime, over 50% of incidents being repeats. Currently only 12% of victims of domestic violence report incidents to the police.

---

[2]   Minister of State, Home Office, HL 2nd Reading (15 December 2003), vol 655, col 951.
[3]   Home Office, July 2003.
[4]   Home Office, 2004.
[5]   See p 8 *Introduction.*
[6]   Home Office Statistical Bulletin 2002/2003.
[7]   2000 British Crime Survey.
[8]   Home Office Statistical Bulletin 18/00; British Crime Survey 2000.
[9]   Clancy, Hough, Aust and Kershaw, Home Office Research Study 223 *Crime, Policing and Justice: The Experience of Ethnic Minorities Findings from the British Crime Survey* (Home Office, 2001).

That consultation paper identified the need to make further provision for victims to ensure that its amount and balance were right. The arrangements proposed in respect of victim compensation have to be viewed as part of a bigger picture, which had in part been set out in the earlier consultation paper.

A better deal for victims and witnesses

6.4 Amongst the positives identified by that earlier consultation paper were the development of victim support since 1997, now helping in excess of one million victims each year, the limitations on cross-examination contained in the Youth Justice and Criminal Evidence Act 1999,[10] the extension of the Witness Service to magistrates' courts, and better training for both police and CPS in identifying vulnerable witnesses. Yet a range of problems remains. The abandonment of cases because witnesses and victims refuse to testify,[11] the intimidatory nature of the trial and of cross-examination, victims and witnesses feeling badly informed and badly treated, and the waste of time being summoned for hearings that never occur because of last-minute changes of plea[12] are each identified as problems. So, too, is the fact that victims and witnesses are not routinely kept up-to-date on the progress of cases or informed of significant events such as the release date of an offender, or the reasons why a case is not being continued. Some of these problems could reflect the fact that responsibility for victims and witnesses is too spread out across the Criminal Justice Service agencies, causing confusion, inefficiency and delay. Whatever the reason, victim satisfaction with the police fell from 67% in 1994 to 58% in 2000.[13]

6.5 The consultation paper noted:

> 'Everyone has the right to justice, including those accused of a crime. But many victims feel that the rights of defendants take precedence over theirs. Public confidence in the CJS is dependant on how people perceive that they, or their family and friends, will be treated as a victim or witness to a crime. Too often the perception is that victims and witnesses are the ones on trial rather than the suspect.
>
> Our reforms are intended to ensure that the needs and rights of victims and witnesses are considered at every stage. Our overall aim is to reduce crime, and so reduce the number of people who are victims in the first place. This particularly applies to those who are subject to repeated crime who are often the most vulnerable people living in the most disadvantaged areas.'

[10] The consultation paper refers specifically to the prohibition of cross-examination by unrepresented defendants in rape cases, but could equally have referred to the range of special measures direction under the 1999 Act.

[11] Some 30,000 during 2001. The problem is party addressed by changes in the hearsay evidence rules contained in Criminal Justice Act 2003, due to come into force in 2005

[12] An issue addressed by new procedures in the Criminal Justice Act 2003 to encourage early indications of guilty plea

[13] See Consultation Paper, p 2.

It proposed a variety of measures, amongst which were:

- the setting of targets to ensure victims and witnesses are at the heart of the system;
- greater powers for the police to impose conditions on bail;
- the encouragement of early guilty pleas, with the introduction of indications on sentence;
- more use of witness statements at trial;
- anonymity for victims of domestic violence;
- exploring the possibility of utilising places other than formal courtrooms for some cases, particularly those involving young and vulnerable defendants, victims and witnesses;
- a clear coherent sentencing framework which will help victims understand what sentence has been passed and its effects;
- new sentences for violent and sexual offenders;
- a formal conditional caution system;
- the tightening up of bail conditions so victims do not see offenders escaping justice;
- reform of enforcement procedures for compensation orders;
- emphasis on reparation and rehabilitation in sentencing policy;
- victim personal statements.

Many of these steps have been put into effect, or the foundation to do so laid, by the passage of legislation, particularly the Criminal Justice Act 2003,[14] or by a range of pilot projects or initiatives, often in liaison with the voluntary sector or inter-agency partnership, or the targeting of particular resource. One good example is that a new national free-phone 24-hour helpline was launched in December 2003 to provide support for the victims of domestic violence, funded to the tune of £1 million each from Government and from Comic Relief.[15]

6.6   It is in this general context that the provisions of the DVCVA 2004 have to be viewed. They are intended:[16]

> 'to give victims the rights to consistent and guaranteed levels of advice, support and information from the criminal justice agencies that they come into contact with, and to give them a powerful voice across Government.'

The range of provisions clearly has as its primary focus the victim's interaction within the criminal justice system. But the needs of victims can extend beyond this. The new Independent Commissioner is intended to be a 'champion' for the needs of victims and witnesses across government. It provides, said

---

[14]   See, on many of these matters, Ward and Davies *The Criminal Justice Act 2003 – A Practitioners' Guide* (Jordans, 2004).

[15]   See Baroness Scotland, Minister of State, Home Office, HL 2nd Reading (15 December 2003), vol 655, col 950.

[16]   Ibid, at col 953.

Baroness Scotland, 'the first focused and holistic response to the all-round needs of victims'.

THE CODE OF PRACTICE

The duty

6.7 Section 32(1) requires the Home Secretary to issue a code of practice as to the services to be provided to a victim of criminal conduct by a person appearing to him to have functions relating to (a) the victims of criminal conduct, or (b) any aspect of the criminal justice system. The Code is intended to define the minimum statutory services that criminal justice agencies should provide to victims of crime. It is meant to build on the pre-existing Victims' Charter, adopted in 1996, 'creating clear rights for all victims, in terms of information, advice, personal support and protection.'[17]

The term 'services' is not defined, despite strenuous efforts made during the parliamentary proceedings to insert a partial definition, which would have included 'protection, personal support, to receive and provide information and to receive explanations'.[18]

'Criminal conduct' means conduct constituting an offence (s 32(7)). That does not presuppose a complaint or conviction,[19] and s 32(6) puts it beyond doubt that prosecution and conviction for the offence is, for this purpose, unnecessary: it is immaterial whether a person has been charged with or convicted of the offence. The code can be restricted to specified descriptions of victims, or victims of specified offences or descriptions of conduct (s 32(2)(a), (b)).

The procedure to be followed in the making of the Code is prescribed by s 33. Interestingly, it does not require consultation beyond either the Attorney-General or Lord Chancellor, although in practice consultation with the various interested bodies within the criminal justice system will occur. It is also likely that the new Commissioner for Victims and Witnesses, an office created by the DVCVA 2004,[20] will also be consulted, although that is not a statutory requirement.[21]The process of amendment and revision of the Code is dealt with by s 33(3). The Home Secretary may not, though, revise the Code if it appears to him that the proposed revisions would result in a significant reduction in the quality or extent of the services to be provided under the Code, or in a

---

[17] Harriet Harman, MP, Solicitor-General, HL Standing Committee (29 June 2004), col 226.
[18] The substantive terms of the amendment, moved by Cheryl Gillam, MP, relying in turn on proposals from Victim Support. See HC Standing Committee (29 June 2004), col 222.
[19] In the context of ss 42-45, this is made explicit by 46(3)).
[20] See para **6.44**.
[21] Paul Goggins, MP, Parliamentary Under-Secretary of Sate for the Department of Home Affairs, HC Standing Committee (29 June 2004), col 232.

significant restriction in the description of persons to whom services are to be provided under the Code. Although one may wonder if any Home Secretary would categorise changes proposed by him as 'significant reductions' the provision is a welcome statement of the priority that victim support is to be given.

6.8   During the passage of the Act, the Government published an Indicative Draft of the proposed Victim's Code of Practice. A copy of that indicative draft is found at Appendix B of this book. Although the detail will change, this indicative draft gives extensive insights as to what is likely to be put in place after commencement. Reference is made to it in this part of the book. The Code is intended to identify a minimum level of service, and additional services may be provided in some areas in accordance with priorities agreed with local Criminal Justice Boards.

The Code will be published in final form for consultation during the early part of 2005. Agencies will be asked to comply with the Code from April 2005, but it is not anticipated that the Code will come into full force until November 2005.[22]

One general issue that will need to be carefully considered when the final version of the Code is adopted is the extent to which the terms of the Code respect the rights of a defendant to a fair trial. This was a matter of concern to the Joint Committee on Human Rights.[23] It recommended careful scrutiny to ensure that this fundamental right is not prejudiced.

To whom does the Code apply?

6.9   The Code may restrict its application to specified persons, or specified descriptions of persons having functions relating to victims or in respect of any aspect of the criminal justice system (s 32(1), (2) (c)). Its requirements may differ in respect of those who have different functions, or in respect of different areas (s 32(4)). What it may not do is require anything to be done by a person acting in a judicial capacity, or by a function of the Crown Prosecution Service involving the exercise of discretion (s 32(5))

The indicative draft Code[24] identifies the following as organisations required to provide services for victims under the Code:

* Court Service/ Magistrates' Courts Committees[25]
* Criminal Cases Review Commission
* Criminal Injuries Compensation Authority

---

[22]   See Criminal Justice Online website www.cjonline.gov.uk.
[23]   3rd Report 2003-2004, at para 2.14.
[24]   See para **6.8**.
[25]   From April 2005 these will be one new Courts Agency.

- Criminal Injuries Compensation Appeals Panel
- Crown Prosecution Service
- all police forces for police areas in England and Wales and the British Transport Police
- Parole Board
- local probation boards
- National Association of Victim Support Schemes
- Youth Offending Teams.

The Code is intended to apply in respect of victims of offences committed in England and Wales, with the person providing the services also in England and Wales.[26]

People entitled to receive services under the Code

6.10 The Indicative Draft Code puts flesh on the skeleton created by s 32. The Code focuses on victims of certain crimes. It requires services to be provided to any person who has made an allegation of an offence to a police officer,[27] or had an application for compensation made on his or her behalf, that he or she has been subjected   to criminal conduct which:

(a) deprived that person of his or hr property, or damaged it, or was likely to do one of these things;
(b) led, or was intended or likely to lead, to the person's death or to cause physical or mental injury; or
(c) constituted a sexual offence against the person. The term 'sexual offence' is not defined in the draft, but the term no doubt bears a wide meaning.[28]

Services under the Code will be provided to the direct victim, not to third parties or indirect victims such as witnesses of violent crime. If the victim is under 17, then the parent or guardian is likewise entitled to receive services, unless under investigation, or charged, in respect of the criminal conduct of which the child or young person is a victim. Where the victim is dead, the family spokesperson (nominated by the close relatives of the deceased)[29] is entitled to receive services.

---

[26] Harriet Harman, Solicitor-General, HC Standing Committee (29 June 2004), col 227.
[27] No allegation is necessary where a person has died as a result of criminal conduct: it is sufficient that a criminal investigation has commenced: Draft Code, para 4.2.
[28] See, eg, DVCVA 2004, s 45(2), which states that an offence is a sexual offence if it is an offence specified in Criminal Justice Act 2003, Sch 15, or one in respect of which the offender is subject to the notification requirements of Part 2 of the Sexual Offences Act 2003.
[29] The Code provides for nomination by the senior investigating officer if the family is unable to do so, or there are no close relatives.

6.11   Businesses with nine or more employees[30] are not entitled to receive services under the code. Nor need services be provided to a person where the criminal conduct amounted to a person driving a motor vehicle in a way which led (or was likely to lead) to physical injury or damage to property. This exclusion is subject to an exception where death results. Thus the Code applies in respect of the family of the victim of a motoring offence where the victim has died), but not to the victim of careless or dangerous driving. A third exception is in respect of criminal conduct the subject of a health and safety investigation.[31]

6.12   A service provider must decide whether a person is entitled to services on the basis of the allegation of criminal conduct made, irrespective of whether the service provider does not believe that allegation, or that no person has been charged, or that a person has been charged with a different offence, or no person has been convicted. On the other hand, if the service provider is satisfied that an allegation of misconduct does not constitute a criminal offence at all, then services need not be provided. Thus a complainant of theft is entitled to services, even if the police conclude that no offence was committed or that it was handling stolen gods, but a complainant whose complaint, if true, amounts to no crime at all is not. A person aggrieved by an incorrect assessment may have recourse to the Parliamentary Commissioner for Administration.[32]

Vulnerable victims

6.13   The obligation to provide certain services extends to vulnerable victims only. A vulnerable victim is a person who is vulnerable by virtue of their personal circumstances or the circumstances of the offence, including but not limited to a victim who:

(a) is under the age of 17;
(b) is suffering from mental disorder, within the meaning of the Mental Health Act 1983;[33]
(c) has experienced domestic violence. Just as with the DVCVA 2004, this term is not defined;
(d) has been the subject of recorded or reported incidents of harassment or bullying. It is not clear why a distinction between recorded or reported incidents is drawn because there is surely a duty to record reported allegations;

---

[30]   The term 'business' includes unincorporated associations, partnerships and not-for-profit organisations, and an 'employee' includes a partner or director.
[31]   Under Health and Safety at Work Act 1974, s 20 or s 39.
[32]   See para **6.43**.
[33]   'Mental disorder' is defined by the MHA 1983, s 1, as meaning 'mental illness, arrested or incomplete development of mind, psychopathic disorder and any other disorder or disability of mind'.

(e) has made an allegation of criminal conduct which constitutes a criminal offence or which is racially aggravated, or aggravated on religious, homophobic or transphobic grounds;

(f) is the family spokesperson of a person who has died;[34]

(g) is likely to be or who has been subject to intimidation in respect of the allegation of criminal conduct which the person has made.

If the person is vulnerable certain duties specifically apply. The police must take all reasonable steps promptly to identify vulnerable witnesses. Where such a person may be called as a witness, and may be eligible for special measures under Youth Justice and Criminal Evidence Act 1999,[35] the police must explain the relevant provisions and record any views the victim expresses about applying for special measures. The CPS must also consider whether or not to make an application for special measures directions, and record the result of that consideration.

6.14 The police must inform a vulnerable victim if the suspect is given bail in circumstances where the police had sought a remand in custody, or made an application for a remand in custody. The vulnerable victim must be informed of any bail conditions which involve or affect the victim, and the steps that victim can take if they are broken. The timescale for doing is within one working day (as defined) after the day when the police receive the information from the court unless the vulnerable victim specifically requests not to be informed or there are good reasons why the information cannot be passed on (in which case a contemporary record must be kept).

6.15 The police must also keep a vulnerable victim, and the probation service victim contact team,[36] informed of the result of an appeal in respect of relevant criminal conduct no later than one working day after the police are notified by the court of the result.

Breaches of the Code

6.16 Section 34 of the DVCVA 2004 makes it clear that a failure to perform a duty imposed by the Code does not, of itself, make the individual or body liable to criminal or civil proceedings. It is, though, admissible in evidence in criminal or civil proceedings and a court may take into account a failure to comply with the code in determining a question in the proceedings.

This provision is, on its face, unexceptionable. It mirrors provisions common in the context of Codes of Practice. Yet it is unclear how this provision may operate. No question arises of liability for breach of statutory duty: if there was any doubt on this question it is removed by the terms of s 34 itself. It is

---

[34] See Indicative Code.
[35] See para **6.10**.
[36] See in particular Youth Justice and Criminal Evidence Act 1999, ss 16-23.

not self-evident when breach of the Code *will* be relevant to a question in the proceedings. That may be the case, perhaps, if there any questions about whether special measures directions should be made, under the Youth Justice and Criminal Evidence Act 1999.

6.17   Where a victim *does* believe there has been a breach of the Code, one remedy where the victim remains dissatisfied following complaint, is the opportunity to have the case examined by the Parliamentary Commissioner for Administration, who is given jurisdiction in such matters by the DVCVA 2004.[37]

The obligations of service providers

6.18   We have already noted that the service level obligations set out by the Code are minima.[38] It may be the case than in some areas they will be augmented or exceeded. The specific duties owed to vulnerable victims have also been noted.[39] Within that framework, the Code sets out the likely obligation of the main players in the criminal justice system. Because we set out in full the provisions of the Indicative Draft, we do not repeat the detail obligations therein set out, and reference to the detail should be made to the Indicative Code, at Appendix 2. However the main thrust of its provisions is to provide obligations on the main players within the criminal justice, especially the Crown Prosecution Service and Police. Amongst the key issues dealt with are notification of dates of hearings, progress reports, notification of sentence and outcome, and of appeals. It also covers issues such as protection (including from intimidation) and information about personal support and advice.

Its effect was described the Government in *Justice for All*[40] as follows:

> 'Under the new Code all the services that come into contact with victims, including the police, the CPS, the courts, the defence, the probation and prison services, the Criminal Injuries Compensation Authority, the Criminal Cases Review Commission and Victim Support ... have new responsibilities to ensure that the needs of victims are met (each of these groups responsibilities will differ depending upon the role within the system).. The police, for example, will be responsible for providing information if a suspect is arrested, cautioned or charged; telling them whether the suspect is on bail; protecting them from intimidation; informing them promptly   of the date of any court hearing; and ensuring that a victim is put in touch with Victim Support Services. The National Probation Service will be responsible for keeping victims informed about a prisoner's release and arrangements for their supervision and any licence conditions.'

---

[37]   See para **6.43**.
[38]   See para **6.8**.
[39]   See para **6.13 – 6.15**.
[40]   Op cit, para 2.43.

A particular role is seen for the Crown Prosecution Service, building on pre-existing initiatives. The Government has already provided £11 million to the CPS to take responsibility for communicating prosecution decisions direct to victims. Under the Scheme the CPS provides victims with an explanation when the prosecution decision is to discontinue the case or to alter the charges substantially. In certain sex offences or racially aggravated crime in serious cases such as those involving a death or child abuse, the CPS offer to meet the victim or victim's family to explain the basis of the decision.[41]

RIGHT OF VICTIMS OF SEXUAL OR VIOLENT OFFENCES TO MAKE REPRESENTATIONS AND RECEIVE INFORMATION

Background

6.19 As already noted,[42] one important factor for victims is to be aware of what is going in respect of 'their crime' and have the right to make representations about the case. The Indicative Code provides a practical framework for this.[43] Part 3, Chapter 2 of the DVCVA 2004 contains a wide range of specific statutory provisions relating to the victims of sexual or violent offences.

6.20 These provisions, added to the Bill during its latter parliamentary stages,[44] are intended 'to achieve a simple aim ... that victims of serious sexual or violent offending should have the right to information about the release of the offender, whether the offender has received a prison sentence or been dealt with under mental health legislation.'[45] Section 69 of the Criminal Justice and Courts Services Act 2000 created that duty in respect of those who receive a prison sentence. The new provisions re-enact that duty, and extend it to the relevant parts of the mental health legislation

Section 45(2) of the DVCVA 2004 states that an offence is a sexual or violent offence if it is any of the following:

(a) murder or an offence specified in Sch 15 to the Criminal Justice Act 2003;[46]
(b) an offence in respect of which the patient or offender is subject to the notification requirements of Part 2 of the Sexual Offences Act 2003;[47]

---

41 *Safety and Justice,* op cit, p 26 – 27; *Justice for All,* op cit, para 2.35.
42 See para **6.4**.
43 See para **6.7**.
44 See HC Deb (27 October) 2004, col 1446.
45 Paul Goggins, Parliamentary Under-Secretary of State for the Home Department, ibid.
46 Sch 15 to the 2003 Act identifies some 65 violent offences, and detailed reference should be made thereto. It includes all of the serious offences of assault, etc.
47 Defined by reference to Sch 3 to the CJA 2003.

(c) an offence against a child within the meaning of Part 2 of the Criminal Justice and Court Services Act 2000.[48]

6.21 One general issue arises in respect of all of the provisions dealt with in this context, namely how much detail is a victim to be given? This is particularly important in the context of the new powers in respect of those detained under mental health legislation, because matters relating to the of the patient's health will be confidential. On being pressed on this, which of course raises Art 8 issues, the Parliamentary Under-Secretary of State observed:[49]

> 'The provisions do not allow for the disclosure of personal medical information or specific information about an individual's mental health. They ensure that the victim has the right to make representations about the conditions that will apply when the offender is released. They can be given simple, factual, information, namely that the individual has been released from hospital or prison and the details of any on prohibitions on contact …. So far as I can tell … there are no strictly enforced legal limitations [on disclosure by the victim of the information] but common sense dictates that the closer the information is kept the better.'

The right of the local probation board to pass to the victim such other information as it considers appropriate[50] must therefore be read subject to this important limitation.

General right to make representations and receive information about matters relating to licence

6.22 Section 35 of the DVCVA 2004 (which replaces s 69 of the Criminal Justice and Courts Services Act 2000) imposes a duty on a local probation board for the area in which the sentence is imposed (ie the area in which the sentencing court is situated) to take all reasonable steps to ascertain whether a person who falls within the terms of the section (a victim or someone who represents the victim) wishes to make representations about matters relating to licence conditions or requirements, or receive information about them.

The section applies where a person is convicted of a sexual or violent offence,[51] and a 'relevant sentence' is imposed on the offender. The term 'relevant sentence' is defined by s 45 and means a sentence of imprisonment for a term of 12 months or more,[52] a sentence of detention during Her Majesty's pleasure, a sentence of detention for a period of 12 months or more under s 91 of the Powers of Criminal Courts (Sentencing) Act 2000,[53] or a detention and training

---

[48] Part 2 of the 2000 Act defines an 'offence against a child' as any offence against a child which falls within paras 1 to 3 of Sch 4 to the CJCSA 2000.

[49] HC Deb (27 October 2004), col 1449.

[50] See para **6.23**.

[51] See para **6.20**.

[52] See para **6.12**.

[53] Section 91 of the Powers of Criminal Courts (Sentencing) Act 2000 provides for detention of offenders under 18 convicted of certain serious offences.

order for a period of 12 months or more.[54] The section does not, though, apply if a court gives a hospital direction and a limitation direction in relation to the offender.[55] In such a case the duty imposed by s 39[56] applies.

6.23 The matters about which representations should be sought are whether the offender should be subject to any licence conditions or supervision requirements in the event of his release and, if so, what conditions or requirements (s 35(4)). The duty is placed on the local board for the area in which the offender is sentenced. That board is also under a duty to ascertain whether the victim wishes to be informed about any such conditions or requirements that are in fact imposed (s 35(3),(5)). The obligation to fulfil the request made under s 35(5) is, though, on the local board for the area where an offender is to be supervised on release or, in any other case, the local board for the area where the prison or other place of detention are situated (s 35(8)).

The procedure to be followed is specified by s 35(6) and (7). If the victim *does* make representations, they must be forwarded to the persons responsible for determining the matter, [57] which may be the court, Home Secretary or Parole Board. If the victim has expressed a wish to receive information about conditions and restrictions, then the local board (as defined above) must do certain things. It must take all reasonable steps:

(a) to inform the victim whether or not the offender is to be subject to any licence conditions or supervision requirements;
(b) if he is, to supply details of any conditions or restrictions which relate to contact with the victim or his family; and
(c) to provide the person with such other information as the relevant local probation board considers appropriate in all the circumstances of the case.

There are no statutory limitations imposed by s 35(7) on what may, or should, be given by way of information pursuant to (c) above. Clearly, information relating to the safety or well-being of the family would be important (for example, that he is living – if that be the case – in the same locality) but, as noted earlier, the power cannot be unlimited. Some information of a medical or personal nature attracts confidentiality and should not (at any rate ordinarily) be disclosed. That in turn raises the question as to what might legitimately be disclosed under para (c) or its equivalents in other sections. The matter will, arguably, be subject to challenge on normal judicial review principles.

---

[54] See Crime and Disorder Act 1998.
[55] 'Hospital direction' has the meaning given by Mental Health Act 1983, s 45A(3)(a); 'limitation direction' the meaning given by s 45(3) (b) of the 1983 Act (DVCVA 2004, s 45(1)). See, further, para **6.24–6.27**.
[56] See para **6.28**.
[57] For current arrangements re licence determination, release conditions and supervision, see, generally Ward and Davis *Criminal Justice Act 2003 – A Practitioner's Guide* (Jordans, 2004).

Information in cases where a hospital order is made

6.24   Section 36 applies where a finding is made of disability under s 4 of the Criminal Procedure (Insanity) Act 1964[58] in a case where it is found that the offender did the act[59] that otherwise would amount to a sexual or violent offence.[60] If in such a case a hospital order[61] with a restriction order[62] is made in respect of the patient by a court dealing with him for the offence, the victim's rights in ss 36(4), 37 and 38 arise.

The local probation board for the area where the court that made the findings summarised above is situated must take all reasonable steps to ascertain whether a person who appears to the board to be a victim of the offence, or to act for the victim of the offence, wishes to make representations. The representations will be as to whether the patient should be subject to any conditions in the event of his discharge from hospital and, if so, what conditions, or to receive information about any conditions to which the patient should be subject in the event of his discharge (s 36(4), (5), (6)). The information that must be supplied is governed by s 37 or s 38.[63]

The duty to make such enquiries may thus be satisfied by contact with a representative, whether it be a solicitor, victim or witness support, or other known support mechanisms. Whatever, the result of any representations made must be forwarded to the persons responsible for determining the matter (s 37(1)), a duty that ends once the restriction order ceases to be in force (s 37(3)).

6.25   Some matters may be within the decision-making power of the Secretary of State. These are decisions as to whether to make a direction lifting restrictions,[64] whether to discharge the patient either absolutely or subject to conditions, or as to whether to vary the conditions subject to which a patient has been discharged. Other matters may be within the remit of the Mental Health Review Tribunal. These are applications concerning restricted patients,[65] or references to the Tribunal made by the Secretary of Sate in respect of restricted patients.[66] In any of these situations the Secretary of State or the Tribunal (as the case may be) must inform the local probation board for the

---

[58]   Section 4 of the 1964 Act provides for any question of fitness to plead to be determined by the court. Under s 4(5) of that Act that determination had to be made by a jury, but see, now s 17 of the DVCVA 2004 and para **5.25**.

[59]   In accordance with 1964 Act, s 4A. See para **5.27**.

[60]   See para **6.20**.

[61]   As defined by Mental Health Act 1983, s 37(4) (DVCVA 2004, s 45(1)).

[62]   As defined by MHA 1983, s 41 (DVCVA 2004, s 45(1)).

[63]   See paras **6.24–6.26**.

[64]   Under MHA 1983, s 42(1).

[65]   Under MHA 1983, s 69, 70 or 75.

[66]   MHA 1983, s 71.

area into which it is proposed to discharge a patient subject to a condition that he reside in that area, or in any other case, the local board for the area where the hospital where the patient is detained is situated (s 37(4), (5), (8)). Having been so informed, then if the victim expressed a wish to make representations about a matter specified by s 36(5),[67] or it appears that the victim has made such representations, then the information supplied by the Secretary of State or Tribunal must be supplied to the victim or someone acting on his behalf (s 37(6), (7)).

6.26 Section 38 governs the information that must be supplied to a victim about the discharge of a patient detained for a sexual or violent offence, in a case where s 36 applies. The duty imposed by s 38 is owed to a victim who has expressed a wish to receive certain information or wishes to make representations. If that victim has expressed the wish to receive information about the conditions to which the patient is to be subject in the event of his discharge from hospital, or has subsequently informed the relevant local board that he or she wishes to receive such information, the board must take all reasonable steps to inform the victim of certain matters. These are whether or not the patient is to be subject to any conditions in the event of his discharge and, if he is, the Board must provide the victim with details of any conditions which relate to contact with the victim or his family (s 38(2),(3)) The victim must also be told of the date on which any restriction order is to cease, and provide the victim with such other information as it considers appropriate in all the circumstances of the case (s 38(3)(c), (d)).

6.27 In respect of such a patient, the Secretary of State is under a duty to supply certain information (specified by s 38(4)) to the relevant local board. So too is a Mental Health Tribunal (in respect of the matters in s 38(5) or (6)). These matters relate to discharge, and conditions to which discharge is subject. The detailed provisions of s 38(5) and (6) govern the question as to whether it is the Secretary of State or the Tribunal that must inform the relevant local board. The board is then under a duty to inform the victim or a person acting on his behalf (s 38(3))

Information in cases where a hospital direction and limitation direction are given

6.28 Sections 39 to 41 of the DVCVA 2004 mirror (subject obviously to necessary textual modifications) the hospital order provisions. Section 39 applies if the offender is convicted of a sexual or violent offence,[68] a relevant sentence[69] is imposed on him, and a hospital direction and a limitation direction are given in relation to him by a court dealing with him for the offence.

---

[67] See para **6.24**.
[68] See para **6.20**.
[69] See para **6.22**.

In such a case the local probation board for the area in which the hospital direction is given must take reasonable steps to ascertain whether the person who appears to be a victim or to act for the victim wishes to make representations about specified matters, or to receive information about them (s 39(2)). The matters specified by s 39(3) are:

(a) whether the offender should, in the event of his discharge from hospital, be subject to any conditions and, if so, what they should be;
(b) whether the offender should, in the event of his release from hospital, be subject to any licence conditions or supervision requirements, and, if so, what they might be;
(c) if the offender is transferred to a prison or other institution in which he might have been detained if he had not been removed to hospital, whether he should, in the event of his release from prison or another institution, be subject to any licence conditions and, if so, what they might be.

The information to which the victim is entitled is information about any conditions to which the offender is to be subject in the event of his discharge, or about any licence conditions or supervision requirements to which the offender is to be subject in the event of his release (s 39(4)).

6.29   Sections 39 and 40 replicate the provisions described earlier in the context of hospital orders, in respect of the duties to communicate representations to the appropriate decision-makers, and impose duties about the supply of information by the Secretary of State or Mental Health Review Tribunal. The information to be supplied to a victim, or person acting on his behalf, is specified by s 41(3), and relates to the matters to which the victim was entitled to make representations.

Victims rights where a transfer direction and a restriction direction

6.30   Sections 42 to 44 of the DVCVA 2004 provide a similar scheme for cases where there is a transfer direction[70] and a restriction direction,[71] subsequent to an offender receiving a relevant sentence in respect of a sexual or violent offence. These provisions, which do not differ in structure or principle from those discussed above, provide the same legislative framework to ensure that victims who wish to make representations, or receive information, about the conditions to which any discharge will be subject, or other date on which any restriction ceases to have effect, or receive any other appropriate information, do so.

[70]   Within the meaning of MHA 1983, s 47(1).
[71]   Within the meaning of MHA 1983, s 49(2).

FINANCIAL SUPPORT TO AID VICTIMS

6.31 Part of the Government's strategy is to address the needs of victims of crime is to focus help (financial and non financial) on their needs. The consultation paper 'Compensation and Support for Victims of Crime'[72] highlighted ways in which could be achieved. One was in respect of changes to the Criminal Injuries Compensation Scheme.[73] But the Government considered that 'it is essential to provide a wider package of support for victims. We therefore want to establish a Victim's Fund in England and Wales to provide the many types of additional support which victims and witnesses need'.[74]

That consultation paper thus reviewed the perceived problems,[75] and made proposals in respect of the Victim's Fund, and with the principle of making offenders pay (already discussed in the context of surcharges to be paid by offenders).[76] It proposed significant changes to the Criminal Injuries Compensation Authority and its ability to recover money from offenders. The DVCVA 2004 in part provides the legislative framework necessary to implement the strategy identified in the consultation paper.

The Victims' Fund

6.32 No direct statutory authority is needed for the establishment of the Victims' Fund,[77] and none is therefore conferred by the DVCVA 2004. Resources for the fund will come from the surcharges imposed following a criminal conviction (for which statutory authority is needed, and therefore conferred by the Act)[78] and from resources released from charges to the Criminal Injuries Compensation Scheme.

6.33 Offenders can be made to pay in a variety of ways, including surcharges. Another source of funding for victims is, of course, compensation paid directly by the offender under a compensation order. Some 14% of those sentenced in the magistrates' court and 7% of those sentenced in the Crown Court are ordered to pay compensation. 28% of those sentenced for violence against the person and 14% of those sentenced for burglary are ordered to pay compensation; but, perhaps unsurprisingly, it is those who are made subject to a community sentence who are most likely to be ordered to pay compensation. In 2001, the average compensation order was £144 at

---

[72] Home Office (January 2004).
[73] See para **6.34**.
[74] *Compensation and Support for Victims of Crime*, op cit, Executive Summary, p 4, para 6.
[75] See para **6.3**.
[76] See para **5.10** et seq.
[77] See para **5.10**.
[78] See para **5.10**.

magistrates' courts and £1444 at the Crown Court.[79] The fact remains that the majority of victims receive nothing from the person who has committed an offence against them.

The consultation paper identified a range of reasons for this.[80] These include the limited means of many offenders, or limited information about those means,[81] the limited amount of payment that can as a result legitimately be ordered, the lack of information about the levels of compensation sought or needed by the victim, and the fact that many who might be ordered to pay compensation are given custodial sentences. Nor is compensation ordered commonly in combination with a fine. The Government wishes to increase the incidence of compensation orders[82] New provisions in the Courts Act 2003 are designed to assist, and new guidance is contemplated. Nothing in the DVCVA 2004 directly impacts on the powers of sentencing courts to make compensation orders or directly encourages them to do so. Rather, the DVCVA 2004, though the Victims' Fund provisions is attempting to address the same problem from a different direction. So, too, with the provisions in the DVCVA 2004 relating to the powers of the Criminal Injuries Compensation Authority.

Criminal Injuries Compensation Authority – powers to recover money from offenders

6.34   Section 57 of the DVCVA 2004 amends the Criminal Injuries Compensation Act 1995 by inserting therein new ss 7A, 7B, 7C and 7D. These provide for the recovery of compensation from offenders. The changes are intended:

> 'to improve the chances of making the offender pay by arming the Criminal Injuries Compensation Authority with powers to get back from offenders money it has paid out in compensation to its victims, as well as the costs of administrating that payment. The state or designated authority is clearly better placed than most individual victims to pursue an offender for damages, and it is right that it should do so when there is a reasonable chance of making a net recovery of public funds...'.

The consultation paper also made a variety of other proposals in respect of a more focused, targeted and efficient criminal injuries compensation scheme. These are not, though, part of the range of measures introduced by the DVCVA 2004.

---

[79]   These and other statistics in this para are taken from Consultation Paper, op cit, p 11.

[80]   Ibid, Ch 3, paras 23–36.

[81]   See, now, Courts Act 2003, which puts the onus on the defendant to declare his or her income and expenditure, and creates a new criminal offence aimed at those who fail to provide information about means.

[82]   Consultation Paper, op cit, Ch 3, para 28.

6.35 At the outset it should be stressed that these provisions do not directly impact on the eligibility of a victim for an award from the authority. Such an award will not be contingent upon recovery being available or made.[83]

6.36 The new s 7A of the Criminal Injuries Compensation Act 1995, inserted by s 57(2) of the DVCVA 2004, empowers the Home Secretary to make regulations which provide for the recovery of a sum equal to all or part of the compensation paid in respect of a criminal injury. That amount will be recovered from an 'appropriate person', defined by s 7A(2) as a person who has been convicted of an offence in respect of a criminal injury. The term 'in respect of' is not defined by these enabling provisions, and could, theoretically, extend not only to the direct perpetrator of the injury but also to a party to that crime, or another crime related to that injury. What, for example of someone convicted of assisting an offender to commit an offence which results in injury or loss? No doubt the regulations made will identify matters of definition of this type. However, the problem may be more theoretical than real in the light of s 7A(3) which provides that the amount recoverable must be determined by reference only to the extent to which the criminal injury is directly attributable to an offence of which he has been convicted. Thus an offender should be liable for an amount only if it is directly linked to *his* offence.

6.37 The regulations made under this power may confer functions on claims officers, or a Scheme manager (s 7A)(4)), but the enabling power contains one important limitation. The regulations may not authorise the recovery of an amount in respect of compensation from a person to the extent that the compensation has been repaid in accordance with the scheme.

6.38 When (under the proposed regulations) it has been determined that an amount is due, a recovery notice must be issue, pursuant to the new s 7B of the Criminal Procedure and Investigations Act 1996 ('CPIA'). That will require the payment of the specified sum, and provide the information specified by s 7B(2).[84] That information is the following:

(a) the reasons for the determination that an amount is recoverable from the person;
(b) the basis on which the amount has been determined;
(c) the way in which and the date before which the amount is required to be paid;
(d) the means by which the amount may be recovered if it is not paid in accordance with the notice;
(e) the grounds on which and the procedure by means of which the offender may seek a review if he objects to the determination, or the amount of the determination.

[83] Paul Goggins, Parliamentary Under Secretary of Sate, Department of Home Affairs, HC Standing Committee (6 July 2004), col 337.
[84] The requirements may be varied by order made by the Home Secretary: see s 7B(3).

Provisions for review of the determination are contained in a new s 7C, and, again, are to be covered by regulations. The Act is strangely silent as to who is to conduct the review. Nor does the consultation paper assist, but the answer given during parliamentary debate[85] suggests that the review is an internal review by the Criminal Injuries Compensation Authority. The detail will, no doubt, be set out in the relevant regulations but, in so far as it is a review within the authority, it surely cannot prevent judicial review of the determination.[86] It raises important issues about independent rights of appeal and, not inconceivably, important issues about adequate redress to satisfy the terms of the European Convention on Human Rights.[87]

6.39   The grounds for review are specified by s 7C(2) and are (only) that:

(a) the person subject to the determination has not been convicted of an offence to which the injury is directly attributable;
(b) the compensation paid was not determined in accordance with the scheme;
(c) the amount determined as recoverable from him was not determined in accordance with the regulations.

The person conducting the review may set aside, or reduce the determination, take no action. He or she may not, however, increase the amount unless it appears to him or her that the interests of justice require the amount to be increased.

The meaning of para (a) is not entirely clear. It might be that it extended to the fact of conviction at all (for example, two people with the same name); alternatively it might relate to questions of direct attribution of the loss to the offence. It could, of course, encompass both and, arguably, should.

6.40   The amount due under the determination is recoverable as a debt (in accordance with normal procedures, subject only to any specific details contained in the regulations), but only if there has been the issue of a recovery notice and a failure to pay (new s 7D(1)). Cases are likely to be pursued only if there is a reasonable prospect of recovering sums that are greater than the costs of so doing.[88]

In such debt recovery procedures, it is a defence for the person who is subject to the recovery notice, to show that:

(a) he has not been convicted of an offence to which the injury is directly attributable;

[85]   Paul Goggins, Parliamentary Under Secretary of State, Department for Home Affairs, HC Select Committee (6 July 2004), col 337.
[86]   Whether the Administrative Court would entertain an application prior to the conclusion of an application for review is somewhat doubtful.
[87]   But see para **6.39-6.40**.
[88]   Paul Goggins, MP, Parliamentary Under-Secretary of State, Department of Home Affairs, HC Standing Committee (6 July 2004), col 343.

(b) the compensation paid was not determined in accordance with the scheme; or

(c) the amount determined was not determined in accordance with the relevant regulations.

These are the *only* permitted grounds of challenge (at this stage) to the determination. No other question may be raised or finding made as to the amount that was, or ought to have been, the subject of the award. Thus if there are grounds to challenge the determination on any other grounds (such as, for the example, the apportionment of the determination between particular joint defendants), those would have to be pursued by means of an application for judicial review,[89] not by way of defence to the debt enforcement proceedings (s 7A(3)). Of course, nothing in s 7D(3) prevents a defence on the grounds that the amount due under the determination has been paid. The limitation therein is confined to challenges to the *award*.

6.41 The proceedings under s 7D are civil proceedings. In so far as they are contested, the normal civil standard of proof will be on those seeking to enforce the debt, and that will therefore require proof of the conviction (if that be needed) by a certificate of conviction, and of the determination. It is arguable that, because of the terms of s 7D(2), there will be no need (initially at any rate) for any evidence of the conviction to be adduced at all, because the fact of conviction is either a matter totally prohibited by s 7D(3) or, alternatively, the wording of s 7D(2)(a) places the obligation in that respect on the defendant (arguably, the preferred construction). Proof of any other matters is placed on the defendant, but only within the limits permitted by s 7D(2)(a),(b) or (c).

The relevant limitation period is specified by s 7D(4).

Grants

6.42 Section 56 provides a further strand in fulfilment of this strategy of targeting greater resources on victims. It permits the Secretary of State to pay such grants to such persons as he considers appropriate in connection with measures which appear to him to be intended to assist victims, witnesses or other persons affected by offences.

INSTITUTIONAL AND PROCEDURAL CHANGES

Parliamentary Commissioner for Administration

6.43 The DVCVA 2004 makes a variety of institutional and procedural changes. It extends the power of the Parliamentary Commissioner and provides

---

[89] Under Civil Procedure Rules, Part 54.

for the Commissioner to investigate complaints made by members of the public in relation to breaches of the Victims' Code issued by the Home Secretary.[90]

It does so in s 47 of and Sch 7 to the DVCVA 2004. The Parliamentary Commissioner, in pursuance of his functions under the Parliamentary Commissioner Act 1967 (which is amended) will be able to investigate and report on complaints of breach of the Victims' Code, and in respect of complaints that a local probation board has failed to disclose information to victims under s 69 of the Criminal Justice and Courts Services Act 2000.[91]

Normally, the Parliamentary Commissioner does not have jurisdiction in respect of matters relating to criminal investigations and proceedings.[92] For obvious reasons, that restriction does not apply in respect these investigations[93] – there would otherwise be no point in the new jurisdiction.

Commissioner for Victims and Witnesses

6.44   Section 48 of and Sch 8 to the DVCVA 2004 provide for the appointment of a Commissioner for Victims and Witnesses. As a corporation sole (s 48(3)) the Commissioner has legal personality, can hold property, employ staff and bring legal proceedings. The functions of the Commissioner are, as noted below, in respect of victims and witnesses. These terms are defined in detail by s 52.

'Victim'

6.45   A victim is the victim of an offence, or of anti-social behaviour. Anti-social behaviour will often constitute a crime, but the wording of s 52(2) puts beyond doubt that the role of the Commissioner extends to such behaviour irrespective of whether it is unlawful, or subject to an anti-social behaviour order.[94] It is irrelevant whether a complaint has been made about an offence, or that no-one has been charged with an offence (s 52(3)).

Witness

6.46   This term is defined by s 52(3), and means a person (other than a defendant, defined by reference to s 52(6)) who:

(a) has witnessed conduct in relation to which he may be or has been called to give evidence in relevant proceedings;

---

[90]   As to which see para **6.7**.
[91]   See para **6.22**.
[92]   Parliamentary Commissioner Act 1967.
[93]   Sch 7, para 4.
[94]   See Anti Social Behaviour Act 2003.

(b) is able to provide or has provided anything that might be used or has been used in evidence in relevant proceedings; or

(c) is able to provide anything mentioned in s 52(5) (whether admissible or not). Subsection (5) specifies matters which might be used in evidence, or tend to confirm evidence, or which might be used as the basis for cross-examination of any person.

'Relevant proceedings' are defined by s 52(7).

6.47 The general functions of the Commissioner are specified by s 49. By s 49(1) the Commissioner must:

(a) promote the interests of victims and witnesses;

(b) take such steps as he considers appropriate with a view to encouraging good practice in the treatment of victims and witnesses;

(c) keep under review the operation of the code of practice.[95]

In performing those duties the Commissioner can make proposals to the Secretary of State for amending the code (either on his own initiative or at the request of the Secretary of State), report to the Secretary of State, make recommendations to an authority within his remit (defined by reference to s 53), undertake or support (financially or otherwise) research, and consult such persons as he considers appropriate (s 49(2)).

The Commissioner must provide advice on issues relating to victims and witnesses when requested to do so by any government minister (s 50).

6.48 Section 51 restricts the functions of the Commissioner in an important respect. He must not exercise any of his functions in relation to:

(a) a particular victim or witness;

(b) the bringing or conduct of particular proceedings;

(c) anything done or ordered to be done by a person acting in a judicial capacity or on the instructions of or on behalf of such a person.

Victims' Advisory Panel

6.49 In the White Paper *Justice for All*[96] the proposal was made for the establishment of a Victims' Advisory Panel. A non-statutory advisory non-departmental public body was then established, and met for the first time on 3 March 2003. The purpose of s 55 is to put the existing arrangements on a statutory footing.

The membership of the current panel comprises[97] 10 voluntary lay members, who must have direct experience of issues relating to victims, three co-opted

---

[95] As to which, see para **6.3**.

[96] Home Office, 2002, para 2.45.

[97] See Explanatory Notes to the Act.

members representing wider victim's interests, representatives of voluntary organisations to which the Government provide core funding to provide direct services to victims and witnesses, and senior officials from criminal justice agencies. It is chaired by the Minister for Criminal Justice and also attended by a minister from the Department for Constitutional Affairs, and the Solicitor-General. This will not be regarded as having been comprised under statute (s 55(7)).

THE SHARING OF INFORMATION

6.50   One key issue if there is to be an integrated response to the needs of victims and witnesses is the need to ensure that there is proper information-sharing between relevant departments and agencies. That does, though, raise issues of disclosure and confidentiality. Section 54 permits the disclosure of information to a relevant authority for the purpose of compliance with the Victims' Code,[98] to facilitate the effective working of the arrangements in respect of the rights to make representations and receive information,[99] and for the carrying out of the functions of the Commissioner.[100]

The relevant authority is any one of the following:

(a)   a person required to do anything under the Code;
(b)   a local probation board;
(c)   the Commissioner;
(d)   an authority within the Commissioner's remit.[101]

Nothing in s 54 authorises the making of a disclosure which would contravene the Data Protection Act 1998.

6.51 The Joint Committee on Human Rights[102] was 'very concerned' about this provision. By expressly preserving duties under the Data Protection Act 1998, whilst excluding any other duties of non disclosure, the effect may be to exclude rights in favour of non disclosure that might be made pursuant to Art 8 of the European Convention on Human Rights, although the Joint Committee did concede that the reference to the Data Protection Act was in fact likely to satisfy the requirements of Art 8.

---

[98]   See para **6.7**.
[99]   See para **6.22** and also the Indicative Code.
[100] See para **6.47**.
[101] See above.
[102] 3rd Report, 2003-2004, at para 2.15–2.19.

DOMESTIC HOMICIDE REVIEWS

6.52   It may perhaps seem incongruous to deal with the establishment of a review process for domestic homicide in the context of discussion of victims. Nonetheless, the establishment, by s 9 of the DVCVA 2004, of a process for multi-agency homicide reviews is seen as a key element in preventing such homicides from occurring. Domestic attacks that result in death are, often, not the first incidence of domestic violence, and may often be the culmination of a long history of violent incidents.[103] For that reason, where systems or professionals went wrong, and what can be changed, are important questions to be answered. For some time, local initiatives have been undertaken. In London, the Metropolitan Police, working in conjunction with other agencies, have carried out reviews of every domestic violence homicide, with similar initiatives elsewhere by the Crown Prosecution Service.[104] These reviews draw on the experience of serious case reviews that occur where abuse or neglect are known or suspected to have been a factor in the death of a child.

A 'domestic violence review' is defined by s 9 as a review of the circumstances in which the death of a person aged 16 or over has, or appears to have, resulted from violence, abuse or neglect by:

(a) a person to whom he was related with whom he was or has been in an intimate personal relationship, or

(b) a member of the same household as himself,

held with a view to establishing the lessons to be learnt from the death.

The Secretary of State has the power, in any given case, to direct a specific person or body to establish, or participate in, such an inquiry (s 9(2)) Those who may be so required are identified by s 9(4). They include the police, local authorities, local probation board, strategic health authorities and primary health care trusts. All concerned will be bound by guidance issued by the Home Secretary (s 9(3)).

---

[103]   *Safety and Justice* op cit, p 37.
[104]   Ibid, at p 38.

Appendix One

DOMESTIC VIOLENCE, CRIME AND VICTIMS ACT 2004

PART 1
DOMESTIC VIOLENCE ETC

Amendments to Part 4 of the Family Law Act 1996

1 Breach of non-molestation order to be a criminal offence

In Part 4 of the Family Law Act 1996 (c 27) (family homes and domestic violence), after section 42 insert—

'42A Offence of breaching non-molestation order

(1)   A person who without reasonable excuse does anything that he is prohibited from doing by a non-molestation order is guilty of an offence.

(2)   In the case of a non-molestation order made by virtue of section 45(1), a person can be guilty of an offence under this section only in respect of conduct engaged in at a time when he was aware of the existence of the order.

(3)   Where a person is convicted of an offence under this section in respect of any conduct, that conduct is not punishable as a contempt of court.

(4)   A person cannot be convicted of an offence under this section in respect of any conduct which has been punished as a contempt of court.

(5)   A person guilty of an offence under this section is liable—
    (a)   on conviction on indictment, to imprisonment for a term not exceeding five years, or a fine, or both;
    (b)   on summary conviction, to imprisonment for a term not exceeding 12 months, or a fine not exceeding the statutory maximum, or both.

(6)   A reference in any enactment to proceedings under this Part, or to an order under this Part, does not include a reference to proceedings for an offence under this section or to an order made in such proceedings.
    'Enactment' includes an enactment contained in subordinate legislation within the meaning of the Interpretation Act 1978 (c 30).'

2 Additional considerations if parties are cohabitants or former cohabitants

(1)   Section 41 of the Family Law Act 1996 (c 27) (which requires a court, when considering the nature of the relationship of cohabitants or former cohabitants, to have regard to their non-married status) is repealed.

(2)   In section 36(6)(e) of that Act (court to have regard to nature of parties' relationship when considering whether to give right to occupy to cohabitant or former cohabitant with no existing right), after 'relationship' insert 'and in particular the level of commitment involved in it'.

3 'Cohabitants' in Part 4 of 1996 Act to include same-sex couples

In section 62(1)(a) of the Family Law Act 1996 (definition of 'cohabitant' for the purposes of Part 4 of that Act), for the words after ' 'cohabitants' are' substitute 'two persons who, although not married to each other, are living together as husband and wife or (if of the same sex) in an equivalent relationship; and'.

4 Extension of Part 4 of 1996 Act to non-cohabiting couples

In section 62(3) of the Family Law Act 1996 (definition of 'associated' persons for the purposes of Part 4 of that Act), after paragraph (e) insert—

> '(ea) they have or have had an intimate personal relationship with each other which is or was of significant duration;' .

Causing or allowing the death of a child or vulnerable adult

5 The offence

(1)   A person ('D') is guilty of an offence if—
    (a)   a child or vulnerable adult ('V') dies as a result of the unlawful act of a person who—
      (i)was a member of the same household as V, and
      (ii)had frequent contact with him,
    (b)   D was such a person at the time of that act,
    (c)   at that time there was a significant risk of serious physical harm being caused to V by the unlawful act of such a person, and
    (d)   either D was the person whose act caused V's death or—
      (i)D was, or ought to have been, aware of the risk mentioned in paragraph (c),
      (ii)D failed to take such steps as he could reasonably have been expected to take to protect V from the risk, and
      (iii)the act occurred in circumstances of the kind that D foresaw or ought to have foreseen.

(2)   The prosecution does not have to prove whether it is the first alternative in subsection (1)(d) or the second (sub-paragraphs (i) to (iii)) that applies.

(3)   If D was not the mother or father of V—
    (a)   D may not be charged with an offence under this section if he was under the age of 16 at the time of the act that caused V's death;
    (b)   for the purposes of subsection (1)(d)(ii) D could not have been expected to take any such step as is referred to there before attaining that age.˜

(4)   For the purposes of this section—
    (a)   a person is to be regarded as a 'member' of a particular household, even if he does not live in that household, if he visits it so often and for such periods of time that it is reasonable to regard him as a member of it;
    (b)   where V lived in different households at different times, 'the same household

as V' refers to the household in which V was living at the time of the act that caused V's death.

(5)   For the purposes of this section an 'unlawful' act is one that—
  (a)   constitutes an offence, or
  (b)   would constitute an offence but for being the act of—
    (i)a person under the age of ten, or
    (ii)a person entitled to rely on a defence of insanity.
  Paragraph (b) does not apply to an act of D.

(6)   In this section—
  'act' includes a course of conduct and also includes omission;
  'child' means a person under the age of 16;
  'serious' harm means harm that amounts to grievous bodily harm for the purposes of the Offences against the Person Act 1861 (c 100);
  'vulnerable adult' means a person aged 16 or over whose ability to protect himself from violence, abuse or neglect is significantly impaired through physical or mental disability or illness, through old age or otherwise.

(7)   A person guilty of an offence under this section is liable on conviction on indictment to imprisonment for a term not exceeding 14 years or to a fine, or to both.

6 Evidence and procedure: England and Wales

(1)   Subsections (2) to (4) apply where a person ('the defendant') is charged in the same proceedings with an offence of murder or manslaughter and with an offence under section 5 in respect of the same death ('the section 5 offence').

(2)   Where by virtue of section 35(3) of the Criminal Justice and Public Order Act 1994 (c 33) a court or jury is permitted, in relation to the section 5 offence, to draw such inferences as appear proper from the defendant's failure to give evidence or refusal to answer a question, the court or jury may also draw such inferences in determining whether he is guilty—
  (a)   of murder or manslaughter, or
  (b)   of any other offence of which he could lawfully be convicted on the charge of murder or manslaughter,

even if there would otherwise be no case for him to answer in relation to that offence.

(3)   The charge of murder or manslaughter is not to be dismissed under paragraph 2 of Schedule 3 to the Crime and Disorder Act 1998 (c 37) (unless the section 5 offence is dismissed).

(4)   At the defendant's trial the question whether there is a case for the defendant to answer on the charge of murder or manslaughter is not to be considered before the close of all the evidence (or, if at some earlier time he ceases to be charged with the section 5 offence, before that earlier time).

(5)   An offence under section 5 is an offence of homicide for the purposes of the following enactments—
  sections 24 and 25 of the Magistrates' Courts Act 1980 (c 43) (mode of trial of child or young person for indictable offence);
  section 51A of the Crime and Disorder Act 1998 (sending cases to the Crown Court: children and young persons);
  section 8 of the Powers of Criminal Courts (Sentencing) Act 2000 (c 6) (power and duty to remit young offenders to youth courts for sentence).

7 Evidence and procedure: Northern Ireland

(1)   Subsections (2) to (4) apply where a person ('the defendant') is charged in the same proceedings with an offence of murder or manslaughter and with an offence under section 5 in respect of the same death ('the section 5 offence').

(2)   Where by virtue of Article 4(4) of the Criminal Evidence (Northern Ireland) Order 1988 (SI 1988/1987 (NI 20)) a court or jury is permitted, in relation to the section 5 offence, to draw such inferences as appear proper from the defendant's failure to give evidence or refusal to answer a question, the court or jury may also draw such inferences in determining whether he is guilty—
   (a)   of murder or manslaughter, or
   (b)   of any other offence of which he could lawfully be convicted on the charge of murder or manslaughter,
even if there would otherwise be no case for him to answer in relation to that offence.

(3)   Where a magistrates' court is considering under Article 37 of the Magistrates' Courts (Northern Ireland) Order 1981 (SI 1981/1675 (NI 26)) whether to commit the defendant for trial for the offence of murder or manslaughter, if there is sufficient evidence to put him upon trial for the section 5 offence there is deemed to be sufficient evidence to put him upon trial for the offence of murder or manslaughter.

(4)   At the defendant's trial the question whether there is a case to answer on the charge of murder or manslaughter is not to be considered before the close of all the evidence (or, if at some earlier time he ceases to be charged with the section 5 offence, before that earlier time).

(5)   An offence under section 5 is an offence of homicide for the purposes of the following provisions—
   Article 17 of the Criminal Justice (Children) (Northern Ireland) Order 1998 (SI 1998/
      1504 (NI 9)) (mode of trial of child for indictable offence);
   Article 32 of that Order (power and duty to remit children to youth courts for
      sentence).

8 Evidence and procedure: courts-martial

(1)   Section 6(1), (2) and (4) has effect in relation to proceedings before courts-martial with the following adaptations.

(2)   A reference to an offence of murder or manslaughter or an offence under section 5 is to be read as a reference to an offence under—
   (a)   section 70 of the Army Act 1955 (3 & 4 Eliz. 2 c 18),
   (b)   section 70 of the Air Force Act 1955 (3 & 4 Eliz. 2 c 19), or
   (c)   section 42 of the Naval Discipline Act 1957 (c 53),

for which the offence referred to in section 6 is the corresponding civil offence (within the meaning of that Act).

(3)   A reference to the court or jury is to be read as a reference to the court.

Domestic homicide reviews

9 Establishment and conduct of reviews

(1)   In this section 'domestic homicide review' means a review of the circumstances in which the death of a person aged 16 or over has, or appears to have, resulted from violence, abuse or neglect by—
   (a) a person to whom he was related or with whom he was or had been in an intimate personal relationship, or
   (b) a member of the same household as himself,

held with a view to identifying the lessons to be learnt from the death.

(2)   The Secretary of State may in a particular case direct a specified person or body within subsection (4) to establish, or to participate in, a domestic homicide review.

(3)   It is the duty of any person or body within subsection (4) establishing or participating in a domestic homicide review (whether or not held pursuant to a direction under subsection (2)) to have regard to any guidance issued by the Secretary of State as to the establishment and conduct of such reviews.

(4)   The persons and bodies within this subsection are—
   (a) in relation to England and Wales—
      chief officers of police for police areas in England and Wales;
      local authorities;
      local probation boards established under section 4 of the Criminal Justice and Court Services Act 2000 (c 43);
      Strategic Health Authorities established under section 8 of the National Health Service Act 1977 (c 49);
      Primary Care Trusts established under Section 16A of that Act.
      Local Health Boards established under section 16BA of that Act;
      NHS trusts established under section 5 of the National Health Service and Community Care Act 1990 (c 19);
   (b) in relation to Northern Ireland—
      the Chief Constable of the Police Service of Northern Ireland;
      the Probation Board for Northern Ireland;
      Health and Social Services Boards established under Article 16 of the Health and Personal Social Services (Northern Ireland) Order 1972 (SI 1972/1265 (NI 14));
      Health and Social Services trusts established under Article 10 of the Health and Personal Social Services (Northern Ireland) Order 1991 (SI 1991/194 (NI 1)).

(5)   In subsection (4)(a) 'local authority' means—
   (a) in relation to England, the council of a district, county or London borough, the Common Council of the City of London and the Council of the Isles of Scilly;
   (b) in relation to Wales, the council of a county or county borough.

(6)   The Secretary of State may by order amend subsection (4) or (5).

PART 2
CRIMINAL JUSTICE

Assault, harassment etc

10 Common assault to be an arrestable offence

(1)   In Schedule 1A to the Police and Criminal Evidence Act 1984 (c 60) (specific offences which are arrestable offences), before paragraph 15 (but after the heading '*Criminal Justice Act 1988*') insert—

'14A

Common assault.'

(2)   In Article 26(2) of the Police and Criminal Evidence (Northern Ireland) Order 1989 (SI 1989/1341 (NI 12)) (specific offences which are arrestable offences), after paragraph (m) insert—

> '(n) an offence under section 42 of the Offences against the Person Act 1861 (c 100) (common assault etc).'

11 Common assault etc as alternative verdict

In section 6 of the Criminal Law Act 1967 (c 58) (trial of offences), after subsection (3) (alternative verdicts on trial on indictment) insert—

'(3A)   For the purposes of subsection (3) above an offence falls within the jurisdiction of the court of trial if it is an offence to which section 40 of the Criminal Justice Act 1988 applies (power to join in indictment count for common assault etc), even if a count charging the offence is not included in the indictment.

(3B)   A person convicted of an offence by virtue of subsection (3A) may only be dealt with for it in a manner in which a magistrates' court could have dealt with him.'

12 Restraining orders: England and Wales

(1)   In section 5 of the Protection from Harassment Act 1997 (c 40) (power to make restraining order where defendant convicted of offence under section 2 or 4 of that Act), in subsection (1) omit 'under section 2 or 4'.

(2)   After subsection (3) of that section insert—

'(3A)   In proceedings under this section both the prosecution and the defence may lead, as further evidence, any evidence that would be admissible in proceedings for an injunction under section 3.'

(3)   After subsection (4) of that section insert—

'(4A)   Any person mentioned in the order is entitled to be heard on the hearing of an application under subsection (4).'

(4)   After subsection (6) of that section insert—

'(7)   A court dealing with a person for an offence under this section may vary or discharge the order in question by a further order.'

(5)   After that section insert—

'5A Restraining orders on acquittal

(1)   A court before which a person ('the defendant') is acquitted of an offence may, if it considers it necessary to do so to protect a person from harassment by the defendant, make an order prohibiting the defendant from doing anything described in the order.

(2)   Subsections (3) to (7) of section 5 apply to an order under this section as they apply to an order under that one.

(3)   Where the Court of Appeal allow an appeal against conviction they may remit the case to the Crown Court to consider whether to proceed under this section.

(4)   Where—
   (a)   the Crown Court allows an appeal against conviction, or
   (b)   a case is remitted to the Crown Court under subsection (3),

the reference in subsection (1) to a court before which a person is acquitted of an offence is to be read as referring to that court.

(5)   A person made subject to an order under this section has the same right of appeal against the order as if—
   (a)   he had been convicted of the offence in question before the court which made the order, and
   (b)   the order had been made under section 5.'

13 Restraining orders: Northern Ireland

(1)   In Article 7 of the Protection from Harassment (Northern Ireland) Order 1997 (SI 1997/1180 (NI 9)) (power to make restraining order where defendant convicted of offence under Article 4 or 6 of that Order), in paragraph (1) omit 'under Article 4 or 6'.

(2)   After paragraph (3) of that Article insert—

'(3A)   In proceedings under this Article both the prosecution and the defence may lead, as further evidence, any evidence that would be admissible in proceedings for an injunction under Article 5.'

(3)   After paragraph (4) of that Article insert—

'(4A)   Any person mentioned in the order is entitled to be heard on the hearing of an application under paragraph (4).'

(4)   After paragraph (6) of that Article insert—A :

'(7)   A court dealing with a person for an offence under this Article may vary or discharge the order in question by a further order.'

(5)   After that Article insert—

'7A Restraining orders on acquittal

(1)   A court before which a person ('the defendant') is acquitted of an offence may, if it

considers it necessary to do so to protect a person from harassment by the defendant, make an order prohibiting the defendant from doing anything described in the order.

(2)   Paragraphs (3) to (7) of Article 7 apply to an order under this Article as they apply to an order under that one.

(3)   Where the Court of Appeal allow an appeal against conviction they may remit the case to the Crown Court to consider whether to proceed under this Article.

(4)   Where—
  (a)   a county court allows an appeal against conviction, or
  (b)   a case is remitted to the Crown Court under paragraph (3),

the reference in paragraph (1) to a court before which a person is acquitted of an offence is to be read as referring to that court.

(5)   A person made subject to an order under this Article has the same right of appeal against the order as if—
  (a)   he had been convicted of the offence in question before the court which made the order, and
  (b)   the order had been made under Article 7.'

Surcharges

14 Surcharge payable on conviction

(1)   In Chapter 1 of Part 12 of the Criminal Justice Act 2003 (c 44) (general provisions about sentencing), after section 161 insert—

'Surcharges

161A Court's duty to order payment of surcharge

(1)   A court when dealing with a person for one or more offences must also (subject to subsections (2) and (3)) order him to pay a surcharge.

(2)   Subsection (1) does not apply in such cases as may be prescribed by an order made by the Secretary of State.

(3)   Where a court dealing with an offender considers—
  (a)   that it would be appropriate to make a compensation order, but
  (b)   that he has insufficient means to pay both the surcharge and appropriate compensation,

the court must reduce the surcharge accordingly (if necessary to nil).

(4)   For the purposes of this section a court does not 'deal with' a person if it—
  (a)   discharges him absolutely, or
  (b)   makes an order under the Mental Health Act 1983 in respect of him.

161B Amount of surcharge

(1)   The surcharge payable under section 161A is such amount as the Secretary of State may specify by order.

(2)   An order under this section may provide for the amount to depend on—
  (a)   the offence or offences committed,

    (b) how the offender is otherwise dealt with (including, where the offender is fined, the amount of the fine),

    (c) the age of the offender.

This is not to be read as limiting section 330(3) (power to make different provision for different purposes etc).'

(2)   In section 164 of that Act (fixing of fines), after subsection (4) insert—

'(4A) In applying subsection (3), a court must not reduce the amount of a fine on account of any surcharge it orders the offender to pay under section 161A, except to the extent that he has insufficient means to pay both.'

(3)   In Part 1 of Schedule 9 to the Administration of Justice Act 1970 (c 31) (cases where payment enforceable as on summary conviction), after paragraph 12 insert—

'13

Where under section 161A of the Criminal Justice Act 2003 a court orders the payment of a surcharge.'

(4)   In Schedule 5 to the Courts Act 2003 (c 39) (collection of fines), in paragraph 1(1) (application of Schedule), after 'a fine' insert 'or a surcharge imposed under section 161A of the Criminal Justice Act 2003'.

(5)   The Secretary of State may by order—

    (a) make provision amending Schedule 5 (collection of fines) or Schedule 6 (discharge of fines by unpaid work) to the Courts Act 2003 in its application by virtue of subsection (3) or (4) to surcharges;

    (b) make provision for any part of Schedule 5, or the whole or any part of Schedule 6, not to apply to surcharges;

    (c) make amendments to any enactment that are consequential on provision made under paragraph (a) or (b).

15 Increase in maximum on-the-spot penalty for disorderly behaviour

(1)   In Chapter 1 of Part 1 of the Criminal Justice and Police Act 2001 (c 16) (on-the-spot penalties for disorderly behaviour), section 3 is amended as follows.

(2)   In subsection (2) (maximum penalty that may be prescribed), at the end insert 'plus a half of the relevant surcharge'.

(3)   After that subsection insert—

'(2A) The 'relevant surcharge', in relation to a person of a given age, is the amount payable by way of surcharge under section 161A of the Criminal Justice Act 2003 by a person of that age who is fined the maximum amount for the offence.'

16 Higher fixed penalty for repeated road traffic offences

(1)   The Road Traffic Offenders Act 1988 (c 53) is amended as follows.

(2)   In section 53 (amount of fixed penalty), after subsection (2) insert—

'(3)   In particular, in relation to England and Wales an order made under subsection (1)(a) may prescribe a higher fixed penalty in a case where, in the period of three years ending with the date of the offence in question, the offender committed an offence for which—

    (a)   he was disqualified from driving, or

    (b)   penalty points were endorsed on the counterpart of any licence held by him.'

(3)   At the end of section 84 (regulations) (which becomes subsection (1)) insert—

'(2)   The Secretary of State may by regulations provide that where—

    (a)   a conditional offer has been issued under section 75 of this Act,

    (b)   the amount of the penalty stated in the offer is not the higher amount applicable by virtue of section 53(3) of this Act, and

    (c)   it subsequently appears that that higher amount is in fact applicable,

the fixed penalty clerk may issue a further notice (a 'surcharge notice') requiring payment of the difference between the two amounts.

(3)   Regulations under subsection (2) above may—

    (a)   provide for this Part of this Act to have effect, in cases to which the regulations apply, with such modifications as may be specified;

    (b)   make provision for the collection and enforcement of amounts due under surcharge notices.'

Trial by jury of sample counts only

17 Application by prosecution for certain counts to be tried without a jury

(1)   The prosecution may apply to a judge of the Crown Court for a trial on indictment to take place on the basis that the trial of some, but not all, of the counts included in the indictment may be conducted without a jury.

(2)   If such an application is made and the judge is satisfied that the following three conditions are fulfilled, he may make an order for the trial to take place on the basis that the trial of some, but not all, of the counts included in the indictment may be conducted without a jury.

(3)   The first condition is that the number of counts included in the indictment is likely to mean that a trial by jury involving all of those counts would be impracticable.

(4)   The second condition is that, if an order under subsection (2) were made, each count or group of counts which would accordingly be tried with a jury can be regarded as a sample of counts which could accordingly be tried without a jury.

(5)   The third condition is that it is in the interests of justice for an order under subsection (2) to be made.

(6)   In deciding whether or not to make an order under subsection (2), the judge must have regard to any steps which might reasonably be taken to facilitate a trial by jury.

(7)   But a step is not to be regarded as reasonable if it could lead to the possibility of a defendant in the trial receiving a lesser sentence than would be the case if that step were not taken.

(8)   An order under subsection (2) must specify the counts which may be tried without a jury.

(9) For the purposes of this section and sections 18 to 20, a count may not be regarded as a sample of other counts unless the defendant in respect of each count is the same person.

18 Procedure for applications under section 17

(1) An application under section 17 must be determined at a preparatory hearing.

(2) Section 7(1) of the 1987 Act and section 29(2) of the 1996 Act are to have effect as if the purposes there mentioned included the purpose of determining an application under section 17.

(3) Section 29(1) of the 1996 Act is to have effect as if the grounds on which a judge of the Crown Court may make an order under that provision included the ground that an application under section 17 has been made.

(4) The parties to a preparatory hearing at which an application under section 17 is to be determined must be given an opportunity to make representations with respect to the application.

(5) Section 9(11) of the 1987 Act and section 35(1) of the 1996 Act are to have effect as if they also provided for an appeal to the Court of Appeal to lie from the determination by a judge of an application under section 17.

(6) In this section—
    'preparatory hearing' means a preparatory hearing within the meaning of the 1987 Act or Part 3 of the 1996 Act;
    'the 1987 Act' means the Criminal Justice Act 1987 (c 38);
    'the 1996 Act' means the Criminal Procedure and Investigations Act 1996 (c 25).

19 Effect of order under section 17(2)

(1) The effect of an order under section 17(2) is that where, in the course of the proceedings to which the order relates, a defendant is found guilty by a jury on a count which can be regarded as a sample of other counts to be tried in those proceedings, those other counts may be tried without a jury in those proceedings.

(2) Where the trial of a count is conducted without a jury because of an order under section 17(2), the court is to have all the powers, authorities and jurisdiction which the court would have had if the trial of that count had been conducted with a jury (including power to determine any question and to make any finding which would be required to be determined or made by a jury).

(3) Except where the context otherwise requires, any reference in an enactment to a jury, the verdict of a jury or the finding of a jury is to be read, in relation to the trial of a count conducted without a jury because of an order under section 17(2), as a reference to the court, the verdict of the court or the finding of the court.

(4) Where the trial of a count is conducted without a jury because of an order under section 17(2) and the court convicts the defendant of that count—
    (a) the court must give a judgment which states the reasons for the conviction at, or as soon as reasonably practicable after, the time of the conviction, and
    (b) the reference in section 18(2) of the Criminal Appeal Act 1968 (c 19) (notice of appeal or of application for leave to appeal to be given within 28 days from date of conviction etc) to the date of the conviction is to be read as a reference to the date of the judgment mentioned in paragraph (a).

(5)   Where, in the case of proceedings in respect of which an order under section 17(2) has been made, a jury convicts a defendant of a count, time does not begin to run under section 18(2) of the Criminal Appeal Act 1968 in relation to an appeal against that conviction until the date on which the proceedings end.

(6)   In determining for the purposes of subsection (5) the date on which proceedings end, any part of those proceedings which takes place after the time when matters relating to sentencing begin to be dealt with is to be disregarded.

(7)   Nothing in this section or section 17, 18 or 20 affects the requirement under section 4A of the Criminal Procedure (Insanity) Act 1964 (c 84) that any question, finding or verdict mentioned in that section be determined, made or returned by a jury.

20 Rules of court

(1)   Rules of court may make such provision as appears to the authority making them to be necessary or expedient for the purposes of sections 17 to 19.

(2)   Without limiting subsection (1), rules of court may in particular make provision for time limits within which applications under section 17 must be made or within which other things in connection with that section or section 18 or 19 must be done.

(3)   Nothing in this section is to be taken as affecting the generality of any enactment conferring powers to make rules of court.

21 Application of sections 17 to 20 to Northern Ireland

(1)   In their application to Northern Ireland, sections 17 to 20 have effect subject to the modifications in Schedule 1.

(2)   Sections 17 to 20 do not apply in relation to a trial to which section 75 of the Terrorism Act 2000 (c 11) (trial without jury for certain offences) applies.

Unfitness to plead and insanity

22 Procedure for determining fitness to plead: England and Wales

(1)   The Criminal Procedure (Insanity) Act 1964 is amended as follows.

(2)   In section 4 (finding of unfitness to plead), in subsection (5) (question of fitness to be determined by a jury), for the words from 'by a jury' to the end substitute 'by the court without a jury'.

(3)   In subsection (6) of that section, for 'A jury' substitute 'The court'.

(4)   In subsection (1) of section 4A (finding that the accused did the act or omission charged against him), for 'jury' substitute 'court'.

(5)   For subsection (5) of that section substitute—

'(5)   Where the question of disability was determined after arraignment of the accused, the determination under subsection (2) is to be made by the jury by whom he was being tried.'

23 Procedure for determining fitness to be tried: Northern Ireland

(1)   The Mental Health (Northern Ireland) Order 1986 (SI 1986/595 (NI 4)) is amended as follows.

(2)   In Article 49 (finding of unfitness to be tried), in paragraph (4) (question of fitness to be determined by a jury), for the words from 'by a jury' to the end substitute 'by the court without a jury'.

(3)   In paragraph (4A) of that Article, for 'A jury' substitute 'The court'.

(4)   In paragraph (1) of Article 49A (finding that the accused did the act or omission charged against him), for 'jury' substitute 'court'.

(5)   For paragraph (5) of that Article substitute—

'(5)   Where the question of fitness to be tried was determined after arraignment of the accused, the determination under paragraph (2) is to be made by the jury by whom he was being tried.'

24 Powers of court on finding of insanity or unfitness to plead etc

(1)   For section 5 of the Criminal Procedure (Insanity) Act 1964 (c 84) substitute—

'5 Powers to deal with persons not guilty by reason of insanity or unfit to plead etc

(1)   This section applies where—
  (a)   a special verdict is returned that the accused is not guilty by reason of insanity; or
  (b)   findings have been made that the accused is under a disability and that he did the act or made the omission charged against him.

(2)   The court shall make in respect of the accused—
  (a)   a hospital order (with or without a restriction order);
  (b)   a supervision order; or
  (c)   an order for his absolute discharge.

(3)   Where—
  (a)   the offence to which the special verdict or the findings relate is an offence the sentence for which is fixed by law, and
  (b)   the court have power to make a hospital order,

the court shall make a hospital order with a restriction order (whether or not they would have power to make a restriction order apart from this subsection).

(4)   In this section—
  'hospital order' has the meaning given in section 37 of the Mental Health Act 1983;
  'restriction order' has the meaning given to it by section 41 of that Act;
  'supervision order' has the meaning given in Part 1 of Schedule 1A to this Act.

5A Orders made under or by virtue of section 5

(1)   In relation to the making of an order by virtue of subsection (2)(a) of section 5 above, section 37 (hospital orders etc) of the Mental Health Act 1983 ('the 1983 Act') shall have effect as if—
  (a)   the reference in subsection (1) to a person being convicted before the Crown Court included a reference to the case where section 5 above applies;
  (b)   the words after 'punishable with imprisonment' and before 'or is convicted' were omitted; and
  (c)   for subsections (4) and (5) there were substituted—

'(4)   Where an order is made under this section requiring a person to be admitted to a hospital ('a hospital order'), it shall be the duty of the managers of the hospital specified in the order to admit him in accordance with it.'

(2)   In relation to a case where section 5 above applies but the court have not yet made one of the disposals mentioned in subsection (2) of that section—

   (a)   section 35 of the 1983 Act (remand to hospital for report on accused's mental condition) shall have effect with the omission of the words after paragraph (b) in subsection (3);

   (b)   section 36 of that Act (remand of accused person to hospital for treatment) shall have effect with the omission of the words ' (other than an offence the sentence for which is fixed by law)' in subsection (2);

   (c)   references in sections 35 and 36 of that Act to an accused person shall be construed as including a person in whose case this subsection applies; and

   (d)   section 38 of that Act (interim hospital orders) shall have effect as if—
       (i)the reference in subsection (1) to a person being convicted before the Crown Court included a reference to the case where section 5 above applies; and
       (ii)the words ' (other than an offence the sentence for which is fixed by law)' in that subsection were omitted.

(3)   In relation to the making of any order under the 1983 Act by virtue of this Act, references in the 1983 Act to an offender shall be construed as including references to a person in whose case section 5 above applies, and references to an offence shall be construed accordingly.

(4)   Where—

   (a)   a person is detained in pursuance of a hospital order which the court had power to make by virtue of section 5(1)(b) above, and

   (b)   the court also made a restriction order, and that order has not ceased to have effect,

the Secretary of State, if satisfied after consultation with the responsible medical officer that the person can properly be tried, may remit the person for trial, either to the court of trial or to a prison.

On the person's arrival at the court or prison, the hospital order and the restriction order shall cease to have effect.

(5)   Schedule 1A to this Act (supervision orders) has effect with respect to the making of supervision orders under subsection (2)(b) of section 5 above, and with respect to the revocation and amendment of such orders.

(6)   In relation to the making of an order under subsection (2)(c) of section 5 above, section 12(1) of the Powers of Criminal Courts (Sentencing) Act 2000 (absolute and conditional discharge) shall have effect as if—

   (a)   the reference to a person being convicted by or before a court of such an offence as is there mentioned included a reference to the case where section 5 above applies; and

   (b)   the reference to the court being of opinion that it is inexpedient to inflict punishment included a reference to it thinking that an order for absolute discharge would be most suitable in all the circumstances of the case.'

(2)   Before Schedule 2 to the Criminal Procedure (Insanity) Act 1964 (c 84) insert the Schedule set out in Schedule 2 to this Act.

(3)   In section 6 of the Criminal Appeal Act 1968 (c 19) (substitution of finding of insanity or findings of unfitness to plead etc) and in section 14 of that Act (substitution of findings of unfitness to plead etc), for subsections (2) and (3) substitute—

'(2)   The Court of Appeal shall make in respect of the accused—

   (a) a hospital order (with or without a restriction order);
   (b) a supervision order; or
   (c) an order for his absolute discharge.

(3) Where—
   (a) the offence to which the appeal relates is an offence the sentence for which is fixed by law, and
   (b) the court have power to make a hospital order,

the court shall make a hospital order with a restriction order (whether or not they would have power to make a restriction order apart from this subsection).

(4) Section 5A of the Criminal Procedure (Insanity) Act 1964 ('the 1964 Act') applies in relation to this section as it applies in relation to section 5 of that Act.

(5) Where the Court of Appeal make an interim hospital order by virtue of this section—
   (a) the power of renewing or terminating it and of dealing with the appellant on its termination shall be exercisable by the court below and not by the Court of Appeal; and
   (b) the court below shall be treated for the purposes of section 38(7) of the Mental Health Act 1983 (absconding offenders) as the court that made the order.

(6) Where the Court of Appeal make a supervision order by virtue of this section, any power of revoking or amending it shall be exercisable as if the order had been made by the court below.

(7) In this section—
   'hospital order' has the meaning given in section 37 of the Mental Health Act 1983;
   'interim hospital order' has the meaning given in section 38 of that Act;
   'restriction order' has the meaning given to it by section 41 of that Act;
   'supervision order' has the meaning given in Part 1 of Schedule 1A to the 1964 Act.'

(4)   Section 14A of the Criminal Appeal Act 1968 (c 19) (power to order admission to hospital where, on appeal against verdict of not guilty by reason of insanity, Court of Appeal substitutes verdict of acquittal) is repealed.

(5)   Section 5 of the Criminal Procedure (Insanity and Unfitness to Plead) Act 1991 (c 25) and Schedules 1 and 2 to that Act are repealed.

25 Appeal against order made on finding of insanity or unfitness to plead etc

After section 16 of the Criminal Appeal Act 1968 insert—

'Appeal against order made in cases of insanity or unfitness to plead

16A Right of appeal against hospital order etc

(1) A person in whose case the Crown Court—
   (a) makes a hospital order or interim hospital order by virtue of section 5 or 5A of the Criminal Procedure (Insanity) Act 1964, or
   (b) makes a supervision order under section 5 of that Act,

may appeal to the Court of Appeal against the order.

(2) An appeal under this section lies only—
   (a) with the leave of the Court of Appeal; or
   (b) if the judge of the court of trial grants a certificate that the case is fit for appeal.

16B Disposal of appeal under s. 16A

(1)   If on an appeal under section 16A of this Act the Court of Appeal consider that the appellant should be dealt with differently from the way in which the court below dealt with him—

    (a)   they may quash any order which is the subject of the appeal; and

    (b)   they may make such order, whether by substitution for the original order or by variation of or addition to it, as they think appropriate for the case and as the court below had power to make.

(2)   The fact that an appeal is pending against an interim hospital order under the Mental Health Act 1983 shall not affect the power of the court below to renew or terminate the order or deal with the appellant on its termination.

(3)   Where the Court of Appeal make an interim hospital order by virtue of this section—

    (a)   the power of renewing or terminating it and of dealing with the appellant on its termination shall be exercisable by the court below and not by the Court of Appeal; and

    (b)   the court below shall be treated for the purposes of section 38(7) of the said Act of 1983 (absconding offenders) as the court that made the order.

(4)   The fact that an appeal is pending against a supervision order under section 5 of the Criminal Procedure (Insanity) Act 1964 shall not affect the power of the court below to revoke the order, or of a magistrates' court to revoke or amend it.

(5)   Where the Court of Appeal make a supervision order by virtue of this section, the power of revoking or amending it shall be exercisable as if the order had been made by the court below.'

26 Courts-martial etc

Schedule 3 (unfitness to stand trial and insanity: courts-martial etc) has effect.

Miscellaneous

27 Powers of authorised officers executing warrants

(1)   After section 125B of the Magistrates' Courts Act 1980 (c 43) insert—

'125BA Powers of persons authorised under section 125A or 125B

Schedule 4A to this Act, which confers powers on persons authorised under section 125A or 125B for the purpose of executing warrants for the enforcement of fines and other orders, shall have effect.'

(2)   After Schedule 4 to that Act insert the Schedule set out in Schedule 4 to this Act.

28 Disclosure orders for purpose of executing warrants

After section 125C of the Magistrates' Courts Act 1980 insert—

'125CA Power to make disclosure order

(1)   A magistrates' court may make a disclosure order if satisfied that it is necessary to do so for the purpose of executing a warrant to which this section applies.

(2)   This section applies to a warrant of arrest, commitment, detention or distress issued by a justice of the peace in connection with the enforcement of a fine or other order imposed or made on conviction.

(3)   A disclosure order is an order requiring the person to whom it is directed to supply the designated officer for the court with any of the following information about the person to whom the warrant relates—

    (a)   his name, date of birth or national insurance number;

    (b)   his address (or any of his addresses).

(4)   A disclosure order may be made only on the application of a person entitled to execute the warrant.

(5)   This section applies to the Crown as it applies to other persons.

125CB Use of information supplied under disclosure order

(1)   Information supplied to a person under a disclosure order, or under this subsection, may be supplied by him to—

    (a)   the applicant for the order or any other person entitled to execute the warrant concerned;

    (b)   any employee of a body or person who, for the purposes of section 125B above, is an approved enforcement agency in relation to the warrant;

    (c)   any justices' clerk or other person appointed under section 2(1) of the Courts Act 2003.

(2)   A person who intentionally or recklessly—

    (a)   discloses information supplied under a disclosure order otherwise than as permitted by subsection (1) above, or

    (b)   uses information so supplied otherwise than for the purpose of facilitating the execution of the warrant concerned,

commits an offence.

(3)   But it is not an offence under subsection (2) above—

    (a)   to disclose any information in accordance with any enactment or order of a court or for the purposes of any proceedings before a court; or

    (b)   to disclose any information which has previously been lawfully disclosed to the public.

(4)   A person guilty of an offence under subsection (2) above is liable—

    (a)   on summary conviction, to a fine not exceeding the statutory maximum;

    (b)   on conviction on indictment, to a fine.

(5)   In this section 'disclosure order' has the meaning given by section 125CA(3) above.'

29 Procedure on breach of community penalty etc

Schedule 5 (procedure on breach of community penalty etc) has effect.

30 Prosecution appeals

(1)   In section 58(13) of the Criminal Justice Act 2003 (c 44) (which defines 'applicable time'), for 'start of the judge's' substitute 'time when the judge starts his'.

(2)   After section 58(13) of that Act insert—

'(14)   The reference in subsection (13) to the time when the judge starts his summing-up to the jury includes the time when the judge would start his summing-up to the jury but for the making of an order under Part 7.'

31 Intermittent custody

Schedule 6 (intermittent custody) has effect.

PART 3
VICTIMS ETC

CHAPTER 1
THE VICTIMS' CODE

32 Code of practice for victims

(1)   The Secretary of State must issue a code of practice as to the services to be provided to a victim of criminal conduct by persons appearing to him to have functions relating to—
  (a)   victims of criminal conduct, or
  (b)   any aspect of the criminal justice system.

(2)   The code may restrict the application of its provisions to—
  (a)   specified descriptions of victims;
  (b)   victims of specified offences or descriptions of conduct;
  (c)   specified persons or descriptions of persons appearing to the Secretary of State to have functions of the kind mentioned in subsection (1).

(3)   The code may include provision requiring or permitting the services which are to be provided to a victim to be provided to one or more others—
  (a)   instead of the victim (for example where the victim has died);
  (b)   as well as the victim.

(4)   The code may make different provision for different purposes, including different provision for—
  (a)   different descriptions of victims;
  (b)   persons who have different functions or descriptions of functions;
  (c)   different areas.

(5)   The code may not require anything to be done by—
  (a)   a person acting in a judicial capacity;
  (b)   a person acting in the discharge of a function of a member of the Crown Prosecution Service which involves the exercise of a discretion.

(6)   In determining whether a person is a victim of criminal conduct for the purposes of this section, it is immaterial that no person has been charged with or convicted of an offence in respect of the conduct.

(7)   In this section—
  'criminal conduct' means conduct constituting an offence;
  'specified' means specified in the code.

33 Procedure

(1)   Subsections (2) to (7) apply in relation to a code of practice required to be issued under section 32.

(2)   The Secretary of State must prepare a draft of the code.

(3)   In preparing the draft the Secretary of State must consult the Attorney General and the Lord Chancellor.

(4)   After preparing the draft the Secretary of State must—

    (a) publish the draft;

    (b) specify a period during which representations about the draft may be made to him.

(5)   The Secretary of State must—

    (a) consider in consultation with the Attorney General and the Lord Chancellor any representations made to him before the end of the specified period about the draft;

    (b) if he thinks it appropriate, modify the draft in the light of any such representations.

(6)   After the Secretary of State has proceeded under subsection (5) he must lay the code before Parliament.

(7)   When he has laid the code before Parliament the Secretary of State must bring it into operation on such day as he appoints by order.

(8)   The Secretary of State may from time to time revise a code previously brought into operation under this section; and subsections (2) to (7) apply to a revised code as they apply to the code as first prepared.

(9)   But the Secretary of State may revise a code under subsection (8) only if it appears to him that the proposed revisions would not result in—

    (a) a significant reduction in the quality or extent of the services to be provided under the code, or

    (b) a significant restriction in the description of persons to whom services are to be provided under the code.

34 Effect of non-compliance

(1)   If a person fails to perform a duty imposed on him by a code issued under section 32, the failure does not of itself make him liable to criminal or civil proceedings.

(2)   But the code is admissible in evidence in criminal or civil proceedings and a court may take into account a failure to comply with the code in determining a question in the proceedings.

CHAPTER 2

REPRESENTATIONS AND INFORMATION

Imprisonment or detention

35 Victims' rights to make representations and receive information

(1)   This section applies if—

    (a) a court convicts a person ('the offender') of a sexual or violent offence, and

    (b) a relevant sentence is imposed on him in respect of the offence.

(2)   But section 39 applies (instead of this section) if a hospital direction and a limitation direction are given in relation to the offender.

(3)   The local probation board for the area in which the sentence is imposed must take all reasonable steps to ascertain whether a person who appears to the board to be the

victim of the offence or to act for the victim of the offence wishes—

    (a) to make representations about the matters specified in subsection (4);

    (b) to receive the information specified in subsection (5).

(4)   The matters are—

    (a) whether the offender should be subject to any licence conditions or supervision requirements in the event of his release;

    (b) if so, what licence conditions or supervision requirements.

(5)   The information is information about any licence conditions or supervision requirements to which the offender is to be subject in the event of his release.

(6)   If a person whose wishes have been ascertained under subsection (3) makes representations to the local probation board mentioned in that subsection or the relevant local probation board about a matter specified in subsection (4), the relevant local probation board must forward those representations to the persons responsible for determining the matter.

(7)   If a local probation board has ascertained under subsection (3) that a person wishes to receive the information specified in subsection (5), the relevant local probation board must take all reasonable steps—

    (a) to inform the person whether or not the offender is to be subject to any licence conditions or supervision requirements in the event of his release,

    (b) if he is, to provide the person with details of any licence conditions or supervision requirements which relate to contact with the victim or his family, and

    (c) to provide the person with such other information as the relevant local probation board considers appropriate in all the circumstances of the case.

(8)   The relevant local probation board is—

    (a) in a case where the offender is to be supervised on release by an officer of a local probation board, that local probation board;

    (b) in any other case, the local probation board for the area in which the prison or other place in which the offender is detained is situated.

Hospital orders

36 Victims' rights: preliminary

(1)   This section applies if the conditions in subsections (2) and (3) are met.

(2)   The first condition is that one of these applies in respect of a person ('the patient') charged with a sexual or violent offence—

    (a) the patient is convicted of the offence;

    (b) a verdict is returned that the patient is not guilty of the offence by reason of insanity;

    (c) a finding is made—

        (i) under section 4 of the Criminal Procedure (Insanity) Act 1964 (c 84) that the patient is under a disability, and

       (ii) under section 4A of that Act that he did the act or made the omission charged against him as the offence.

(3)   The second condition is that a hospital order with a restriction order is made in respect of the patient by a court dealing with him for the offence.

(4)   The local probation board for the area in which the determination mentioned in subsection (2)(a), (b) or (c) is made must take all reasonable steps to ascertain whether a person who appears to the board to be the victim of the offence or to act for the victim of the offence wishes—

(a)   to make representations about the matters specified in subsection (5);

(b)   to receive the information specified in subsection (6).

(5)   The matters are—

(a)   whether the patient should be subject to any conditions in the event of his discharge from hospital;

(b)   if so, what conditions.

(6)   The information is information about any conditions to which the patient is to be subject in the event of his discharge from hospital.

37 Representations

(1)   This section applies if section 36 applies.

(2)   If—

(a)   a person makes representations about a matter specified in section 36(5) to the local probation board mentioned in section 36(4) or the relevant local probation board, and

(b)   it appears to the relevant local probation board that the person is the victim of the offence or acts for the victim of the offence,

the relevant local probation board must forward the representations to the persons responsible for determining the matter.

(3)   The duty in subsection (2) applies only while the restriction order made in respect of the patient is in force.

(4)   The Secretary of State must inform the relevant local probation board if he is considering—

(a)   whether to give a direction in respect of the patient under section 42(1) of the Mental Health Act 1983 (c 20) (directions lifting restrictions),

(b)   whether to discharge the patient under section 42(2) of that Act, either absolutely or subject to conditions, or

(c)   if the patient has been discharged subject to conditions, whether to vary the conditions.

(5)   A Mental Health Review Tribunal must inform the relevant local probation board if—

(a)   an application is made to the tribunal by the patient under section 69, 70 or 75 of the Mental Health Act 1983 (applications concerning restricted patients), or

(b)   the Secretary of State refers the patient's case to the tribunal under section 71 of that Act (references concerning restricted patients).

(6)   Subsection (7) applies if—

(a)   the relevant local probation board receives information under subsection (4) or (5), and

(b)   a person who appears to the relevant local probation board to be the victim of the offence or to act for the victim of the offence—

(i)   when his wishes were ascertained under section 36(4), expressed a wish to make representations about a matter specified in section 36(5), or

    (ii) has made representations about such a matter to the relevant local probation board or the local probation board mentioned in section 36(4).

(7)   The relevant local probation board must provide the information to the person.

(8)   The relevant local probation board is—
    (a) if the patient is to be discharged subject to a condition that he reside in a particular area, the local probation board for the area;
    (b) in any other case, the local probation board for the area in which the hospital in which the patient is detained is situated.

38 Information

(1)   This section applies if section 36 applies.

(2)   Subsection (3) applies if a person who appears to the relevant local probation board to be the victim of the offence or to act for the victim of the offence—
    (a) when his wishes were ascertained under section 36(4), expressed a wish to receive the information specified in section 36(6), or
    (b) has subsequently informed the relevant local probation board that he wishes to receive that information.

(3)   The relevant local probation board must take all reasonable steps—
    (a) to inform that person whether or not the patient is to be subject to any conditions in the event of his discharge;
    (b) if he is, to provide that person with details of any conditions which relate to contact with the victim or his family;
    (c) if the restriction order in respect of the patient is to cease to have effect, to notify that person of the date on which it is to cease to have effect;
    (d) to provide that person with such other information as the board considers appropriate in all the circumstances of the case.

(4)   The Secretary of State must inform the relevant local probation board—
    (a) whether the patient is to be discharged;
    (b) if he is, whether he is to be discharged absolutely or subject to conditions;
    (c) if he is to be discharged subject to conditions, what the conditions are to be;
    (d) if he has been discharged subject to conditions—
       (i)of any variation of the conditions by the Secretary of State;
       (ii)of any recall to hospital under section 42(3) of the Mental Health Act 1983 (c 20);
    (e) if the restriction order is to cease to have effect by virtue of action to be taken by the Secretary of State, of the date on which the restriction order is to cease to have effect.

(5)   Subsections (6) and (7) apply (instead of subsection (4)) if—
    (a) an application is made to a Mental Health Review Tribunal by the patient under section 69, 70 or 75 of the Mental Health Act 1983 (c 20) (applications concerning restricted patients), or
    (b) the Secretary of State refers the patient's case to a Mental Health Review Tribunal under section 71 of that Act (references concerning restricted patients).

(6)   The tribunal must inform the relevant local probation board—
    (a) of the matters specified in subsection (4)(a) to (c);
    (b) if the patient has been discharged subject to conditions, of any variation of the conditions by the tribunal;

(c) if the restriction order is to cease to have effect by virtue of action to be taken by the tribunal, of the date on which the restriction order is to cease to have effect.

(7) The Secretary of State must inform the relevant local probation board of the matters specified in subsection (4)(d) and (e).

(8) The duties in subsections (3) to (7) apply only while the restriction order is in force.

(9) The relevant local probation board has the meaning given in section 37(8).

Hospital directions

39 Victims' rights: preliminary

(1) This section applies if—
   (a) a person ('the offender') is convicted of a sexual or violent offence,
   (b) a relevant sentence is imposed on him in respect of the offence, and
   (c) a hospital direction and a limitation direction are given in relation to him by a court dealing with him for the offence.

(2) The local probation board for the area in which the hospital direction is given must take all reasonable steps to ascertain whether a person who appears to the board to be the victim of the offence or to act for the victim of the offence wishes—
   (a) to make representations about the matters specified in subsection (3);
   (b) to receive the information specified in subsection (4).

(3) The matters are—
   (a) whether the offender should, in the event of his discharge from hospital, be subject to any conditions and, if so, what conditions;
   (b) whether the offender should, in the event of his release from hospital, be subject to any licence conditions or supervision requirements and, if so, what licence conditions or supervision requirements;
   (c) if the offender is transferred to a prison or other institution in which he might have been detained if he had not been removed to hospital, whether he should, in the event of his release from prison or another such institution, be subject to any licence conditions or supervision requirements and, if so, what licence conditions or supervision requirements.

(4) The information is—
   (a) information about any conditions to which the offender is to be subject in the event of his discharge;
   (b) information about any licence conditions or supervision requirements to which the offender is to be subject in the event of his release.

40 Representations

(1) This section applies if section 39 applies.

(2) If—
   (a) a person makes representations about a matter specified in section 39(3) to the local probation board mentioned in section 39(2) or the relevant local probation board, and

(b) it appears to the relevant local probation board that the person is the victim of the offence or acts for the victim of the offence,

the relevant local probation board must forward the representations to the persons responsible for determining the matter.

(3)   If the representations are about a matter specified in section 39(3)(a), the duty in subsection (2) applies only while the limitation direction given in relation to the offender is in force.

(4)   The Secretary of State must inform the relevant local probation board if he is considering—
(a) whether to give a direction in respect of the offender under section 42(1) of the Mental Health Act 1983 (c 20) (directions lifting restrictions),
(b) whether to discharge the offender under section 42(2) of that Act, either absolutely or subject to conditions, or
(c) if the offender has been discharged subject to conditions, whether to vary the conditions.

(5)   A Mental Health Review Tribunal must inform the relevant local probation board if—
(a) an application is made to the tribunal by the offender under section 69, 70 or 75 of the Mental Health Act 1983 (applications concerning restricted patients), or
(b) the Secretary of State refers the offender's case to the tribunal under section 71 of that Act (references concerning restricted patients).

(6)   Subsection (7) applies if—
(a) the relevant local probation board receives information under subsection (4) or (5), and
(b) a person who appears to the relevant local probation board to be the victim of the offence or to act for the victim of the offence—
(i)when his wishes were ascertained under section 39(2), expressed a wish to make representations about a matter specified in section 39(3)(a), or
(ii)has made representations about such a matter to the relevant local probation board or the local probation board mentioned in section 39(2).

(7)   The relevant local probation board must provide the information to the person.

(8)   The relevant local probation board is—
(a) if the offender is to be discharged from hospital subject to a condition that he reside in a particular area, the local probation board for the area;
(b) if the offender is to be supervised on release by an officer of a local probation board, that local probation board;
(c) in any other case, the local probation board for the area in which the hospital, prison or other place in which the offender is detained is situated.

41 Information

(1)   This section applies if section 39 applies.

(2)   Subsection (3) applies if a person who appears to the relevant local probation board to be the victim of the offence or to act for the victim of the offence—
(a) when his wishes were ascertained under section 39(2), expressed a wish to receive the information specified in section 39(4), or
(b) has subsequently informed the relevant local probation board that he wishes to receive that information.

(3)　The relevant local probation board must take all reasonable steps—

    (a)　to inform that person whether or not the offender is to be subject to any conditions in the event of his discharge;

    (b)　if he is, to provide that person with details of any conditions which relate to contact with the victim or his family;

    (c)　if the limitation direction in respect of the offender is to cease to have effect, to notify that person of the date on which it is to cease to have effect;

    (d)　to inform that person whether or not the offender is to be subject to any licence conditions or supervision requirements in the event of his release;

    (e)　if he is, to provide that person with details of any licence conditions or supervision requirements which relate to contact with the victim or his family;

    (f)　to provide that person with such other information as the board considers appropriate in all the circumstances of the case.

(4)　The Secretary of State must inform the relevant local probation board—

    (a)　whether the offender is to be discharged;

    (b)　if he is, whether he is to be discharged absolutely or subject to conditions;

    (c)　if he is to be discharged subject to conditions, what the conditions are to be;

    (d)　if he has been discharged subject to conditions—

        (i)of any variation of the conditions by the Secretary of State;

        (ii)of any recall to hospital under section 42(3) of the Mental Health Act 1983 (c 20);

    (e)　if the limitation direction is to cease to have effect by virtue of action to be taken by the Secretary of State, of the date on which the limitation direction is to cease to have effect.

(5)　Subsections (6) and (7) apply (instead of subsection (4)) if—

    (a)　an application is made to a Mental Health Review Tribunal by the offender under section 69, 70 or 75 of the Mental Health Act 1983 (c 20) (applications concerning restricted patients), or

    (b)　the Secretary of State refers the offender's case to a Mental Health Review Tribunal under section 71 of that Act (references concerning restricted patients).

(6)　The tribunal must inform the relevant local probation board—

    (a)　of the matters specified in subsection (4)(a) to (c);

    (b)　if the offender has been discharged subject to conditions, of any variation of the conditions by the tribunal;

    (c)　if the limitation direction is to cease to have effect by virtue of action to be taken by the tribunal, of the date on which the limitation direction is to cease to have effect.

(7)　The Secretary of State must inform the relevant local probation board of the matters specified in subsection (4)(d) and (e).

(8)　The duties in subsections (3)(a) to (c) and (4) to (7) apply only while the limitation direction is in force.

(9)　The relevant local probation board has the meaning given in section 40(8).

Transfer directions

42 Victims' rights: preliminary

(1)　This section applies if—

(a)   a person ('the offender') is convicted of a sexual or violent offence,

(b)   a relevant sentence is imposed on him in respect of the offence, and

(c)   while the offender is serving the sentence, the Secretary of State gives a transfer direction and a restriction direction in respect of him.

(2)   The local probation board for the area in which the hospital specified in the transfer direction is situated must take all reasonable steps to ascertain whether a person who appears to the board to be the victim of the offence or to act for the victim of the offence wishes—

(a)   to make representations about the matters specified in subsection (3);

(b)   to receive the information specified in subsection (4).

(3)   The matters are—

(a)   whether the offender should be subject to any conditions in the event of his discharge from hospital;

(b)   if so, what conditions.

(4)   The information is information about any conditions to which the offender is to be subject in the event of his discharge from hospital.

43 Representations

(1)   This section applies if section 42 applies.

(2)   If—

(a)   a person makes representations about a matter specified in section 42(3) to the local probation board mentioned in section 42(2) or the relevant local probation board, and

(b)   it appears to the relevant local probation board that the person is the victim of the offence or acts for the victim of the offence,

the relevant local probation board must forward the representations to the persons responsible for determining the matter.

(3)   The duty in subsection (2) applies only while the restriction direction given in respect of the offender is in force.

(4)   The Secretary of State must inform the relevant local probation board if he is considering—

(a)   whether to give a direction in respect of the offender under section 42(1) of the Mental Health Act 1983 (c 20) (directions lifting restrictions),

(b)   whether to discharge the offender under section 42(2) of that Act, either absolutely or subject to conditions, or

(c)   if the offender has been discharged subject to conditions, whether to vary the conditions.

(5)   A Mental Health Review Tribunal must inform the relevant local probation board if—

(a)   an application is made to the tribunal by the offender under section 69, 70 or 75 of the Mental Health Act 1983 (applications concerning restricted patients), or

(b)   the Secretary of State refers the offender's case to the tribunal under section 71 of that Act (references concerning restricted patients).

(6)   Subsection (7) applies if—

(a)   the relevant local probation board receives information under subsection (4) or (5), and

   (b) a person who appears to the relevant local probation board to be the victim of the offence or to act for the victim of the offence—

      (i) when his wishes were ascertained under section 42(2), expressed a wish to make representations about a matter specified in section 42(3), or

      (ii) has made representations about such a matter to the relevant local probation board or the local probation board mentioned in section 42(2).

(7)   The relevant local probation board must provide the information to the person.

(8)   The relevant local probation board is—

   (a) if the offender is to be discharged subject to a condition that he reside in a particular area, the local probation board for the area;

   (b) in any other case, the local probation board for the area in which the hospital in which the offender is detained is situated.

44 Information

(1)   This section applies if section 42 applies.

(2)   Subsection (3) applies if a person who appears to the relevant local probation board to be the victim of the offence or to act for the victim of the offence—

   (a) when his wishes were ascertained under section 42(2), expressed a wish to receive the information specified in section 42(4), or

   (b) has subsequently informed the relevant local probation board that he wishes to receive that information.

(3)   The relevant local probation board must take all reasonable steps—

   (a) to inform that person whether or not the offender is to be subject to any conditions in the event of his discharge;

   (b) if he is, to provide that person with details of any conditions which relate to contact with the victim or his family;

   (c) if the restriction direction in respect of the offender is to cease to have effect, to notify that person of the date on which it is to cease to have effect;

   (d) to provide that person with such other information as the board considers appropriate in all the circumstances of the case.

(4)   The Secretary of State must inform the relevant local probation board—

   (a) whether the offender is to be discharged;

   (b) if he is, whether he is to be discharged absolutely or subject to conditions;

   (c) if he is to be discharged subject to conditions, what the conditions are to be;

   (d) if he has been discharged subject to conditions—

      (i) of any variation of the conditions by the Secretary of State;

      (ii) of any recall to hospital under section 42(3) of the Mental Health Act 1983 (c 20);

   (e) if the restriction direction is to cease to have effect by virtue of action to be taken by the Secretary of State, of the date on which the restriction direction is to cease to have effect.

(5)   Subsections (6) and (7) apply (instead of subsection (4)) if—

   (a) an application is made to a Mental Health Review Tribunal by the offender under section 69, 70 or 75 of the Mental Health Act 1983 (applications concerning restricted patients), or

   (b) the Secretary of State refers the offender's case to a Mental Health Review Tribunal under section 71 of that Act (references concerning restricted patients).

(6)   The tribunal must inform the relevant local probation board—

(a) of the matters specified in subsection (4)(a) to (c);

(b) if the offender has been discharged subject to conditions, of any variation of the conditions by the tribunal;

(c) if the restriction direction is to cease to have effect by virtue of action to be taken by the tribunal, of the date on which the restriction direction is to cease to have effect.

(7)   The Secretary of State must inform the relevant local probation board of the matters specified in subsection (4)(d) and (e).

(8)   The duties in subsections (3) to (7) apply only while the restriction direction is in force.

(9)   The relevant local probation board has the meaning given in section 43(8).

Interpretation

45 Interpretation: sections 35 to 44

(1)   In sections 35 to 44—

'court' does not include a court-martial or the Courts-Martial Appeal Court;

'hospital direction' has the meaning given in section 45A(3)(a) of the Mental Health Act 1983 (c 20);

'hospital order' has the meaning given in section 37(4) of that Act;

'licence condition' means a condition in a licence;

'limitation direction' has the meaning given in section 45A(3)(b) of the Mental Health Act 1983;

'local probation board' means a local probation board established under section 4 of the Criminal Justice and Court Services Act 2000 (c 43);

'relevant sentence' means any of these—

(a)a sentence of imprisonment for a term of 12 months or more;

(b)a sentence of detention during Her Majesty's pleasure;

(c)a sentence of detention for a period of 12 months or more under section 91 of the Powers of Criminal Courts (Sentencing) Act 2000 (c 6) (offenders under 18 convicted of certain serious offences);

(d)a detention and training order for a term of 12 months or more;

'restriction direction' has the meaning given in section 49(2) of the Mental Health Act 1983;

'restriction order' has the meaning given in section 41(1) of that Act;

'supervision requirements' means requirements specified in a notice under section 103(6) of the Powers of Criminal Courts (Sentencing) Act 2000;

'transfer direction' has the meaning given in section 47(1) of the Mental Health Act 1983.

(2)   For the purposes of sections 35 to 44, an offence is a sexual or violent offence if it is any of these—

(a) murder or an offence specified in Schedule 15 to the Criminal Justice Act 2003 (c 44);

(b) an offence in respect of which the patient or offender is subject to the notification requirements of Part 2 of the Sexual Offences Act 2003 (c 42));

(c) an offence against a child within the meaning of Part 2 of the Criminal Justice and Court Services Act 2000.

Northern Ireland

46 Victims of mentally disordered persons

(1)   The Justice (Northern Ireland) Act 2002 (c 26) is amended as follows.

(2)   After section 69 (views on temporary release) insert—

'69A Information about discharge and leave of absence of mentally disordered persons

(1)   The Secretary of State must make a scheme requiring the Secretary of State to make available to persons falling within subsection (2) information about—
    (a)   the discharge from hospital of, or
    (b)   the grant of leave of absence from hospital to,

persons in respect of whom relevant determinations have been made.

(2)   The persons referred to in subsection (1) are victims of the offences in respect of which the determinations were made who wish to receive the information.

(3)   A relevant determination is made in respect of a person if—
    (a)   a hospital order with a restriction order is made in respect of him by a court dealing with him for an offence, or
    (b)   a transfer direction and a restriction direction are given in respect of him while he is serving a sentence of imprisonment in respect of an offence.

(4)   The Secretary of State may from time to time make a new scheme or alterations to a scheme.

(5)   The information to be made available under a scheme must include information as to any relevant conditions to which a person in respect of whom a relevant determination has been made is to be subject in the event of—
    (a)   his discharge from hospital, or
    (b)   the grant of leave of absence from hospital to him.

(6)   A condition is relevant for the purposes of subsection (5) if it appears to the Secretary of State that it might affect a victim of an offence in respect of which the determination was made.

(7)   A scheme may require the Secretary of State to take all reasonable steps to ascertain whether a person who appears to him to be the victim of an offence in respect of which a relevant determination has been made wishes to make representations about the matters specified in subsection (8).

(8)   The matters are—
    (a)   whether the person in respect of whom the determination has been made should be subject to any conditions in the event of his discharge from hospital or the grant of leave of absence from hospital to him;
    (b)   if so, what conditions.

(9)   A scheme that includes provision such as is mentioned in subsection (7) must specify how the representations are to be made.

(10)   A scheme may require other information in relation to the discharge of, or the grant of leave of absence to, persons in respect of whom relevant determinations are made to be made available under the scheme.

(11)   The other information may include, in cases of a description specified by the scheme or in which the Secretary of State considers it appropriate, the date on which it is anticipated that a person in respect of whom a relevant determination has been made will be discharged or granted leave of absence from hospital.

(12)   Subsections (5) to (8) of section 68 apply in relation to a scheme made under this section as they apply in relation to a scheme made under that section.C:

(13)   A scheme may make different provision in relation to different descriptions of persons in respect of whom a relevant determination is made.

69B Views on leave of absence

(1)   If a person who is the victim of an offence in respect of which a relevant determination has been made makes to the Secretary of State representations falling within subsection (2) the Secretary of State has the obligations specified in subsection (3).

(2)   Representations fall within this subsection if they are to the effect that the grant of leave of absence to the person in respect of whom the determination has been made would threaten the safety, or otherwise adversely affect the well-being, of—
    (a)   the actual victim of the offence in respect of which the determination was made, or
    (b)   a person who is regarded for the purposes of a scheme under section 69A as a victim of that offence by virtue of section 68(5) (as applied by section 69A(12)).

(3)   The Secretary of State must—
    (a)   have regard to the representations in deciding whether he should give his consent to leave of absence being granted, and
    (b)   inform the victim of any such decision.

(4)   Section 69A(3) (relevant determination) applies for the purposes of this section.'

(3)   In section 70 (supplementary), after subsection (3) insert—

'(4)   In sections 68 and 69 references to a person serving a sentence of imprisonment in Northern Ireland include a person detained in hospital pursuant to a transfer direction and a restriction direction.

(5)   In subsection (4) and section 69A(3)—
    'restriction direction' has the meaning given in Article 55(2) of the Mental Health (Northern Ireland) Order 1986;
    'transfer direction' has the meaning given in Article 53(2) of that Order.

(6)   In section 69A(3)—
    'hospital order' has the meaning given in Article 44(1) of the Mental Health (Northern Ireland) Order 1986;
    'restriction order' has the meaning given in Article 47(1) of that Order;
    'sentence of imprisonment' has the meaning given in Article 53(5) of that Order.

(7)   In sections 69A and 69B 'leave of absence' means leave of absence under Article 15 of the Mental Health (Northern Ireland) Order 1986.'

(4)   In section 90(5) (statutory rules), in paragraph (b) after 'section 68' insert 'or 69A'.

CHAPTER 3
OTHER MATTERS RELATING TO VICTIMS ETC

Parliamentary Commissioner

47 Investigations by Parliamentary Commissioner

Schedule 7 (which amends the Parliamentary Commissioner Act 1967 (c 13)) has effect.

48 Commissioner for Victims and Witnesses

(1)   The Secretary of State must appoint a Commissioner for Victims and Witnesses (referred to in this Part as the Commissioner).

(2)   Before appointing the Commissioner the Secretary of State must consult the Attorney General and the Lord Chancellor as to the person to be appointed.

(3)   The Commissioner is a corporation sole.

(4)   The Commissioner is not to be regarded—
    (a)   as the servant or agent of the Crown, or
    (b)   as enjoying any status, immunity or privilege of the Crown.

(5)   The Commissioner's property is not to be regarded as property of, or held on behalf of, the Crown.

(6)   Schedule 8 (which make further provision in connection with the Commissioner) has effect.

49 General functions of Commissioner

(1)   The Commissioner must—
    (a)   promote the interests of victims and witnesses;
    (b)   take such steps as he considers appropriate with a view to encouraging good practice in the treatment of victims and witnesses;
    (c)   keep under review the operation of the code of practice issued under section 32.

(2)   The Commissioner may, for any purpose connected with the performance of his duties under subsection (1)—
    (a)   make proposals to the Secretary of State for amending the code (at the request of the Secretary of State or on his own initiative);
    (b)   make a report to the Secretary of State;
    (c)   make recommendations to an authority within his remit;
    (d)   undertake or arrange for or support (financially or otherwise) the carrying out of research;
    (e)   consult any person he thinks appropriate.

(3)   If the Commissioner makes a report to the Secretary of State under subsection (2)(b)—
    (a)   the Commissioner must send a copy of the report to the Attorney General and the Lord Chancellor;
    (b)   the Secretary of State must lay a copy of the report before Parliament and arrange for the report to be published.

50 Advice

(1)   If he is required to do so by a Minister of the Crown, the Commissioner must give advice to the Minister of the Crown in connection with any matter which—
    (a)   is specified by the Minister, and
    (b)   relates to victims or witnesses.

(2)   If he is required to do so by or on behalf of an authority within his remit, the Commissioner must give advice to the authority in connection with the information provided or to be provided by or on behalf of the authority to victims or witnesses.

(3) In this section 'Minister of the Crown' includes the Treasury.

51 Restrictions on exercise of functions

The Commissioner must not exercise any of his functions in relation to—
- (a) a particular victim or witness;
- (b) the bringing or conduct of particular proceedings;
- (c) anything done or omitted to be done by a person acting in a judicial capacity or on the instructions of or on behalf of such a person.

52 'Victims' and 'witnesses'

(1) This section applies for the purposes of sections 48 to 51.

(2) 'Victim' means—
- (a) a victim of an offence, or
- (b) a victim of anti-social behaviour.

(3) It is immaterial for the purposes of subsection (2)(a) that—
- (a) no complaint has been made about the offence;
- (b) no person has been charged with or convicted of the offence.

(4) 'Witness' means a person (other than a defendant)—
- (a) who has witnessed conduct in relation to which he may be or has been called to give evidence in relevant proceedings;
- (b) who is able to provide or has provided anything which might be used or has been used as evidence in relevant proceedings; or
- (c) who is able to provide or has provided anything mentioned in subsection (5) (whether or not admissible in evidence in relevant proceedings).

(5) The things referred to in subsection (4)(c) are—
- (a) anything which might tend to confirm, has tended to confirm or might have tended to confirm evidence which may be, has been or could have been admitted in relevant proceedings;
- (b) anything which might be, has been or might have been referred to in evidence given in relevant proceedings by another person;
- (c) anything which might be, has been or might have been used as the basis for any cross examination in the course of relevant proceedings.

(6) For the purposes of subsection (4)—
- (a) a person is a defendant in relation to any criminal proceedings if he might be, has been or might have been charged with or convicted of an offence in the proceedings;
- (b) a person is a defendant in relation to any other relevant proceedings if he might be, has been or might have been the subject of an order made in those proceedings.

(7) In subsections (4) to (6) 'relevant proceedings' means—
- (a) criminal proceedings;
- (b) proceedings of any other kind in respect of anti-social behaviour.

(8) For the purposes of this section—
- (a) 'anti-social behaviour' means behaviour by a person which causes or is likely to cause harassment, alarm or distress to one or more persons not of the same household as the person;

    (b) a person is a victim of anti-social behaviour if the behaviour has caused him harassment, alarm or distress and he is not of the same household as the person who engages in the behaviour.

53 Authorities within Commissioner's remit

(1)   For the purposes of this Part the authorities within the Commissioner's remit are those specified in Schedule 9.

(2)   An authority specified in Schedule 9 that has functions in relation to an area outside England and Wales is within the Commissioner's remit only to the extent that it discharges its functions in relation to England and Wales.

(3)   Subsection (2) does not apply in relation to the Foreign and Commonwealth Office.

(4)   The Secretary of State may by order amend Schedule 9 by—
    (a) adding an authority appearing to him to exercise functions of a public nature;
    (b) omitting an authority;
    (c) changing the description of an authority.

(5)   In preparing a draft of an order under subsection (4) the Secretary of State must consult the Attorney General and the Lord Chancellor.

Disclosure of information

54 Disclosure of information

(1)   A person may disclose information to a relevant authority for a purpose specified in subsection (2).

(2)   The purposes are purposes connected with any of these—
    (a) compliance with the code issued under section 32;
    (b) compliance with sections 35 to 44;
    (c) the carrying out of the functions of the Commissioner.

(3)   These are relevant authorities—
    (a) a person required to do anything under the code issued under section 32;
    (b) a local probation board established under section 4 of the Criminal Justice and Court Services Act 2000 (c 43);
    (c) the Commissioner;
    (d) an authority within the Commissioner's remit.

(4)   The Secretary of State may by order—
    (a) amend subsection (2) by adding any purpose appearing to him to be connected with the assistance of victims of offences or anti-social behaviour, witnesses of offences or anti-social behaviour or other persons affected by offences or anti-social behaviour;
    (b) amend subsection (3) by adding any authority appearing to him to exercise functions of a public nature.

(5)   The reference in subsection (4)(a) to persons affected by offences does not include persons accused or convicted of offences.

(6)   The Secretary of State may exercise the power in subsection (4) only after consulting the Attorney General and the Lord Chancellor.

(7)   Nothing in this section authorises the making of a disclosure which contravenes the Data Protection Act 1998 (c 29).

(8)   This section does not affect a power to disclose which exists apart from this section.

Victims' Advisory Panel

55 Victims' Advisory Panel

(1)   The Secretary of State must appoint persons to form a panel, to be known as the Victims' Advisory Panel.

(2)   The Secretary of State must consult the Attorney General and the Lord Chancellor before—
   (a)   appointing a person to the Panel, or
   (b)   removing a person from the Panel.

(3)   The Secretary of State must consult the Panel at such times and in such manner as he thinks appropriate on matters appearing to him to relate to victims of offences or anti-social behaviour or witnesses of offences or anti-social behaviour.

(4)   The Secretary of State may reimburse the members of the Panel for such of their travelling and other expenses as he thinks appropriate.

(5)   If the Secretary of State consults the Panel under subsection (3) in a particular year, he must arrange for the Panel to prepare a report for the year—
   (a)   summarising what the Panel has done in response to the consultation, and
   (b)   dealing with such other matters as the Panel consider appropriate.

(6)   If a report is prepared under subsection (5), the Secretary of State must—
   (a)   arrange for it to be published, and
   (b)   lay it before Parliament.

(7)   The non-statutory Victims' Advisory Panel is to be treated as having been established in accordance with this section.

(8)   If the Secretary of State consults the non-statutory Victims' Advisory Panel on a matter mentioned in subsection (3) before the date on which this section comes into force, the consultation is to be treated as taking place under subsection (3).

(9)   The non-statutory Victims' Advisory Panel is the unincorporated body of persons known as the Victims' Advisory Panel established by the Secretary of State before the date on which this section comes into force.

(10)   In this section 'year' means a period of 12 months beginning on 1 April.

Grants

56 Grants for assisting victims, witnesses etc

(1)   The Secretary of State may pay such grants to such persons as he considers appropriate in connection with measures which appear to him to be intended to assist victims, witnesses or other persons affected by offences.

(2)   The Secretary of State may make a grant under this section subject to such conditions as he considers appropriate.

Criminal injuries compensation

57 Recovery of criminal injuries compensation from offendersr:

(1)   The Criminal Injuries Compensation Act 1995 (c 53) is amended as follows.

(2)   After section 7 insert—

'7A Recovery of compensation from offenders: general

(1)   The Secretary of State may, by regulations made by statutory instrument, make provision for the recovery from an appropriate person of an amount equal to all or part of the compensation paid in respect of a criminal injury.

(2)   An appropriate person is a person who has been convicted of an offence in respect of the criminal injury.

(3)   The amount recoverable from a person under the regulations must be determined by reference only to the extent to which the criminal injury is directly attributable to an offence of which he has been convicted.

(4)   The regulations may confer functions in respect of recovery on—
   (a)   claims officers;
   (b)   if a Scheme manager has been appointed, persons appointed by the Scheme manager under section 3(4)(a).

(5)   The regulations may not authorise the recovery of an amount in respect of compensation from a person to the extent that the compensation has been repaid in accordance with the Scheme.

7B Recovery notices

(1)   If, under regulations made under section 7A(1), an amount has been determined as recoverable from a person, he must be given a notice (a 'recovery notice') in accordance with the regulations which—
   (a)   requires him to pay that amount, and
   (b)   contains the information mentioned in subsection (2).

(2)   The information is—
   (a)   the reasons for the determination that an amount is recoverable from the person;
   (b)   the basis on which the amount has been determined;
   (c)   the way in which and the date before which the amount is required to be paid;
   (d)   the means by which the amount may be recovered if it is not paid in accordance with the notice;
   (e)   the grounds on which and the procedure by means of which he may seek a review if he objects to—
      (i)the determination that an amount is recoverable from him;
      (ii)the amount determined as recoverable from him.

(3)   The Secretary of State may by order made by statutory instrument amend subsection (2) by—
   (a)   adding information;
   (b)   omitting information;
   (c)   changing the description of information.

7C Review of recovery determinations

(1)   Regulations under section 7A(1) shall include provision for the review, in such circumstances as may be prescribed by the regulations, of—
  (a)   a determination that an amount is recoverable from a person;l:
  (b)   the amount determined as recoverable from a person.

(2)   A person from whom an amount has been determined as recoverable under the regulations may seek such a review only on the grounds—
  (a)   that he has not been convicted of an offence to which the injury is directly attributable;
  (b)   that the compensation paid was not determined in accordance with the Scheme;
  (c)   that the amount determined as recoverable from him was not determined in accordance with the regulations.

(3)   Any such review must be conducted by a person other than the person who made the determination under review.

(4)   The person conducting any such review may—
  (a)   set aside the determination that the amount is recoverable;
  (b)   reduce the amount determined as recoverable;
  (c)   increase the amount determined as recoverable;
  (d)   determine to take no action under paragraphs (a) to (c).

(5)   But the person conducting any such review may increase the amount determined as recoverable if (but only if) it appears to that person that the interests of justice require the amount to be increased.

7D Recovery proceedings

(1)   An amount determined as recoverable from a person under regulations under section 7A(1) is recoverable from him as a debt due to the Crown if (but only if)—
  (a)   he has been given a recovery notice in accordance with the regulations which complies with the requirements of section 7B, and
  (b)   he has failed to pay the amount in accordance with the notice.

(2)   In any proceedings for the recovery of the amount from a person, it is a defence for the person to show—
  (a)   that he has not been convicted of an offence to which the injury is directly attributable;
  (b)   that the compensation paid was not determined in accordance with the Scheme; or
  (c)   that the amount determined as recoverable from him was not determined in accordance with regulations under section 7A.

(3)   In any such proceedings, except for the purposes of subsection (2)(b), no question may be raised or finding made as to the amount that was, or ought to have been, the subject of an award.

(4)   For the purposes of section 9 of the Limitation Act 1980 (time limit for actions for sums recoverable by statute to run from date on which cause of action accrued) the cause of action to recover that amount shall be taken to have accrued—
  (a)   on the date on which the compensation was paid; or
  (b)   if later, on the date on which a person from whom an amount is sought to be recovered was convicted of an offence to which the injury is directly attributable.

(5)   If that person is convicted of more than one such offence and the convictions are made on different dates, the reference in subsection (4)(b) to the date on which he was convicted of such an offence shall be taken to be a reference to the earlier or earliest (as the case may be) of the dates on which he was convicted of such an offence.' .

(3)   In section 9(7) (financial provisions: sums payable into Consolidated Fund), after 'section 3(1)(c)' insert ', or by virtue of regulations made under section 7A(1),'.

(4)   In section 11, after subsection (8) insert—

'(8A)   No regulations under section 7A(1) or order under section 7B(3) shall be made unless a draft of the regulations or order has been laid before Parliament and approved by a resolution of each House.'

PART 4
SUPPLEMENTARY

58 Amendments and repeals

(1)   Schedule 10 (minor and consequential amendments) has effect.

(2)   The provisions mentioned in Schedule 11 are repealed or revoked to the extent specified.

59 Transitional and transitory provisions

Schedule 12 (transitional and transitory provisions) has effect.

60 Commencement

The preceding provisions of this Act come into force in accordance with provision made by the Secretary of State by order.

61 Orders

(1)   An order under this Act—
   (a)   may make different provision for different purposes;
   (b)   may include supplementary, incidental, saving or transitional provisions.

(2)   Any power to make an order under this Act is exercisable by statutory instrument.

(3)   A statutory instrument containing an order under section 9(6) or 33(7) is subject to annulment in pursuance of a resolution of either House of Parliament.

(4)   No order may be made under section 14(5), 53(4) or 54(4) unless a draft of the order has been laid before Parliament and approved by a resolution of each House.

62 Extent

(1)   Subject to the following provisions of this section, Parts 1 to 3 extend to England and Wales only.

(2)   The following provisions extend also to Northern Ireland—
   section 5;
   section 9;
   sections 17 to 21;
   Schedule 1;
   section 56;

(3)   The following provisions extend to Northern Ireland only—
   section 7;
   section 10(2);
   section 13;
   section 23;
   section 46.

(4)   Section 8, so far as relating to proceedings before courts-martial constituted under a particular Act mentioned in subsection (2) of that section, has the same extent as that Act.

(5)   An amendment, repeal or revocation in Schedule 3, 7, 8, 10 or 11 has the same extent as the provision to which it relates.

63 Short title

This Act may be cited as the Domestic Violence, Crime and Victims Act 2004.

SCHEDULE 1
MODIFICATION OF SECTIONS 17 TO 20 FOR NORTHERN IRELAND

Section 21

1   For section 18 substitute—

'18 Procedure for applications under section 17

(1)   An application under section 17 must be determined—
   (a)   at a preparatory hearing (within the meaning of the 1988 Order), or
   (b)   at a hearing specified in, or for which provision is made by, Crown Court rules.

(2)   The parties to a hearing mentioned in subsection (1) at which an application under section 17 is to be determined must be given an opportunity to make representations with respect to the application.

(3)   Article 6(1) of the 1988 Order (which sets out the purposes of preparatory hearings) is to have effect as if the purposes there mentioned included the purpose of determining an application under section 17.

(4)   Article 8(11) of the 1988 Order (appeal to Court of Appeal) is to have effect as if it also provided for an appeal to the Court of Appeal to lie from the determination by a judge of an application under section 17.

(5)   In this section 'the 1988 Order' means the Criminal Justice (Serious Fraud) (Northern Ireland) Order 1988.

18A Appeals in respect of hearings under section 18(1)(b)

(1)   An appeal shall lie to the Court of Appeal from the refusal by a judge at a hearing mentioned in section 18(1)(b) of an application under section 17 or from an order of a judge at such a hearing under section 17(2) which is made on the determination of such an application.

(2)   Such an appeal may be brought only with the leave of the judge or the Court of Appeal.

(3)   An order or a refusal of an application from which an appeal under this section lies is not to take effect—
   (a)   before the expiration of the period for bringing an appeal under this section, or
   (b)   if such an appeal is brought, before the appeal is finally disposed of or abandoned.

(4)   On the termination of the hearing of an appeal under this section, the Court of Appeal may—
   (a)   where the appeal is from an order, confirm or revoke the order, or

(b)   where the appeal is from a refusal of an application, confirm the refusal or make the order which is the subject of the application.

(5)   In section 31(1) of the Criminal Appeal (Northern Ireland) Act 1980 (right of appeal to House of Lords) for 'Act or' substitute 'Act, section 18A of the Domestic Violence, Crime and Victims Act 2004,'.

(6)   In section 35 of that Act (bail) after 'appeal under' insert 'section 18A of the Domestic Violence, Crime and Victims Act 2004,'.

(7)   The Secretary of State may make an order containing provision, in relation to proceedings before the Court of Appeal under this section, which corresponds to any provision, in relation to appeals or other proceedings before that court, which is contained in the Criminal Appeal (Northern Ireland) Act 1980 (subject to any specified modifications).

(8)   A statutory instrument containing an order under subsection (7) is subject to annulment in pursuance of a resolution of either House of Parliament.

18B Reporting restrictions

(1)   Sections 41 and 42 of the Criminal Procedure and Investigations Act 1996 are to apply in relation to—
   (a)   a hearing of the kind mentioned in section 18(1)(b), and
   (b)   any appeal or application for leave to appeal relating to such a hearing,

as they apply in relation to a ruling under section 40 of that Act, but subject to the following modifications.

(2)   Section 41(2) of that Act is to have effect as if for paragraphs (a) to (d) there were substituted—

   '(a)   a hearing of the kind mentioned in section 18(1)(b) of the Domestic Violence, Crime and Victims Act 2004;
   (b)   any appeal or application for leave to appeal relating to such a hearing.'

(3)   Section 41(3) of that Act is to have effect as if—
   (a)   for ' (2)' there were substituted ' (2)(a) or an application to that judge for leave to appeal to the Court of Appeal', and
   (b)   after 'matter', in the second place where it occurs, there were inserted 'or application'.

(4)   Section 41 of that Act is to have effect as if after subsection (3) there were inserted—

   '(3A)   The Court of Appeal may order that subsection (1) shall not apply, or shall not apply to a specified extent, to a report of—
   (a)   an appeal to that Court, or
   (b)   an application to that Court for leave to appeal.

(3B)   The House of Lords may order that subsection (1) shall not apply, or shall not apply to a specified extent, to a report of—
   (a)   an appeal to that House, or
   (b)   an application to that House for leave to appeal.'

(5)   Section 41(4) of that Act is to have effect as if for ' (3) the judge' there were substituted ' (3), (3A) or (3B), the judge, the Court of Appeal or the House of Lords'.

(6)   Section 41(5) of that Act is to have effect as if for ' (3) the judge' there were substituted ' (3), (3A) or (3B), the judge, the Court of Appeal or the House of Lords'.'

2   In section 19(3) after 'enactment' insert ' (including any provision of Northern Ireland legislation)'.

3   In section 19(4)(b) for the words from 'section' to 'etc)' substitute 'section 16(1) of the Criminal Appeal (Northern Ireland) Act 1980 (notice of appeal or application for leave)'.

4   In section 19(5) for 'section 18(2) of the Criminal Appeal Act 1968' substitute 'section 16(1) of the Criminal Appeal (Northern Ireland) Act 1980'.

5   For section 19(7) substitute—

'(7)   Nothing in this section or section 17, 18, 18A, 18B or 20 affects the requirement under Article 49A of the Mental Health (Northern Ireland) Order 1986 that any question, finding or verdict mentioned in that Article be determined, made or returned by a jury.'

6   For section 20(2) substitute—

'(2)   Without limiting subsection (1), rules of court may in particular make provision—
   (a)   for time limits within which applications under section 17 must be made or within which other things in connection with that section or sections 18 to 19 must be done;
   (b)   in relation to hearings of the kind mentioned in section 18(1)(b).'

7   In section 20(3)—
   (a)   after 'section' insert 'or section 18(1)(b)';
   (b)   after 'enactment' insert ' (including any provision of Northern Ireland legislation)'.

SCHEDULE 2
SUPERVISION ORDERS ON FINDING OF INSANITY
OR UNFITNESS TO PLEAD ETC

Section 24

The following is the Schedule inserted before Schedule 2 to the Criminal Procedure (Insanity) Act 1964 (c 84)—

'SCHEDULE 1A
SUPERVISION ORDERS

Section 5A

PART 1
PRELIMINARY

1   (1)   In this Schedule 'supervision order' means an order which requires the person in respect of whom it is made ('the supervised person') to be under the supervision of a social worker or an officer of a local probation board ('the supervising officer') for a period specified in the order of not more than two years.

(2)   A supervision order may, in accordance with paragraph 4 or 5 below, require the supervised

person to submit, during the whole of that period or such part of it as may be specified in the order, to treatment by or under the direction of a registered medical practitioner.

(3)   The Secretary of State may by order direct that sub-paragraph (1) above shall be amended by substituting, for the period for the time being specified there, such period as may be specified in the order.

(4)   An order under sub-paragraph (3) above may make in paragraph 11(2) below any amendment which the Secretary of State thinks necessary in consequence of any substitution made by the order.

(5)   The power of the Secretary of State to make orders under sub-paragraph (3) above shall be exercisable by statutory instrument which shall be subject to annulment in pursuance of a resolution of either House of Parliament.

PART 2
MAKING AND EFFECT OF ORDERS

Circumstances in which orders may be made

2   (1)   The court shall not make a supervision order unless it is satisfied that, having regard to all the circumstances of the case, the making of such an order is the most suitable means of dealing with the accused or appellant.

(2)   The court shall not make a supervision order unless it is also satisfied—
  (a)   that the supervising officer intended to be specified in the order is willing to undertake the supervision; and
  (b)   that arrangements have been made for the treatment intended to be specified in the order.

Making of orders and general requirements

3   (1)   A supervision order shall either—
  (a)   specify the local social services authority area in which the supervised person resides or will reside, and require him to be under the supervision of a social worker of the local social services authority for that area; or
  (b)   specify the local justice area in which that person resides or will reside, and require him to be under the supervision of an officer of a local probation board appointed for or assigned to that area.

(2)   Before making such an order, the court shall explain to the supervised person in ordinary language—
  (a)   the effect of the order (including any requirements proposed to be included in the order in accordance with paragraph 4, 5 or 8 below); and
  (b)   that a magistrates' court has power under paragraphs 9 to 11 below to review the order on the application either of the supervised person or of the supervising officer.

(3)   After making such an order, the court shall forthwith give copies of the order to an officer of a local probation board assigned to the court, and he shall give a copy—
  (a)   to the supervised person; and
  (b)   to the supervising officer.

(4)   After making such an order, the court shall also send to the designated officer for the local justice area in which the supervised person resides or will reside ('the local justice area concerned')—
  (a)   a copy of the order; and

(b)   such documents and information relating to the case as it considers likely to be of assistance to a court acting for that area in the exercise of its functions in relation to the order.

(5)   Where such an order is made, the supervised person shall keep in touch with the supervising officer in accordance with such instructions as he may from time to time be given by that officer and shall notify him of any change of address.

Requirements as to medical treatment

4   (1)   A supervision order may, if the court is satisfied as mentioned in sub-paragraph (2) below, include a requirement that the supervised person shall submit, during the whole of the period specified in the order or during such part of that period as may be so specified, to treatment by or under the direction of a registered medical practitioner with a view to the improvement of his mental condition.

(2)   The court may impose such a requirement only if satisfied on the written or oral evidence of two or more registered medical practitioners, at least one of whom is duly registered, that the mental condition of the supervised person—
(a)   is such as requires and may be susceptible to treatment; but
(b)   is not such as to warrant the making of a hospital order within the meaning of the Mental Health Act 1983.

(3)   The treatment required under this paragraph by any such order shall be such one of the following kinds of treatment as may be specified in the order, that is to say—
(a)   treatment as a non-resident patient at such institution or place as may be specified in the order; and
(b)   treatment by or under the direction of such registered medical practitioner as may be so specified;

but the nature of the treatment shall not be specified in the order except as mentioned in paragraph (a) or (b) above.

5   (1)   This paragraph applies where the court is satisfied on the written or oral evidence of two or more registered medical practitioners that—
(a)   because of his medical condition, other than his mental condition, the supervised person is likely to pose a risk to himself or others; and
(b)   the condition may be susceptible to treatment.

(2)   The supervision order may (whether or not it includes a requirement under paragraph 4 above) include a requirement that the supervised person shall submit, during the whole of the period specified in the order or during such part of that period as may be so specified, to treatment by or under the direction of a registered medical practitioner with a view to the improvement of the condition.

(3)   The treatment required under this paragraph by any such order shall be such one of the following kinds of treatment as may be specified in the order, that is to say—
(a)   treatment as a non-resident patient at such institution or place as may be specified in the order; and
(b)   treatment by or under the direction of such registered medical practitioner as may be so specified;

but the nature of the treatment shall not be specified in the order except as mentioned in paragraph (a) or (b) above.

6   (1)   Where the medical practitioner by whom or under whose direction the supervised person is being treated in pursuance of a requirement under paragraph 4 or 5 above is of the opinion that part of the treatment can be better or more conveniently given in or at an institution or place which—

(a)   is not specified in the order, and

(b)   is one in or at which the treatment of the supervised person will be given by or under the direction of a registered medical practitioner,

he may, with the consent of the supervised person, make arrangements for him to be treated accordingly.

(2)   Such arrangements may provide for the supervised person to receive part of his treatment as a resident patient in an institution or place of any description.

(3)   Where any such arrangements are made for the treatment of a supervised person—

(a)   the medical practitioner by whom the arrangements are made shall give notice in writing to the supervising officer, specifying the institution or place in or at which the treatment is to be carried out; and

(b)   the treatment provided for by the arrangements shall be deemed to be treatment to which he is required to submit in pursuance of the supervision order.

7   While the supervised person is under treatment as a resident patient in pursuance of arrangements under paragraph 6 above, the supervising officer shall carry out the supervision to such extent only as may be necessary for the purpose of the revocation or amendment of the order.

Requirements as to residence

8   (1)   Subject to sub-paragraph (2) below, a supervision order may include requirements as to the residence of the supervised person.

(2)   Before making such an order containing any such requirement, the court shall consider the home surroundings of the supervised person.

PART 3
REVOCATION AND AMENDMENT OF ORDERS

Revocation of order

9   (1)   Where a supervision order is in force in respect of any person and, on the application of the supervised person or the supervising officer, it appears to a magistrates' court acting for the local justice area concerned that, having regard to circumstances which have arisen since the order was made, it would be in the interests of the health or welfare of the supervised person that the order should be revoked, the court may revoke the order.

(2)   The court by which a supervision order was made may of its own motion revoke the order if, having regard to circumstances which have arisen since the order was made, it considers that it would be inappropriate for the order to continue.

Amendment of order by reason of change of residence

10   (1)   This paragraph applies where, at any time while a supervision order is in force in respect of any person, a magistrates' court acting for the local justice area concerned is satisfied that the supervised person proposes to change, or has changed, his residence from the area specified in the order to another local social services authority area or local justice area.

(2)   Subject to sub-paragraph (3) below, the court may, and on the application of the supervising officer shall, amend the supervision order by substituting the other area for the area specified in the order.

(3)   The court shall not amend under this paragraph a supervision order which contains requirements which, in the opinion of the court, cannot be complied with unless the supervised person continues to reside in the area specified in the order unless, in accordance with paragraph 11 below, it either—

  (a)   cancels those requirements; or

  (b)   substitutes for those requirements other requirements which can be complied with if the supervised person ceases to reside in that area.

Amendment of requirements of order

11   (1)   Without prejudice to the provisions of paragraph 10 above, but subject to sub-paragraph (2) below, a magistrates' court for the local justice area concerned may, on the application of the supervised person or the supervising officer, by order amend a supervision order—

  (a)   by cancelling any of the requirements of the order; or

  (b)   by inserting in the order (either in addition to or in substitution for any such requirement) any requirement which the court could include if it were the court by which the order was made and were then making it.

(2)   The power of a magistrates' court under sub-paragraph (1) above shall not include power to amend an order by extending the period specified in it beyond the end of two years from the day of the original order.

Amendment of requirements in pursuance of medical report

12   (1)   Where the medical practitioner by whom or under whose direction the supervised person is being treated for his mental condition in pursuance of any requirement of a supervision order—

  (a)   is of the opinion mentioned in sub-paragraph (2) below, or

  (b)   is for any reason unwilling to continue to treat or direct the treatment of the supervised person,

he shall make a report in writing to that effect to the supervising officer and that officer shall apply under paragraph 11 above to a magistrates' court for the local justice area concerned for the variation or cancellation of the requirement.

(2)   The opinion referred to in sub-paragraph (1) above is—

  (a)   that the treatment of the supervised person should be continued beyond the period specified in the supervision order;

  (b)   that the supervised person needs different treatment, being treatment of a kind to which he could be required to submit in pursuance of such an order;

  (c)   that the supervised person is not susceptible to treatment; or

  (d)   that the supervised person does not require further treatment.

Supplemental

13   (1)   On the making under paragraph 9 above of an order revoking a supervision order, the designated officer for the local justice area concerned, or (as the case may be) the Crown Court, shall forthwith give copies of the revoking order to the supervising officer.

(2)   A supervising officer to whom in accordance with sub-paragraph (1) above copies of a revoking order are given shall give a copy to the supervised person and to the person in charge of any institution in which the supervised person is residing.

14   (1)   On the making under paragraph 10 or 11 above of any order amending a supervision

order, the designated officer for the local justice area concerned shall forthwith—

   (a)   if the order amends the supervision order otherwise than by substituting a new area or a new place for the one specified in the supervision order, give copies of the amending order to the supervising officer;

   (b)   if the order amends the supervision order in the manner excepted by paragraph (a) above, send to the designated officer for the new local justice area concerned—

      (i)copies of the amending order; and

      (ii)such documents and information relating to the case as he considers likely to be of assistance to a court acting for that area in exercising its functions in relation to the order;

and in a case falling within paragraph (b) above, the designated officer for that area shall give copies of the amending order to the supervising officer.

(2)   Where the designated officer for the court making the order is also the designated officer for the new local justice area—

   (a)   sub-paragraph (1)(b) above does not apply; but

   (b)   the designated officers shall give copies of the amending order to the supervising officer.

(3)   Where in accordance with sub-paragraph (1) or (2) above copies of an order are given to the supervising officer, he shall give a copy to the supervised person and to the person in charge of any institution in which the supervised person is or was residing.'

SCHEDULE 3
UNFITNESS TO STAND TRIAL AND INSANITY: COURTS-MARTIAL ETC

Section 26

Army Act 1955 (3 & 4 Eliz 2 c 18) and Air Force Act 1955 (3 & 4 Eliz 2 c 19)

1   For section 116 of the Army Act 1955 and of the Air Force Act 1955 (provisions where accused found insane) substitute—

'Findings of unfitness to stand trial and insanity

115A Fitness to stand trial

(1)   This section applies where on a trial by court-martial of a person the question arises (at the instance of the defence or otherwise) whether the accused is fit to stand trial.

(2)   For the purposes of this Act a person is unfit to stand trial if he is under a disability such that apart from the Criminal Procedure (Insanity) Act 1964 it would constitute a bar to his being tried on indictment in England and Wales.

(3)   If, having regard to the nature of the supposed disability, the judge advocate is of opinion that it is expedient to do so and in the interests of the accused, he may postpone consideration of the question of fitness to stand trial until any time up to the opening of the case for the defence.

(4)   If, before the question of fitness to stand trial falls to be determined, the court finds the accused not guilty on the charge or each of the charges on which he is being tried, that question shall not be determined.

(5)   Subject to subsections (3) and (4) above, the question of fitness to stand trial shall be determined as soon as it arises.

(6)   The question of fitness to stand trial shall be determined by the judge advocate sitting alone.

(7)   A judge advocate shall not make a determination under subsection (6) above except on the written or oral evidence of two or more registered medical practitioners at least one of whom is duly approved.

115B Finding that the accused did the act or made the omission charged

(1)   This section applies where in accordance with section 115A(6) above it is determined by a judge advocate that the accused is unfit to stand trial.

(2)   The trial shall not proceed or further proceed but it shall be determined by the court—
   (a)   on the evidence (if any) already given in the trial, and
   (b)   on such evidence as may be adduced or further adduced by the prosecution, or adduced by a person appointed by the judge advocate under this section to put the case for the defence,

whether it is satisfied, as respects the charge or each of the charges on which the accused was to be or was being tried, that he did the act or made the omission charged against him as the offence.

(3)   If as respects that charge or any of those charges the court is satisfied as mentioned in subsection (2) above, it shall make a finding that the accused did the act or made the omission charged against him.

(4)   If as respects that charge or any of those charges the court is not so satisfied, the court shall find the accused not guilty as if on the charge in question the trial had proceeded to a conclusion.

(5)   Where the question of fitness to stand trial was determined after arraignment of the accused, the determination under subsection (2) above shall be made by the court-martial by whom he was being tried.

116 Findings of insanity

(1)   Where, on the trial of a person by court-martial, the court is satisfied, as respects the charge or any of the charges on which he is being tried, that the accused did the act or made the omission charged against him as the offence but that at the time of that act or omission he was insane, the court shall find that the accused was not guilty of that offence by reason of insanity.

(2)   No finding under subsection (1) above shall be made except on the written or oral evidence of two or more registered medical practitioners at least one of whom is duly approved.

116A Powers to deal with person unfit to stand trial or not guilty by reason of insanity

(1)   This section applies where, on a trial of a person by a court-martial—
   (a)   the accused is found to be unfit to stand trial and to have done the act or made the omission charged against him; or
   (b)   the accused is found not guilty by reason of insanity.

(2)   The court shall make in respect of the accused—
   (a)   a hospital order (with or without a restriction order);
   (b)   a supervision order; or
   (c)   an order for his absolute discharge.

(3)   Where—
   (a)   the offence to which the finding relates is an offence the sentence for which is fixed by law, and
   (b)   the court has power to make a hospital order,

the court shall make a hospital order with a restriction order (whether or not it would have power to make a restriction order apart from this subsection).

(4)   The functions of the court under this section shall be exercised by the judge advocate (or, where subsection (5) below applies, the judicial officer) sitting alone, and section 95(2) and (3) above shall not apply.

(5)   Any function of the court under this section exercisable after an adjournment or an appeal shall be exercisable by a judicial officer if—

(a)   the court ordering the adjournment, or (as the case may be) the Courts-Martial Appeal Court, so orders; or

(b)   the Judge Advocate General so directs.

(6)   In this Act—

'hospital order' has the meaning given in section 37 of the Mental Health Act 1983;

'restriction order' has the meaning given to it by section 41 of that Act;

'supervision order' means an order which requires the person in respect of whom it is made ('the supervised person') to be under the supervision of a person ('the supervising officer') for a period specified in the order of not more than two years.

116B Orders under the Mental Health Act

(1)   In relation to the making of an order by virtue of subsection (2)(a) of section 116A above, section 37 (hospital orders etc) of the Mental Health Act 1983 ('the 1983 Act') shall have effect as if—

(a)   the reference in subsection (1) to a person being convicted before the Crown Court included a reference to the case where section 116A above applies;

(b)   the words after 'punishable with imprisonment' and before 'or is convicted' were omitted; and

(c)   for subsections (4) and (5) there were substituted—

'(4)   Where an order is made under this section requiring a person to be admitted to a hospital ('a hospital order'), it shall be the duty of the managers of the hospital specified in the order to admit him in accordance with it.'

(2)   In relation to a case where section 116A above applies but the court has not yet made one of the disposals mentioned in subsection (2) of that section—

(a)   section 35 of the 1983 Act (remand to hospital for report on accused's mental condition) shall have effect with the omission of the words after paragraph (b) in subsection (3);

(b)   section 36 of that Act (remand of accused person to hospital for treatment) shall have effect with the omission of the words ' (other than an offence the sentence for which is fixed by law)' in subsection (2);

(c)   references in sections 35 and 36 of that Act to an accused person shall be construed as including a person in whose case this subsection applies; and

(d)   section 38 of that Act (interim hospital orders) shall have effect as if—

(i)   the reference in subsection (1) to a person being convicted before the Crown Court included a reference to the case where section 116A above applies; and

(ii)   the words ' (other than an offence the sentence for which is fixed by law)' in that subsection were omitted.

(3)   In relation to the making of any order under the 1983 Act by virtue of this Act, that Act shall apply—

(a)   as if references to the Crown Court were references to a court-martial;

(b)   as if references to an offender were references to a person in whose case section 116A above applies (references to an offence being construed accordingly); and

(c)   with such further modifications as may be prescribed.

(4)   The Secretary of State may by regulations make provision with respect to the admission to, detention in, and release from, hospital of any person in respect of whom an order is made under the 1983 Act by virtue of this Act.

Regulations under this subsection may in particular make provision for a person in respect of whom such an order has been made to be conveyed to, and detained in, a place of safety pending his admission to hospital.

(5) Where—
    (a) a person is detained in pursuance of a hospital order which the court had power to make by virtue of section 116A(1)(a) above, and
    (b) the court also made a restriction order, and that order has not ceased to have effect,

the Secretary of State, if satisfied after consultation with the responsible medical officer that the person can properly be tried, may either remit the person for trial before a court-martial or direct that he be tried before a civil court.

In this subsection 'responsible medical officer' means the registered medical practitioner in charge of the person's treatment.

(6) The Secretary of State may by regulations make provision supplementing subsection (5) above, including in particular—
    (a) provision for a person in whose case that subsection applies to be conveyed to a court or place of detention and to be detained in such a place;
    (b) provision for the hospital order and the restriction order to cease to have effect at such time as may be prescribed.

116C Supervision orders

(1) The court shall not make an order under section 116A(2)(b) above unless it is satisfied—
    (a) that, having regard to all the circumstances of the case, the making of a supervision order is the most suitable means of dealing with the accused;
    (b) that the supervising officer intended to be specified in the order is willing to undertake the supervision; and
    (c) that arrangements have been made for any treatment which (under subsection (2) below) is intended to be specified in the order.

(2) An order under section 116A(2)(b) above may, in accordance with regulations under subsection (3) below, require the supervised person to submit, during the whole of that period or such part of it as may be specified in the order, to treatment by or under the direction of a registered medical practitioner.

(3) The Secretary of State may—
    (a) by order direct that the definition of 'supervision order' in section 116A(6) above shall be amended by substituting, for the period for the time being specified there, such period as may be specified in the order under this subsection;
    (b) by regulations make further provision in relation to supervision orders.

(4) Regulations under subsection (3) above may in particular make provision—
    (a) as to the procedure to be followed by a court-martial making a supervision order;
    (b) as the requirements which may be specified in such an order;
    (c) as to the descriptions of supervising officer who may be so specified;
    (d) for treatment to be provided at a place other than the place specified in the order in accordance with arrangements made by the medical practitioner by whom or under whose direction the supervised person is being treated;
    (e) for the amendment and revocation of any supervision order.

116D Provisions supplementary to sections 115A to 116C

(1) In this section and sections 115A to 116C above—
    'duly approved' means approved for the purposes of section 12 of the Mental Health Act 1983 by the Secretary of State as having special experience in the diagnosis and treatment of mental disorder (within the meaning of that Act);

'prescribed' means prescribed by regulations made by the Secretary of State.

(2)   For the purposes of the provisions of sections 115A and 116 of this Act which permit a court to act on the written evidence of a registered medical practitioner or a registered medical practitioner who is duly approved, a report in writing purporting to be signed by a registered medical practitioner or a registered medical practitioner who is duly approved may, subject to subsection (3) below, be received in evidence without proof of the signature of the practitioner and without proof that he has the requisite qualifications or is duly approved; but the court may require the signatory of any such report to be called to give oral evidence.

(3)   Where, in pursuance of a direction of the court, any such report is tendered in evidence otherwise than by or on behalf of the accused, then—
    (a)   if the accused is represented by counsel or a solicitor, a copy of the report shall be given to his counsel or solicitor;
    (b)   if the accused is not so represented, the substance of the report shall be disclosed to him; and
    (c)   the accused may require the signatory of the report to be called to give oral evidence, and evidence to rebut the evidence contained in the report may be called by the accused or on his behalf.

(4)   The power of the Secretary of State to make regulations under sections 116A to 116C above, and orders under section 116C(3) above, shall be exercisable by statutory instrument which shall be subject to annulment in pursuance of a resolution of either House of Parliament.'

2   In section 225(1) of the Army Act 1955 and in section 223(1) of the Air Force Act 1955 (general provisions as to interpretation) insert at the appropriate places—

"hospital order' has the meaning assigned to it by section 116A(6) of this Act;';

"restriction order' has the meaning assigned to it by section 116A(6) of this Act;';

"supervision order' has the meaning assigned to it by section 116A(6) of this Act;'.

Naval Discipline Act 1957 (c 53)

3   For section 63 of the Naval Discipline Act 1957 (provisions where accused found insane) substitute—

'Findings of unfitness to stand trial and insanity

62A Fitness to stand trial

(1)   This section applies where on a trial by court-martial of a person the question arises (at the instance of the defence or otherwise) whether the accused is fit to stand trial.

(2)   For the purposes of this Act a person is unfit to stand trial if he is under a disability such that apart from the Criminal Procedure (Insanity) Act 1964 it would constitute a bar to his being tried on indictment in England and Wales.

(3)   If, having regard to the nature of the supposed disability, the judge advocate is of opinion that it is expedient to do so and in the interests of the accused, he may postpone consideration of the question of fitness to stand trial until any time up to the opening of the case for the defence.

(4)   If, before the question of fitness to stand trial falls to be determined, the court finds the accused not guilty on the charge or each of the charges on which he is being tried, that question shall not be determined.

(5)   Subject to subsections (3) and (4) above, the question of fitness to stand trial shall be determined as soon as it arises.

(6)   The question of fitness to stand trial shall be determined by the judge advocate sitting alone.

(7)   A judge advocate shall not make a determination under subsection (6) above except on the written or oral evidence of two or more registered medical practitioners at least one of whom is duly approved.

62B Finding that the accused did the act or made the omission charged

(1)   This section applies where in accordance with section 62A(6) above it is determined by a judge advocate that the accused is unfit to stand trial.

(2)   The trial shall not proceed or further proceed but it shall be determined by the court—
   (a)   on the evidence (if any) already given in the trial, and
   (b)   on such evidence as may be adduced or further adduced by the prosecution, or adduced by a person appointed by the judge advocate under this section to put the case for the defence,

whether it is satisfied, as respects the charge or each of the charges on which the accused was to be or was being tried, that he did the act or made the omission charged against him as the offence.

(3)   If as respects that charge or any of those charges the court is satisfied as mentioned in subsection (2) above, it shall make a finding that the accused did the act or made the omission charged against him.

(4)   If as respects that charge or any of those charges the court is not so satisfied, the court shall find the accused not guilty as if on the charge in question the trial had proceeded to a conclusion.

(5)   Where the question of fitness to stand trial was determined after arraignment of the accused, the determination under subsection (2) above shall be made by the court-martial by whom he was being tried.

63 Findings of insanity

(1)   Where, on the trial of a person by court-martial, the court is satisfied, as respects the charge or any of the charges on which he is being tried, that the accused did the act or made the omission charged against him as the offence but that at the time of that act or omission he was insane, the court shall find that the accused was not guilty of that offence by reason of insanity.

(2)   No finding under subsection (1) above shall be made except on the written or oral evidence of two or more registered medical practitioners at least one of whom is duly approved.

63A Powers to deal with person unfit to stand trial or not guilty by reason of insanity

(1)   This section applies where, on a trial of a person by a court-martial—
   (a)   the accused is found to be unfit to stand trial and to have done the act or made the omission charged against him; or
   (b)   the accused is found not guilty by reason of insanity.

(2)   The court shall make in respect of the accused—
   (a)   a hospital order (with or without a restriction order);
   (b)   a supervision order; or
   (c)   an order for his absolute discharge.

(3)   Where—
   (a)   the offence to which the finding relates is an offence the sentence for which is fixed by law, and
   (b)   the court has power to make a hospital order,

the court shall make a hospital order with a restriction order (whether or not it would have power to make a restriction order apart from this subsection).

(4)   The functions of the court under this section shall be exercised by the judge advocate (or, where subsection (5) below applies, the judicial officer) sitting alone, and sections 56A(3) and 57 above shall not apply.

(5)   Any function of the court under this section exercisable after an adjournment or an appeal shall be exercisable by a judicial officer if—
   (a)   the court ordering the adjournment, or (as the case may be) the Courts-Martial Appeal Court, so orders; or
   (b)   the Judge Advocate of Her Majesty's Fleet so directs.

(6)   In this Act—
   'hospital order' has the meaning given in section 37 of the Mental Health Act 1983;
   'restriction order' has the meaning given to it by section 41 of that Act;
   'supervision order' means an order which requires the person in respect of whom it is made ('the supervised person') to be under the supervision of a person ('the supervising officer') for a period specified in the order of not more than two years.

63B Orders under the Mental Health Act

(1)   In relation to the making of an order by virtue of subsection (2)(a) of section 63A above, section 37 (hospital orders etc) of the Mental Health Act 1983 ('the 1983 Act') shall have effect as if—
   (a)   the reference in subsection (1) to a person being convicted before the Crown Court included a reference to the case where section 63A above applies;
   (b)   the words after 'punishable with imprisonment' and before 'or is convicted' were omitted; and
   (c)   for subsections (4) and (5) there were substituted—

'(4)   Where an order is made under this section requiring a person to be admitted to a hospital ('a hospital order'), it shall be the duty of the managers of the hospital specified in the order to admit him in accordance with it.'

(2)   In relation to a case where section 63A above applies but the court has not yet made one of the disposals mentioned in subsection (2) of that section—
   (a)   section 35 of the 1983 Act (remand to hospital for report on accused's mental condition) shall have effect with the omission of the words after paragraph (b) in subsection (3);
   (b)   section 36 of that Act (remand of accused person to hospital for treatment) shall have effect with the omission of the words ' (other than an offence the sentence for which is fixed by law)' in subsection (2);
   (c)   references in sections 35 and 36 of that Act to an accused person shall be construed as including a person in whose case this subsection applies; and
   (d)   section 38 of that Act (interim hospital orders) shall have effect as if—
      (i)the reference in subsection (1) to a person being convicted before the Crown Court included a reference to the case where section 63A above applies; and
      (ii)the words ' (other than an offence the sentence for which is fixed by law)' in that subsection were omitted.

(3)   In relation to the making of any order under the 1983 Act by virtue of this Act, that Act shall apply—
   (a)   as if references to the Crown Court were references to a court-martial;
   (b)   as if references to an offender were references to a person in whose case section 63A above applies (references to an offence being construed accordingly); and
   (c)   with such further modifications as may be prescribed.

(4)   The Secretary of State may by regulations make provision with respect to the admission

to, detention in, and release from, hospital of any person in respect of whom an order is made under the 1983 Act by virtue of this Act.

Regulations under this subsection may in particular make provision for a person in respect of whom such an order has been made to be conveyed to, and detained in, a place of safety pending his admission to hospital.

(5)   Where—
    (a) a person is detained in pursuance of a hospital order which the court had power to make by virtue of section 63A(1)(a) above, and
    (b) the court also made a restriction order, and that order has not ceased to have effect,

the Secretary of State, if satisfied after consultation with the responsible medical officer that the person can properly be tried, may either remit the person for trial before a court-martial or direct that he be tried before a civil court.

In this subsection 'responsible medical officer' means the registered medical practitioner in charge of the person's treatment.

(6)   The Secretary of State may by regulations make provision supplementing subsection (5) above, including in particular—
    (a) provision for a person in whose case that subsection applies to be conveyed to a court or place of detention and to be detained in such a place;
    (b) provision for the hospital order and the restriction order to cease to have effect at such time as may be prescribed.

63C Supervision orders

(1)   The court shall not make an order under section 63A(2)(b) above unless it is satisfied—
    (a) that, having regard to all the circumstances of the case, the making of a supervision order is the most suitable means of dealing with the accused;
    (b) that the supervising officer intended to be specified in the order is willing to undertake the supervision; and
    (c) that arrangements have been made for any treatment which (under subsection (2) below) is intended to be specified in the order.

(2)   An order under section 63A(2)(b) above may, in accordance with regulations under subsection (3) below, require the supervised person to submit, during the whole of that period or such part of it as may be specified in the order, to treatment by or under the direction of a registered medical practitioner.

(3)   The Secretary of State may—
    (a) by order direct that the definition of 'supervision order' in section 63A(6) above shall be amended by substituting, for the period for the time being specified there, such period as may be specified in the order under this subsection;
    (b) by regulations make further provision in relation to supervision orders.

(4)   Regulations under subsection (3) above may in particular make provision—
    (a) as to the procedure to be followed by a court-martial making a supervision order;
    (b) as the requirements which may be specified in such an order;
    (c) as to the descriptions of supervising officer who may be so specified;
    (d) for treatment to be provided at a place other than the place specified in the order in accordance with arrangements made by the medical practitioner by whom or under whose direction the supervised person is being treated;
    (e) for the amendment and revocation of any supervision order.

63D Provisions supplementary to sections 62A to 63C

(1)   In this section and sections 62A to 63C above—

'duly approved' means approved for the purposes of section 12 of the Mental Health Act 1983 by the Secretary of State as having special experience in the diagnosis and treatment of mental disorder (within the meaning of that Act);

'prescribed' means prescribed by regulations made by the Secretary of State.

(2)   For the purposes of the provisions of sections 62A and 63 of this Act which permit a court to act on the written evidence of a registered medical practitioner or a registered medical practitioner who is duly approved, a report in writing purporting to be signed by a registered medical practitioner or a registered medical practitioner who is duly approved may, subject to subsection (3) below, be received in evidence without proof of the signature of the practitioner and without proof that he has the requisite qualifications or is duly approved; but the court may require the signatory of any such report to be called to give oral evidence.

(3)   Where, in pursuance of a direction of the court, any such report is tendered in evidence otherwise than by or on behalf of the accused, then—

(a)   if the accused is represented by counsel or a solicitor, a copy of the report shall be given to his counsel or solicitor;

(b)   if the accused is not so represented, the substance of the report shall be disclosed to him; and

(c)   the accused may require the signatory of the report to be called to give oral evidence, and evidence to rebut the evidence contained in the report may be called by the accused or on his behalf.

(4)   The power of the Secretary of State to make regulations under sections 63A to 63C above, and orders under section 63C(3) above, shall be exercisable by statutory instrument which shall be subject to annulment in pursuance of a resolution of either House of Parliament.'

4   In the proviso to section 56(3) of that Act (court-martial not to be adjourned for more than six days), after 'except with the consent of the accused and the prosecuting authority' insert ', or for the purpose of exercising powers under section 63A of this Act,'.

5   In section 135(1) of that Act (general provisions as to interpretation) insert at the appropriate places—

"hospital order' has the meaning assigned to it by section 63A(6) of this Act;';

"restriction order' has the meaning assigned to it by section 63A(6) of this Act;';

"supervision order' has the meaning assigned to it by section 63A(6) of this Act;'.

Courts-Martial (Appeals) Act 1968 (c 20)

6   The Courts-Martial (Appeals) Act 1968 is amended as follows.

7   For section 16 substitute—

'16 Substitution of finding of insanity or findings of unfitness to stand trial etc

(1)   This section applies where, on an appeal against conviction, the Appeal Court, on the written or oral evidence of two or more registered medical practitioners at least one of whom is duly approved, are of opinion—

(a)   that the proper finding would have been one of not guilty by reason of insanity; or

(b)   that the case is not one where there should have been a finding of not guilty, but that there should have been findings that the accused was unfit to stand trial and that he did the act or made the omission charged against him.

(2)   The Appeal Court shall make in respect of the appellant—

(a)   a hospital order (with or without a restriction order);

(b)   a supervision order; or

(c)   an order for his absolute discharge.

(3)   Where—

    (a)   the offence to which the appeal relates is an offence the sentence for which is fixed by law, and

    (b)   the Appeal Court have power to make a hospital order,

the Appeal Court shall make a hospital order with a restriction order (whether or not they would have power to make a restriction order apart from this subsection).

(4)   The provisions of, or made under, the sections specified below shall apply (with any necessary modifications) in relation to the Appeal Court as they apply in relation to a court-martial.

The sections are—

    (c)   where the relevant Service Act is the Army Act, sections 116B to 116D of that Act;

    (d)   where the relevant Service Act is the Air Force Act, sections 116B to 116D of that Act;

    (e)   where the relevant Service Act is the Naval Discipline Act, sections 63B to 63D of that Act.

(5)   Where the Appeal Court make an interim hospital order by virtue of this section—

    (a)   the power of renewing or terminating it and of dealing with the appellant on its termination shall be exercisable by a judicial officer and not by the Appeal Court; and

    (b)   section 38(7) of the Mental Health Act 1983 (absconding offenders) shall have effect as if the reference to the court that made the order were a reference to a judicial officer.

(6)   Where the Appeal Court make a supervision order by virtue of this section, any power of revoking or amending it shall be exercisable by a judicial officer and not by the Appeal Court.'

8   In section 21 (appeal against finding of not guilty by reason of insanity), in subsection (1), after 'except' insert 'section 8(2) and'.

9   In section 22 (consequences where appeal under section 21 allowed), at the beginning of subsection (4) insert 'Subject to section 23 below,'.

10   For section 23 substitute—

'23 Substitution of findings of unfitness to stand trial etc

(1)   This section applies where, on an appeal under section 21 of this Act, the Appeal Court, on the written or oral evidence of two or more registered medical practitioners at least one of whom is duly approved, are of opinion that—

    (a)   the case is not one where there should have been a finding of not guilty; but

    (b)   there should have been findings that the accused was unfit to stand trial and that he did the act or made the omission charged against him.

(2)   The Appeal Court shall make in respect of the appellant—

    (a)   a hospital order (with or without a restriction order);

    (b)   a supervision order; or

    (c)   an order for his absolute discharge.

(3)   Where—

    (a)   the offence to which the appeal relates is an offence the sentence for which is fixed by law, and

    (b)   the Appeal Court have power to make a hospital order,

the Appeal Court shall make a hospital order with a restriction order (whether or not they would have power to make a restriction order apart from this subsection).

(4)   The provisions of, or made under, the sections specified below shall apply (with any necessary modifications) in relation to the Appeal Court as they apply in relation to a court-martial.

The sections are—
(c)   where the relevant Service Act is the Army Act, sections 116B to 116D of that Act;
(d)   where the relevant Service Act is the Air Force Act, sections 116B to 116D of that Act;
(e)   where the relevant Service Act is the Naval Discipline Act, sections 63B to 63D of that Act.

(5)   Where the Appeal Court make an interim hospital order by virtue of this section—
(a)   the power of renewing or terminating it and of dealing with the appellant on its termination shall be exercisable by a judicial officer and not by the Appeal Court; and
(b)   section 38(7) of the Mental Health Act 1983 (absconding offenders) shall have effect as if the reference to the court that made the order were a reference to a judicial officer.

(6)   Where the Appeal Court make a supervision order by virtue of this section, any power of revoking or amending it shall be exercisable by a judicial officer and not by the Appeal Court.'

11   (1)   Section 24 (appeal against finding of unfitness to stand trial) is amended as follows.

(2)   In subsection (1)—
(a)   for 'his trial' substitute 'trial and to have done the act or made the omission charged against him';
(b)   for 'the finding' substitute 'either or both of those findings'.

(3)   In subsection (2), after 'except' insert 'section 8(2) and'.

12   For section 25 substitute—

'25 Disposal of appeal under s. 24

(1)   This section applies to appeals under section 24 of this Act.

(2)   Where the Appeal Court allow an appeal against a finding that the appellant is unfit to stand trial—
(a)   the appellant may be tried accordingly for the offence with which he was charged; and
(b)   the Court may make such orders as appear to them necessary or expedient pending any such trial for the custody, release or continued detention of the appellant.

(3)   Where, otherwise than in a case falling within subsection (2) above, the Appeal Court allow an appeal against a finding that the appellant did the act or made the omission charged against him, the Court shall, in addition to quashing the finding, direct a finding of not guilty to be recorded (but not a finding of not guilty by reason of insanity).'

13   After that section insert—

'Appeal against order made in cases of insanity or unfitness to stand trial

25A Right of appeal against hospital order etc

(1)   A person in whose case a court-martial—
(a)   makes a hospital order or interim hospital order by virtue of the relevant Service Act, or
(b)   makes a supervision order under the relevant Service Act,

may appeal to the Appeal Court against the order.

(2)   An appeal under this section lies only with the leave of the Appeal Court.

25B Disposal of appeal under s. 25A

(1)   If on an appeal under section 25A of this Act the Appeal Court consider that the appellant should be dealt with differently from the way in which the court below dealt with him—

  (a)   they may quash any order which is the subject of the appeal; and

  (b)   they may make such order, whether by substitution for the original order or by variation of or addition to it, as they think appropriate for the case and as the court below had power to make.

(2)   The fact that an appeal is pending against an interim hospital order under the Mental Health Act 1983 shall not affect the power of the court below to renew or terminate the order or deal with the appellant on its termination.

(3)   Where the Appeal Court make an interim hospital order by virtue of this section—

  (a)   the power of renewing or terminating it and of dealing with the appellant on its termination shall be exercisable by a judicial officer and not by the Appeal Court; and

  (b)   section 38(7) of the said Act of 1983 (absconding offenders) shall have effect as if the reference to the court that made the order were a reference to a judicial officer.

(4)   The fact that an appeal is pending against a supervision order under the relevant Service Act shall not affect any power conferred on any other court to revoke or amend the order.

(5)   Where the Appeal Court make a supervision order by virtue of this section, any power of revoking or amending it shall be exercisable by a judicial officer and not by the Appeal Court.'

14   (1)   Section 57 (interpretation) is amended as follows.

(2)   In subsection (1) insert at the relevant places—

  "duly approved' means approved for the purposes of section 12 of the Mental Health Act 1983 by the Secretary of State as having special experience in the diagnosis and treatment of mental disorder (within the meaning of that Act);';

  "hospital order' has the meaning given in section 37 of the Mental Health Act 1983;';

  "interim hospital order' has the meaning given in section 38 of that Act;';

  "judicial officer' has the same meaning as in the relevant Service Act;';

  "restriction order' has the meaning given to it by section 41 of the Mental Health Act 1983;';

  "supervision order' means an order which requires the person in respect of whom it is made to be under the supervision of another person for a period specified in the order of not more than two years.'

(3)   After subsection (2) insert—

'(2A)   For the purposes of the provisions of sections 16 and 23 of this Act which permit the Appeal Court to act on the written evidence of a registered medical practitioner or a registered medical practitioner who is duly approved, a report in writing purporting to be signed by a registered medical practitioner or a registered medical practitioner who is duly approved may, subject to subsection (2B) below, be received in evidence without proof of the signature of the practitioner and without proof that he has the requisite qualifications or is duly approved; but the Appeal Court may require the signatory of any such report to be called to give oral evidence.

(2B)   Where, in pursuance of a direction of the Appeal Court, any such report is tendered in evidence otherwise than by or on behalf of the appellant, then—

(a) if the appellant is represented by counsel or a solicitor, a copy of the report shall be given to his counsel or solicitor;

(b) if the appellant is not so represented, the substance of the report shall be disclosed to him; and

(c) the appellant may require the signatory of the report to be called to give oral evidence, and evidence to rebut the evidence contained in the report may be called by the appellant or on his behalf.'

15   (1)   Schedule 3 (modifications in relation to prisoners of war) is amended as follows.

(2)   In paragraph 3—
   (a) in paragraph (a), for 'or 15' substitute ', 14A, 15 or 25A';
   (b) omit paragraph (b).

(3)   After paragraph 3 insert—

'3A   In relation to a protected prisoner of war, sections 16 and 23 of this Act shall each have effect as if the following subsection were substituted for subsection (4)—

'(4)   The provisions of a Royal Warrant shall apply (with any necessary modifications) in relation to the Appeal Court as they apply in relation to a court-martial."

SCHEDULE 4
POWERS OF AUTHORISED OFFICERS EXECUTING WARRANTS

Section 27

The following is the Schedule inserted after Schedule 4 to the Magistrates' Courts Act 1980 (c 43)—

'SCHEDULE 4A
POWERS OF AUTHORISED OFFICERS EXECUTING WARRANTS^:

Section 125BA

Meaning of 'authorised officer' etc

1   In this Schedule—
   'authorised officer', in relation to a warrant, means a person who is entitled to execute the warrant by virtue of—
      (a) section 125A of this Act (civilian enforcement officers); or
      (b) section 125B of this Act (approved enforcement agencies);
   'premises' includes any place and, in particular, includes—
      (a) any vehicle, vessel, aircraft or hovercraft;
      (b) any offshore installation within the meaning of the Mineral Workings (Offshore Installations) Act 1971; and
      (c) any tent or movable structure.

Entry to execute warrant of arrest etc

2   (1)   An authorised officer may enter and search any premises for the purpose of executing

a warrant of arrest, commitment or detention issued in proceedings for or in connection with any criminal offence.

(2)   The power may be exercised—
   (a)   only to the extent that it is reasonably required for that purpose; and
   (b)   only if the officer has reasonable grounds for believing that the person whom he is seeking is on the premises.

(3)   In relation to premises consisting of two or more separate dwellings, the power is limited to entering and searching—
   (a)   any parts of the premises which the occupiers of any dwelling comprised in the premises use in common with the occupiers of any other such dwelling; and
   (b)   any such dwelling in which the officer has reasonable grounds for believing that the person whom he is seeking may be.

Entry to levy distress

3   (1)   An authorised officer may enter and search any premises for the purpose of executing a warrant of distress issued under section 76 of this Act for default in paying a sum adjudged to be paid by a conviction.

(2)   The power may be exercised only to the extent that it is reasonably required for that purpose.

Searching arrested persons

4   (1)   This paragraph applies where a person is arrested in pursuance of a warrant of arrest, commitment or detention issued in proceedings for or in connection with any criminal offence.

(2)   An authorised officer may search the arrested person, if he has reasonable grounds for believing that the arrested person may present a danger to himself or others.

(3)   An authorised officer may also search the arrested person for anything which he might use to assist him to escape from lawful custody.

(4)   The power conferred by sub-paragraph (3) above may be exercised—
   (a)   only if the officer has reasonable grounds for believing that the arrested person may have concealed on him anything of a kind mentioned in that sub-paragraph; and
   (b)   only to the extent that it is reasonably required for the purpose of discovering any such thing.

(5)   The powers conferred by this paragraph to search a person are not to be read as authorising the officer to require a person to remove any of his clothing in public other than an outer coat, a jacket or gloves; but they do authorise the search of a person's mouth.

(6)   An officer searching a person under sub-paragraph (2) above may seize and retain anything he finds, if the officer has reasonable grounds for believing that the person searched might use it to cause physical injury to himself or to any other person.

(7)   An officer searching a person under sub-paragraph (3) above may seize and retain anything he finds, if he has reasonable grounds for believing that the person might use it to assist him to escape from lawful custody.

Use of force

5   An authorised officer may use reasonable force, if necessary, in the exercise of a power conferred on him by this Schedule.'

SCHEDULE 5
PROCEDURE ON BREACH OF COMMUNITY PENALTY ETC

Section 29

Interpretation

1   In this Schedule—
'the Sentencing Act' means the Powers of Criminal Courts (Sentencing) Act 2000 (c
6);
'the 2003 Act' means the Criminal Justice Act 2003 (c 44).

Detention and training orders

2   (1)   Section 104 of the Sentencing Act (breach of supervision requirements of
detention and training order) is amended as follows.

(2)   In subsection (1) (issue of summons or warrant by justice of the peace)—
  (a)   omit the words 'acting for a relevant petty sessions area';
  (b)   in paragraph (a), omit the words 'before a youth court acting for the area';
  (c)   in paragraph (b), omit the words 'requiring him to be brought before such a
        court'.

(3)   For subsection (2) substitute—

'(2)   Any summons or warrant issued under this section shall direct the offender to appear or
be brought—
  (a)   before a youth court acting for the petty sessions area in which the offender resides; or
  (b)   if it is not known where the offender resides, before a youth court acting for same petty
        sessions area as the justice who issued the summons or warrant.'

Suspended sentence supervision orders

3   (1)   Section 123 of the Sentencing Act (breach of requirement of suspended
sentence supervision order) is amended as follows.

(2)   In subsection (1) (issue of summons or warrant by justice of the peace) omit the
words 'acting for the petty sessions area for the time being specified in the order'.

(3)   For subsection (2) substitute—

'(2)   Any summons or warrant issued under this section shall direct the offender to appear or
be brought—
  (a)   before a magistrates' court for the petty sessions area in which the offender resides; or
  (b)   if it is not known where the offender resides, before a magistrates' court acting for the
        petty sessions area for the time being specified in the suspended sentence supervision
        order.'

(4)   After subsection (4) insert—

'(5)   Where a magistrates' court dealing with an offender under this section would not otherwise
have the power to amend the suspended sentence supervision order under section 124(3) below
(amendment by reason of change of residence), that provision has effect as if the reference to a

magistrates' court acting for the petty sessions area for the time being specified in the suspended sentence supervision order were a reference to the court dealing with the offender.'

Community orders under the Sentencing Act

4   (1)   Schedule 3 to the Sentencing Act (breach, revocation and amendment of certain community orders), as it has effect on the day on which this Act is passed, is amended as follows.

(2)   In paragraph 3(1) (issue of summons or warrant by justice of the peace) omit the words 'acting for the petty sessions area concerned'.

(3)   In paragraph 3(2) (court before which offender to appear or be brought), for paragraph (c) substitute—

'(c)   in the case of a relevant order which is not an order to which paragraph (a) or (b) applies, before a magistrates' court acting for the petty sessions area in which the offender resides or, if it is not known where he resides, before a magistrates' court acting for the petty sessions area concerned.'

(4)   In paragraph 4 (powers of magistrates' court to deal with breach), after sub-paragraph (3) insert—

'(3A)   Where a magistrates' court dealing with an offender under sub-paragraph (1)(a), (b) or (c) above would not otherwise have the power to amend the relevant order under paragraph 18 below (amendment by reason of change of residence), that paragraph has effect as if the reference to a magistrates' court acting for the petty sessions area concerned were a reference to the court dealing with the offender. ' ~

Curfew orders and exclusion orders

5   (1)   Schedule 3 to the Sentencing Act (breach, revocation and amendment of curfew orders and exclusion orders), as substituted by paragraph 125 of Schedule 32 to the 2003 Act, is amended as follows.

(2)   In paragraph 3(1) (issue of summons or warrant by justice of the peace) omit the words 'acting for the petty sessions area concerned'.

(3)   In paragraph 3(2) (court before which offender to appear or be brought), for paragraph (b) substitute—

'(b)   in the case of a relevant order which is not an order to which paragraph (a) above applies, before a magistrates' court acting for the petty sessions area in which the offender resides or, if it is not known where he resides, before a magistrates' court acting for the petty sessions area concerned.'

(4)   In paragraph 4 (powers of magistrates' court to deal with breach), after sub-paragraph (4) insert—

'(4A)   Where a magistrates' court dealing with an offender under sub-paragraph (2)(a) or (b) above would not otherwise have the power to amend the relevant order under paragraph 15 below (amendment by reason of change of residence), that paragraph has effect as if the reference to a magistrates' court acting for the petty sessions area concerned were a reference to the court dealing with the offender.'

Attendance centre orders

6   (1)   Schedule 5 to the Sentencing Act (breach, revocation and amendment of attendance centre orders) is amended as follows.

(2)   In paragraph 1(1) (issue of summons or warrant by justice of the peace), omit the words—
   (a)   'acting for a relevant petty sessions area';
   (b)   'before a magistrates' court acting for the area';
   (c)   'requiring him to be brought before such a court'.

(3)   For paragraph 1(2) substitute—

'(2)   Any summons or warrant issued under this paragraph shall direct the offender to appear or be brought—
   (a)   before a magistrates' court acting for the petty sessions area in which the offender resides; or
   (b)   if it is not known where the offender resides, before a magistrates' court acting for the petty sessions area in which is situated the attendance centre which the offender is required to attend by the order or by virtue of an order under paragraph 5(1)(b) below.'

(4)   In paragraph 2 (powers of magistrates' court to deal with breach), after sub-paragraph (5) insert—

'(5A)   Where a magistrates' court dealing with an offender under sub-paragraph (1)(a) above would not otherwise have the power to amend the order under paragraph 5(1)(b) below (substitution of different attendance centre), that paragraph has effect as if references to an appropriate magistrates' court were references to the court dealing with the offender.'

Community orders under the 2003 Act

7   (1)   Schedule 8 to the 2003 Act (breach, revocation or amendment of community order) is amended as follows.

(2)   In paragraph 7(2) (issue of summons or warrant by justice of the peace) omit the words 'acting for the petty sessions area concerned'.

(3)   In paragraph 7(3) (court before which offender to appear or be brought), for paragraph (b) substitute—

   '(b)   in any other case, before a magistrates' court acting for the petty sessions area in which the offender resides or, if it is not known where he resides, before a magistrates' court acting for the petty sessions area concerned.'

(4)   In paragraph 9 (powers of magistrates' court to deal with breach), after sub-paragraph (5) insert—

'(5A)   Where a magistrates' court dealing with an offender under sub-paragraph (1)(a) would not otherwise have the power to amend the community order under paragraph 16 (amendment by reason of change of residence), that paragraph has effect as if the references to the appropriate court were references to the court dealing with the offender.'

(5)   In paragraph 27 (provision of copies of orders), at the end of sub-paragraph (1)(c) insert

   ', and

(d)   where the court acts for a petty sessions area other than the one specified in the order prior to the revocation or amendment, provide a copy of the revoking or amending order to a magistrates' court acting for the area so specified.'

Suspended sentence orders under the 2003 Act

8   (1)   Schedule 12 to the 2003 Act (breach or amendment of suspended sentence order, and effect of further conviction) is amended as follows.

(2)   In paragraph 6(2) (issue of summons or warrant by justice of the peace) omit the words 'acting for the petty sessions area concerned'.

(3)   In paragraph 6(3) (court before which offender to appear or be brought), for paragraph (b) substitute—

'(b)   in any other case, before a magistrates' court acting for the petty sessions area in which the offender resides or, if it is not known where he resides, before a magistrates' court acting for the petty sessions area concerned.'

(4)   In paragraph 8 (powers of magistrates' court to deal with breach), after sub-paragraph (4) insert—

'(4A)   Where a magistrates' court dealing with an offender under sub-paragraph (2)(c) would not otherwise have the power to amend the suspended sentence order under paragraph 14 (amendment by reason of change of residence), that paragraph has effect as if the references to the appropriate court were references to the court dealing with the offender.'

(5)   In paragraph 22 (provision of copies of orders), at the end of sub-paragraph (1)(c) insert

', and
(d)   where the court acts for a petty sessions area other than the one specified in the order prior to the revocation or amendment, provide a copy of the revoking or amending order to a magistrates' court acting for the area so specified.'

9   In Schedule 13 to the 2003 Act (transfer of suspended sentence orders to Scotland or Northern Ireland), in paragraph 12 (modifications of Schedule 12), after sub-paragraph (5) insert—

'(5A)   In paragraph 6(3)(b), the words 'before a magistrates' court acting for the petty sessions area in which the offender resides or, if it is not known where he resides,' are omitted.'

Local justice areas

10   The power conferred by section 109(5)(b) of the Courts Act 2003 (c 39) to amend or repeal any enactment, other than one contained in an Act passed in a later session, includes power to amend any such enactment as amended by this Schedule, but only for the purpose of making consequential provision in connection with the establishment of local justice areas under section 8 of that Act.

SCHEDULE 6
INTERMITTENT CUSTODY

Section 31

1   The Criminal Justice Act 2003 (c 44) is amended as follows.

2   In section 244 (duty to release prisoners), in subsection (3)—
   (a) in paragraph (c), for the words from 'which is not' to 'section 183(3)' substitute 'which for the purposes of section 183 (as read with section 263(2) or 264A(2) in the case of concurrent or consecutive sentences) is not a licence period';
   (b) in paragraph (d), after 'consecutive sentences' insert 'none of which falls within paragraph (c)'.

3   In section 246 (power to release prisoners on licence before required to do so), in the definition of 'the required custodial days' in subsection (6)—
   (a) in paragraph (b), after 'custody' insert 'which are consecutive';
   (b) at the end of that paragraph insert

   ', or
   (c) in the case of two or more sentences of intermittent custody which are wholly or partly concurrent, the aggregate of the numbers so specified less the number of days that are to be served concurrently;'.

4   In section 249 (duration of licence), at the end of subsection (3) insert 'and subsection (2) has effect subject to section 264A(3) (consecutive terms: intermittent custody)'.

5   In section 250 (licence conditions), in subsection (7), for 'and section 264(3) and (4) (consecutive terms)' substitute ', section 264(3) and (4) (consecutive terms) and section 264A(3) (consecutive terms: intermittent custody)'.

6   In section 264 (consecutive terms), in subsection (1), after paragraph (b) insert

   ', and
   (c) none of those terms is a term to which an intermittent custody order relates.'

7   After that section insert—

'264A Consecutive terms: intermittent custody

(1) This section applies where—
   (a) a person ('the offender') has been sentenced to two or more terms of imprisonment which are to be served consecutively on each other,
   (b) the sentences were passed on the same occasion or, where they were passed on different occasions, the person has not been released under this Chapter at any time during the period beginning with the first and ending with the last of those occasions, and
   (c) each of the terms is a term to which an intermittent custody order relates.

(2) The offender is not to be treated as having served all the required custodial days in relation to any of the terms of imprisonment until he has served the aggregate of all the required custodial days in relation to each of them.

(3) After the number of days served by the offender in prison is equal to the aggregate of the required custodial days in relation to each of the terms of imprisonment, the offender is to be on licence until the relevant time and subject to such conditions as are required by this Chapter in respect of any of the terms of imprisonment, and none of the terms is to be regarded for any purpose as continuing after the relevant time.

(4) In subsection (3) 'the relevant time' means the time when the offender would, but for his release, have served a term equal in length to the aggregate of—

(a) all the required custodial days in relation to the terms of imprisonment, and

(b) the longest of the total licence periods in relation to those terms.

(5) In this section—

'total licence period', in relation to a term of imprisonment to which an intermittent custody order relates, means a period equal in length to the aggregate of all the licence periods as defined by section 183 in relation to that term;

'the required custodial days', in relation to such a term, means the number of days specified under that section.'

SCHEDULE 7
INVESTIGATIONS BY PARLIAMENTARY COMMISSIONER

Section 47

1   The Parliamentary Commissioner Act 1967 (c 13) is amended as follows.

2   (1)   Section 5 (matters subject to investigation) is amended as follows.

(2)   After subsection (1) insert—

'(1A)   Subsection (1C) of this section applies if—

(a) a written complaint is duly made to a member of the House of Commons by a member of the public who claims that a person has failed to perform a relevant duty owed by him to the member of the public, and

(b) the complaint is referred to the Commissioner, with the consent of the person who made it, by a member of the House of Commons with a request to conduct an investigation into it.

(1B)   For the purposes of subsection (1A) of this section a relevant duty is a duty imposed by any of these—

(a) a code of practice issued under section 32 of the Domestic Violence, Crime and Victims Act 2004 (code of practice for victims), or

(b) sections 35 to 44 of that Act (duties of local probation boards in connection with victims of sexual or violent offences).

(1C)   If this subsection applies, the Commissioner may investigate the complaint.'

(3)   In subsection (3) for 'investigation under this Act' substitute 'investigation under subsection (1) of this section'.

(4)   After subsection (4) insert—

'(4A)   Without prejudice to subsection (2) of this section, the Commissioner shall not conduct an investigation pursuant to a complaint under subsection (1A) of this section in respect of—

(a) action taken by or with the authority of the Secretary of State for the purposes of protecting the security of the State, including action so taken with respect to passports, or

(b) any action or matter described in any of paragraphs 1 to 4 and 6A to 11 of Schedule 3 to this Act.

(4B)   Her Majesty may by Order in Council amend subsection (4A) of this section so as to exclude from paragraph (a) or (b) of that subsection such actions or matters as may be described in the Order.

(4C)   Any statutory instrument made by virtue of subsection (4B) of this section shall be subject to annulment in pursuance of a resolution of either House of Parliament.'

3 (1)   Section 7 (procedure in respect of investigations) is amended as follows.

(2)   In subsection (1) after 'complaint under' insert 'section 5(1) of'.

(3)   After subsection (1) insert—

'(1A)   Where the Commissioner proposes to conduct an investigation pursuant to a complaint under section 5(1A) of this Act, he shall give the person to whom the complaint relates an opportunity to comment on any allegations contained in the complaint.'

(4)   In subsection (2) for 'such investigation' substitute 'investigation under this Act'.

(5)   In subsection (4)—
    (a)   after 'authority concerned' insert 'or the person to whom the complaint relates';
    (b)   for 'that department or authority' substitute 'that department, authority or person'.

4 (1)   Section 8 (evidence) is amended as follows.

(2)   In subsection (1) after 'investigation under' insert 'section 5(1) of'.

(3)   After subsection (1) insert—

'(1A)   For the purposes of an investigation pursuant to a complaint under section 5(1A) of this Act the Commissioner may require any person who in his opinion is able to furnish information or produce documents relevant to the investigation to furnish any such information or produce any such document.'

(4)   In subsection (2) for 'such investigation' substitute 'investigation under this Act'.

5 (1)   Section 10 (reports by Commissioner) is amended as follows.

(2)   In subsection (2), after 'investigation under' insert 'section 5(1) of'.

(3)   After subsection (2) insert—

'(2A)   In any case where the Commissioner conducts an investigation pursuant to a complaint under section 5(1A) of this Act, he shall also send a report of the results of the investigation to the person to whom the complaint relates.'

(4)   In subsection (3) after 'investigation under' insert 'section 5(1) of'.

(5)   After subsection (3) insert—

'(3A)   If, after conducting an investigation pursuant to a complaint under section 5(1A) of this Act, it appears to the Commissioner that—
    (a)   the person to whom the complaint relates has failed to perform a relevant duty owed by him to the person aggrieved, and
    (b)   the failure has not been, or will not be, remedied,

the Commissioner may, if he thinks fit, lay before each House of Parliament a special report upon the case.

(3B)   For the purposes of subsection (3A) of this section 'relevant duty' has the meaning given by section 5(1B) of this Act.'

(6)   In subsection (5)(d) after 'subsection (2)' insert 'or (2A)'.

6   In section 12(1) (interpretation) for the definition of 'person aggrieved' substitute—

"person aggrieved'—

    (a)   in relation to a complaint under section 5(1) of this Act, means the person who claims or is alleged to have sustained such injustice as is mentioned in section 5(1)(a) of this Act;

    (b)   in relation to a complaint under section 5(1A) of this Act, means the person to whom the duty referred to in section 5(1A)(a) of this Act is or is alleged to be owed;'.

SCHEDULE 8
COMMISSIONER FOR VICTIMS AND WITNESSES

Section 48

Deputy Commissioner

1   (1)   The Secretary of State must appoint a Deputy Commissioner for Victims and Witnesses (referred to in this Schedule as the Deputy Commissioner).

(2)   Before appointing the Deputy Commissioner the Secretary of State must consult the Attorney General and the Lord Chancellor as to the person to be appointed.

(3)   The Deputy Commissioner must act as the Commissioner—

    (a)   during any period when the office of Commissioner is vacant;

    (b)   at any time when the Commissioner is absent or is unable toact.

(4)   The Deputy Commissioner is not to be regarded—

    (a)   as the servant or agent of the Crown, or

    (b)   as enjoying any status, immunity or privilege of the Crown.

Terms of appointment

2   (1)   This paragraph applies in relation to a person appointed as the Commissioner or the Deputy Commissioner.

(2)   The period for which the person is appointed must not exceed 5 years.

(3)   Subject to sub-paragraph (4), the person is eligible for re-appointment.

(4)   The person must not hold office for more than 10 years in total.

(5)   The person may at any time resign from office by giving notice in writing to the Secretary of State.

(6)   The Secretary of State may at any time remove the person from office if he is satisfied that the person—

    (a)   has become bankrupt, has had his estate sequestrated or has made a composition or arrangement with, or granted a trust deed for, his creditors, or

    (b)   is otherwise unable or unfit to carry out his functions.

(7)   The Secretary of State must consult the Attorney General and the Lord Chancellor before removing the person from office.

(8)   Subject to sub-paragraphs (2) to (7), the person holds office on the terms specified by the Secretary of State after consulting the Attorney General and the Lord Chancellor.

Staff

3   (1)   The Commissioner may appoint such persons as members of his staff as he thinks fit.

(2)   The Commissioner must obtain the approval of the Secretary of State to—
  (a)   the number of persons appointed as members of his staff, and
  (b)   their terms and conditions of service.

(3)   No member of the staff of the Commissioner is to be regarded—
  (a)   as the servant or agent of the Crown, or
  (b)   as enjoying any status, immunity or privilege of the Crown.

Delegation

4   The Commissioner may authorise any member of his staff or the Deputy Commissioner to carry out any of his functions.

Pensions

5   (1)   Schedule 1 to the Superannuation Act 1972 (c 11) (kinds of employment and offices to which a scheme under section 1 of that Act may apply) is amended as set out in sub-paragraphs (2) and (3).

(2)   At the end of the list headed 'Other Bodies' insert—

'Employment as a member of the staff of the Commissioner for Victims and Witnesses.'

(3)   In the list headed 'Offices', in the appropriate places, insert—

'Commissioner for Victims and Witnesses.'

'Deputy Commissioner for Victims and Witnesses.'

(4)   The Secretary of State must pay to the Minister for the Civil Service, at such times as the Minister for the Civil Service may direct, such sums as the Minister for the Civil Service may determine in respect of the increase attributable to sub-paragraphs (1) to (3) in the sums payable out of money provided by Parliament under the Superannuation Act 1972.

Finance

6   The Secretary of State must pay—
  (a)   the remuneration of the Commissioner and the Deputy Commissioner;
  (b)   such sums as he thinks fit in respect of the expenses of the Commissioner and the Deputy Commissioner.

Accounts

7   (1)   The Commissioner must—
  (a)   keep proper accounts and proper records in relation to the accounts;

(b) prepare a statement of accounts in respect of each financial year, in the form directed by the Secretary of State;

(c) send copies of the statement to the Secretary of State and the Comptroller and Auditor General, not later than the 31 August following the end of the financial year to which it relates.

(2)   The Comptroller and Auditor General must—

(a) examine, certify and report on the statement of accounts;

(b) lay copies of the statement and of his report before Parliament.

Annual plan

8   (1)   The Commissioner must, before the beginning of each financial year apart from the first, prepare a plan setting out how he intends to exercise his functions during the financial year (an annual plan).

(2)   In preparing the plan, the Commissioner must consider whether to deal in the plan with any issues specified by the Secretary of State.

(3)   The Commissioner must send a copy of the plan to the Secretary of State for his approval.

(4)   The Secretary of State must consult the Attorney General and the Lord Chancellor in deciding whether to approve the plan.

(5)   If the Secretary of State does not approve the plan—

(a) he must give the Commissioner his reasons for not approving it, and

(b) the Commissioner must revise the plan.

(6)   Sub-paragraphs (2) to (5) apply to a revised plan as they apply to the plan as first prepared.

Annual report

9   (1)   The Commissioner must, as soon as possible after the end of each financial year, prepare a report on how he has exercised his functions during the financial year.

(2)   The report for any financial year apart from the first must include—

(a) the Commissioner's annual plan for the financial year, and

(b) an assessment of the extent to which the plan has been carried out.

(3)   The Commissioner must send a copy of the report to—

(a) the Secretary of State,

(b) the Attorney General, and

(c) the Lord Chancellor.

(4)   The Secretary of State must—

(a) lay a copy of the report before Parliament;

(b) arrange for the report to be published.

Disqualification Acts

10   (1)   In Part 3 of Schedule 1 to the House of Commons Disqualification Act 1975 (c 24) (offices the holders of which are disqualified) at the appropriate places insert—

'Commissioner for Victims and Witnesses.'

'Deputy Commissioner for Victims and Witnesses.'

(2)   In Part 3 of Schedule 1 to the Northern Ireland Assembly Disqualification Act 1975 (c 25) (offices the holders of which are disqualified) at the appropriate places insert—

'Commissioner for Victims and Witnesses.'

'Deputy Commissioner for Victims and Witnesses.'

Meaning of 'financial year'

11   In this Schedule 'financial year' means—
  (a) the period beginning on the day on which section 48 comes into force and ending on the next 31 March (which is the first financial year), and
  (b) each subsequent period of 12 months beginning on 1 April.

SCHEDULE 9
AUTHORITIES WITHIN COMMISSIONER'S REMIT

Section 53

Government departments

1   The Department for Constitutional Affairs.

2   The Department for Education and Skills.

3   The Department of Health.

4   The Department of Trade and Industry.

5   The Department for Transport.

6   The Department for Work and Pensions.

7   The Foreign and Commonwealth Office.

8   The Home Office.

9   The Office of the Deputy Prime Minister.

Customs and Excise

10   The Commissioners of Customs and Excise.

Police forces etc

11   A police force for a police area in England or Wales.

12   The Serious Fraud Office.

13   The National Criminal Intelligence Service.

14   The National Crime Squad.

15   The force of constables appointed under section 53 of the British Transport Commission Act 1949 (c xxix).

16   The Ministry of Defence Police.

Criminal injuries compensation

17   The Criminal Injuries Compensation Appeals Panel.

18   The Criminal Injuries Compensation Authority.

Health and safety

19   The Health and Safety Commission.

20   The Health and Safety Executive.

Legal services

21   The Legal Services Commission.

Court administration

22   Persons exercising functions relating to the carrying on of the business of a court.

Criminal justice system

23   The Criminal Cases Review Commission.

24   The Crown Prosecution Service.

25   A local probation board established under section 4 of the Criminal Justice and Court Services Act 2000 (c 43).

26   The Parole Board.

27   The Prison Service.

28   The Youth Justice Board for England and Wales.

29   A youth offending team established under section 39 of the Crime and Disorder Act 1998 (c 37).

Maritime and coastguards

30   The Maritime and Coastguard Agency.

SCHEDULE 10
MINOR AND CONSEQUENTIAL AMENDMENTS

Section 58(1)

Colonial Prisoners Removal Act 1884 (c 31)

1   In section 10 of the Colonial Prisoners Removal Act 1884 (application of Act to removal of criminal lunatics), in subsection (3), in paragraph (a) for the words from 'give' to the end substitute 'by warrant direct that he is to be detained in such hospital, within the meaning given by section 145(1) of the Mental Health Act 1983, as may be specified in the direction; and any such direction shall have the same effect as a hospital order under section 37 of that Act together with a restriction order under section 41 of that Act, made without limitation of time;'.

Children and Young Persons Act 1933 (c 12)

2   In Schedule 1 to the Children and Young Persons Act 1933 (offences against children and young persons with respect to which special provisions of the Act apply), after 'Infanticide' insert—

'An offence under section 5 of the Domestic Violence, Crime and Victims Act 2004, in respect of a child or young person.'

Criminal Procedure (Insanity) Act 1964 (c 84)

3   In section 8(2) of the Criminal Procedure (Insanity) Act 1964 (interpretation), after the definition of 'duly approved' insert—

"local probation board' means a local probation board established under section 4 of the Criminal Justice and Court Services Act 2000;'.

Criminal Appeal Act 1968 (c 19)

4   In section 15 of the Criminal Appeal Act 1968 (right of appeal against finding of disability), in subsection (1), for the words 'the jury has returned' substitute 'there have been'.

5   In section 37 of that Act (detention of defendant on appeal by the Crown to House of Lords), in subsection (4), for paragraph (b) substitute—

'(b) a hospital order made by virtue of section 5(2)(a) of the Criminal Procedure (Insanity) Act 1964 (powers to deal with persons not guilty by reason of insanity or unfit to plead etc),'.

6   In section 51 of that Act (interpretation), in subsection (2A), for '6, 14 or 14A' substitute '6 or 14'.

Children and Young Persons Act (Northern Ireland) 1968 (c 34 (NI))

7   In Schedule 1 to the Children and Young Persons Act (Northern Ireland) 1968 (offences against children and young persons with respect to which special provisions of the Act apply), after 'Infanticide' insert—

'An offence under section 5 of the Domestic Violence, Crime and Victims Act 2004, in respect of a child or young person.'

Juries Act 1974 (c 23)

8   (1)   Section 11 of the Juries Act 1974 (ballot and swearing of jurors) is amended as follows.

(2)   In subsection (5) omit paragraph (b).

(3)   In subsection (6) omit ', (b)'.

Rehabilitation of Offenders Act 1974 (c 53)

9   In section 1(3) of the Rehabilitation of Offenders Act 1974 (meaning of 'sentence' for the purposes of that Act), after 'other than' insert—

'(za) a surcharge imposed under section 161A of the Criminal Justice Act 2003;'.

Magistrates' Courts Act 1980 (c 43)

10   In section 108 of the Magistrates' Courts Act 1980 (right of appeal to Crown Court), after subsection (3) insert—

'(4)   Subsection (3)(d) above does not prevent an appeal against a surcharge imposed under section 161A of the Criminal Justice Act 2003.'

11   In section 139 of that Act (disposal of sums adjudged to be paid by conviction)—
       (a)   after paragraph (a) insert—

'(aa) in the second place in payment to the fund mentioned in paragraph (c) below of surcharges imposed under section 161A of the Criminal Justice Act 2003;';

       (b)   in paragraph (b), for 'second' substitute 'third'.

Criminal Appeal (Northern Ireland) Act 1980 (c 47)

12   In section 13A of the Criminal Appeal (Northern Ireland) Act 1980 (appeal against finding of unfitness to be tried), in subsection (1), for 'the jury has returned' substitute 'there has been'.

13   In section 19(1A)(a) of that Act (legal aid), after 'appeal under' insert 'section 18A of the Domestic Violence, Crime and Victims Act 2004,'.

Supreme Court Act 1981 (c 54)

14   In section 55 of the Supreme Court Act 1981 (constitution of criminal division of Court of Appeal), in subsection (4)(a)(iii) omit the words 'of a jury'.

15   In section 81 of that Act (power of Crown Court to grant bail), in subsection (1A), for 'or 15' substitute ', 15 or 16A'.

Criminal Justice Act 1982 (c 48)

16   In Schedule 1 to the Criminal Justice Act 1982 (offences excluded from early release provisions), in Part 2, after the entry relating to the Sexual Offences Act 2003 (c 42) insert—

'*Domestic Violence, Crime and Victims Act 2004*

Section 5 (causing or allowing the death of a child or vulnerable adult).'

Representation of the People Act 1983 (c 2

17   In section 3A of the Representation of the People Act 1983 (disenfranchisement of offenders detained in mental hospitals), for subsection (5) substitute—

'(5)   As respects any part of the United Kingdom, this section applies to any person in respect of whom a hospital order has been made by virtue of—
   (a)   section 116A of the Army Act 1955 or the Air Force Act 1955 or section 63A of the Naval Discipline Act 1957, or
   (b)   section 16 or 23 of the Courts-Martial (Appeals) Act 1968.'

Mental Health Act 1983 (c 20)

18   In section 47 of the Mental Health Act 1983 (removal to hospital of persons serving sentences of imprisonment, etc), in subsection (5)(a), for the words 'under any enactment to which section 46 applies' substitute 'made in consequence of a finding of insanity or unfitness to stand trial'.

19   In section 69 of that Act (application to tribunals concerning patients subject to hospital orders etc), in subsection (2)(a)—
   (a)   for 'below,' substitute 'below or';
   (b)   omit 'or section 5(1) of the Criminal Procedure (Insanity) Act 1964'.

20   In section 71 of that Act (references by Home Secretary concerning restricted patients) omit subsections (5) and (6).

21   In section 79 of that Act (interpretation of Part 5), in subsection (1)—
   (a)   for paragraph (a) substitute—
   '(a)   is treated by virtue of any enactment as subject to a hospital order and a restriction order; or';
   (b)   omit paragraph (b).

22   In section 84 of that Act (removal to England and Wales of offenders found insane in Channel Islands and Isle of Man), in subsection (2), for the words from 'had been' to the end substitute 'were subject to a hospital order together with a restriction order, made without limitation of time'.

23   (1)   Schedule 5 to that Act (transitional and saving provisions) is amended as follows.

(2)   For paragraph 21 substitute—

'21

Any direction to which section 71(4) of the Mental Health Act 1959 applied immediately before the commencement of this Act shall have the same effect as a hospital order together with a restriction order, made without limitation of time.'

(3)   In paragraph 37(2), for 'direction under section 46 of this Act' substitute 'hospital order together with a restriction order, made without limitation of time'.

Police and Criminal Evidence Act 1984 (c 60)

24   In Schedule 5 to the Police and Criminal Evidence Act 1984 (serious arrestable offences), in Part 2, after paragraph 23 insert—

'*Domestic Violence, Crime and Victims Act 2004*

24   Section 5 (causing or allowing the death of a child or vulnerable adult).'

Prosecution of Offences Act 1985 (c 23)

25   In section 16 of the Prosecution of Offences Act 1985 (defence costs), in subsection (4) (power of Court of Appeal to make defendant's costs order), after paragraph (c) insert

'or
(d)   allows, to any extent, an appeal under section 16A of that Act (appeal against order made in cases of insanity or unfitness to plead);' .

Coroners Act 1988 (c 13)

26   In section 16 of the Coroners Act 1988 (adjournment of inquest in event of criminal proceedings), in subsection (1)(a), after sub-paragraph (iii) insert—

'(iv) an offence under section 5 of the Domestic Violence, Crime and Victims Act 2004 (causing or allowing the death of a child or vulnerable adult); or' .

27   In section 17 of that Act (coroner to be informed of result of criminal proceedings), in subsections (1) and (2), at the end of paragraph (c) insert

'; or
(d)   an offence under section 5 of the Domestic Violence, Crime and Victims Act 2004 (causing or allowing the death of a child or vulnerable adult),' .

Criminal Justice Act 1988 (c 33)

28   In section 41 of the Criminal Justice Act 1988 (power of Crown Court to deal with summary offence where person committed for either way offence), after subsection (4) insert—

'(4A)   The committal of a person under this section in respect of an offence to which section 40 above applies shall not prevent him being found guilty of that offence under section 6(3) of the Criminal Law Act 1967 (alternative verdicts on trial on indictment); but where he is convicted under that provision of such an offence, the functions of the Crown Court under this section in relation to the offence shall cease.'

Police and Criminal Evidence (Northern Ireland) Order 1989 (SI 1989/1341 (NI 12))

29   In Schedule 5 to the Police and Criminal Evidence (Northern Ireland) Order 1989 (serious arrestable offences), in Part 2, after paragraph 14 insert—

'*Domestic Violence, Crime and Victims Act 2004*

15   Section 5 (causing or allowing the death of a child or vulnerable adult).'

Criminal Justice Act 1991 (c 53)

30   In section 24 of the Criminal Justice Act 1991 (recovery of fines etc by deductions from income support), after subsection (3) insert—

'(3A)   This section applies in relation to a surcharge imposed under section 161A of the Criminal Justice Act 2003 as if any reference in subsection (1) or (3) above to a fine included a reference to a surcharge.'

Criminal Appeal Act 1995 (c 35)

31   In section 9 of the Criminal Appeal Act 1995 (references by Criminal Cases Review Commission to Court of Appeal), in subsection (6), for the words 'a jury in England and Wales has returned' substitute 'in England and Wales there have been'.

32   In section 10 of that Act (which makes equivalent provision for Northern Ireland), in subsection (7), for the words 'a jury in Northern Ireland has returned' substitute 'in Northern Ireland there has been'.

Law Reform (Year and a Day Rule) Act 1996 (c 19)

33   In section 2 of the Law Reform (Year and a Day Rule) Act 1996 (restriction on institution of proceedings for fatal offence), in subsection (3), at the end of paragraph (b) insert

' , or
(c)   an offence under section 5 of the Domestic Violence, Crime and Victims Act 2004 (causing or allowing the death of a child or vulnerable adult).'

Family Law Act 1996 (c 27)

34   (1)   Section 36 of the Family Law Act 1996 (one cohabitant or former cohabitant with no existing right to occupy) is amended as follows.

(2)   In subsection (1)(c), for the words from 'live together as' to the end substitute 'cohabit or a home in which they at any time cohabited or intended to cohabit'.

(3)   In subsection (6)(f), for 'lived together as husband and wife' substitute 'cohabited'.

35   In section 38 of that Act (neither cohabitant or former cohabitant entitled to occupy), in subsection (1)(a), for 'live or lived together as husband and wife' substitute 'cohabit or cohabited'.

36   (1)   Section 42 of that Act (non-molestation orders) is amended as follows.

(2)   After subsection (4) insert—

'(4A)   A court considering whether to make an occupation order shall also consider whether to exercise the power conferred by subsection (2)(b).

(4B)   In this Part 'the applicant', in relation to a non-molestation order, includes (where the context permits) the person for whose benefit such an order would be or is made in exercise of the power conferred by subsection (2)(b).'

(3)   In subsection (5)(a) omit the words from 'or' to 'made'.

37   (1)   Section 46 of that Act (undertakings) is amended as follows.

(2)   In subsection (3), after 'under subsection (1)' insert 'instead of making an occupation order'.

(3)   After that subsection insert—

'(3A)   The court shall not accept an undertaking under subsection (1) instead of making a non-molestation order in any case where it appears to the court that—
   (a)   the respondent has used or threatened violence against the applicant or a relevant child; and
   (b)   for the protection of the applicant or child it is necessary to make a non-molestation order so that any breach may be punishable under section 42A.'

(4)   In subsection (4), for 'it were an order of the court' substitute 'the court had made an occupation order or a non-molestation order in terms corresponding to those of the undertaking'.

38   (1)   Section 47 of that Act (arrest for breach of occupation order or non-molestation order) is amended as follows.

(2)   Omit subsection (1).

(3)   In subsections (2) and (4), for 'a relevant order' substitute 'an occupation order'.

(4)   In subsections (3) and (5), for 'the relevant order' substitute 'the occupation order'.

(5)   In subsection (8), for the words up to the end of paragraph (b) substitute—

'If the court—
   (a)   has made a non-molestation order, or
   (b)   has made an occupation order but has not attached a power of arrest under subsection

(2) or (3) to any provision of the order, or has attached that power only to certain provisions of the order,' .

39   In section 49 of that Act (variation and discharge of orders), in subsection (4) omit 'or non-molestation order'.

40   In section 62 of that Act (definitions), in subsection (1)(b), for ' 'former cohabitants' is to be read accordingly, but' substitute ' 'cohabit' and 'former cohabitants' are to be read accordingly, but the latter expression'.

41   (1)   In section 63 of that Act (interpretation of Part 4), subsection (1) is amended as follows.

(2)   At the beginning of the definition of 'cohabitant' and 'former cohabitant' insert ' 'cohabit',' .

(3)   In the definition of 'relative'—
   (a)   for 'or nephew' in paragraph (b) substitute ', nephew or first cousin';
   (b)   for 'is living or has lived with another person as husband and wife' substitute 'is cohabiting or has cohabited with another person'.

42   (1)   Schedule 7 to that Act (transfer of certain tenancies on divorce etc or on separation of cohabitants) is amended as follows.

(2)   In paragraph 3(2), for 'to live together as husband and wife' substitute 'to cohabit'.

(3)   In paragraph 4(b), for 'lived together as husband and wife' substitute 'cohabited'.

Protection from Harassment Act 1997 (c 40)

43   (1)   Section 5 of the Protection from Harassment Act 1997 (power to make restraining order where defendant convicted of offence under section 2 or 4 of that Act) is amended as follows.

(2)   In the heading, at the end insert '**on conviction**'.

(3)   In subsection (2) omit 'further'.

44   In section 7 of that Act (interpretation), in subsection (1), for 'sections 1 to 5' substitute 'sections 1 to 5A'.

Crime (Sentences) Act 1997 (c 43)

45   (1)   Section 47 of the Crime (Sentences) Act 1997 (power to specify hospital units) is amended as follows.

(2)   Omit subsections (1)(d) and (2)(c).

(3)   For subsection (4) substitute—

'(4)   A reference in this section to section 37 or 41 of the 1983 Act includes a reference to that section as it applies by virtue of—
   (a)   section 5 of the Criminal Procedure (Insanity) Act 1964,
   (b)   section 6 or 14 of the Criminal Appeal Act 1968,
   (c)   section 116A of the Army Act 1955 or the Air Force Act 1955 or section 63A of the Naval Discipline Act 1957, or
   (d)   section 16 or 23 of the Courts-Martial (Appeals) Act 1968.'

46   (1)   Schedule 1 to that Act (transfers of prisoners within the British Islands) (as amended by Schedule 32 to the Criminal Justice Act 2003) is amended as follows.

(2)   In paragraph 8 (restricted transfers from England and Wales to Scotland), in sub-paragraphs (2)(a) and (4)(a), for '264' substitute '264A'.

(3)   In paragraph 9 (restricted transfers from England and Wales to Northern Ireland), in sub-paragraphs (2)(a) and (4)(a), for '264' substitute '264A'.

Protection from Harassment (Northern Ireland) Order 1997 (SI 1997/1180 (NI 9))

47   (1)   Article 7 of the Protection from Harassment (Northern Ireland) Order 1997 (power to make restraining order where defendant convicted of offence under Article 4 or 6 of that Act) is amended as follows.

(2)   In the heading, at the end insert '**on conviction**'.

(3)   In paragraph (2) omit 'further'.

Crime and Disorder Act 1998 (c 37)

48   In section 32 of the Crime and Disorder Act 1998 (racially or religiously aggravated harassment etc) omit subsection (7) (which is superseded by provision made by section 12(1) above).

Powers of Criminal Courts (Sentencing) Act 2000 (c 6)

49   In section 132 of the Powers of Criminal Courts (Sentencing) Act 2000 (compensation orders: appeals etc), after subsection (4) insert—

'(4A)   Where an order is made in respect of a person under subsection (3) or (4) above, the Court of Appeal or House of Lords shall make such order for the payment of a surcharge under section 161A of the Criminal Justice Act 2003, or such variation of the order of the Crown Court under that section, as is necessary to secure that the person's liability under that section is the same as it would be if he were being dealt with by the Crown Court.'

50   In section 136 of that Act (power to order statement as to financial circumstances of parent or guardian), in subsection (1), for 'or compensation' substitute ', compensation or surcharge'.

51   (1)   Section 137 of that Act (power to order parent or guardian to pay fine, costs or compensation) is amended as follows.

(2)   In the heading, for '**or compensation**' substitute '**, compensation or surcharge**'.

(3)   After subsection (1) insert—

'(1A)   Where but for this subsection a court would order a child or young person to pay a surcharge under section 161A of the Criminal Justice Act 2003, the court shall order that the surcharge be paid by the parent or guardian of the child or young person instead of by the child or young person himself, unless the court is satisfied—
   (a)   that the parent or guardian cannot be found; or
   (b)   that it would be unreasonable to make an order for payment, having regard to the circumstances of the case.'

(4)   In subsection (3), for 'subsections (1) and (2)' substitute 'subsections (1) to (2)'.

52   (1)   Section 138 of that Act (fixing of fine or compensation to be paid by parent or guardian) is amended as follows.

(2)   In the heading, for '**or compensation**' substitute '**, compensation or surcharge**'.

(3)   Before paragraph (a) of subsection (1) insert—

'(za) subsection (3) of section 161A of the Criminal Justice Act 2003 (surcharges) and subsection (4A) of section 164 of that Act (fixing of fines) shall have effect as if any reference in those subsections to the offender's means were a reference to those of the parent or guardian;'.

53   In section 142(1) of that Act (power of Crown Court to order search of persons before it)—
   (a)   before paragraph (a) insert—

'(za) the Crown Court orders a person to pay a surcharge under section 161A of the Criminal Justice Act 2003,';

   (b)   in paragraph (d), for 'or compensation' substitute ', compensation or surcharge'.

Criminal Justice and Court Services Act 2000 (c 43)

54   The Criminal Justice and Court Services Act 2000 is amended as follows.

55   Section 69 (duties in connection with victims of certain offences) (which is superseded by section 35 of this Act) is repealed.

56   In Schedule 4 (offences against children for the purposes of disqualification orders), in paragraph 3, after paragraph (sa) insert—

'(sb) he commits an offence under section 5 of the Domestic Violence, Crime and Victims Act 2004 (causing or allowing the death of a child or vulnerable adult) in respect of a child.'

Sexual Offences Act 2003 (c 42)

57   (1)   Section 133 of the Sexual Offences Act 2003 (general interpretation of Part 2) is amended as follows.

(2)   In subsection (1)—
   (a)   in the definition of 'admitted to a hospital', for paragraph (c) substitute—

'(c)   section 46 of the Mental Health Act 1983, section 69 of the Mental Health (Scotland) Act 1984 or Article 52 of the Mental Health (Northern Ireland) Order 1986;';

   (b)   in the definition of 'detained in a hospital', for paragraph (c) substitute—

'(c)   section 46 of the Mental Health Act 1983, section 69 of the Mental Health (Scotland) Act 1984 or Article 52 of the Mental Health (Northern Ireland) Order 1986;';

   (c)   in the definition of 'restriction order', for paragraph (c) substitute—

'(c)   a direction under section 46 of the Mental Health Act 1983, section 69 of the Mental Health (Scotland) Act 1984 or Article 52 of the Mental Health (Northern Ireland) Order 1986;'.

(3)   After that subsection insert—

'(1A)   A reference to a provision specified in paragraph (a) of the definition of 'admitted to a hospital', 'detained in a hospital' or 'restriction order' includes a reference to the provision as it applies by virtue of—

(a)   section 5 of the Criminal Procedure (Insanity) Act 1964,

(b)   section 6 or 14 of the Criminal Appeal Act 1968,

(c)   section 116A of the Army Act 1955 or the Air Force Act 1955 or section 63A of the Naval Discipline Act 1957, or

(d)   section 16 or 23 of the Courts-Martial (Appeals) Act 1968.'

58   In section 135 of that Act (interpretation: mentally disordered offenders), omit subsection (4)(c).

59   (1)   Schedule 5 to that Act (other offences for the purposes of sexual offences prevention orders) is amended as follows.

(2)   After paragraph 63 insert—

'63A   An offence under section 5 of the Domestic Violence, Crime and Victims Act 2004 (causing or allowing the death of a child or vulnerable adult).'

(3)   After paragraph 171 insert—

'171A   An offence under section 5 of the Domestic Violence, Crime and Victims Act 2004 (causing or allowing the death of a child or vulnerable adult).'

(4)   In paragraph 172, for '63' substitute '63A'.

Criminal Justice Act 2003 (c 44)

60   In section 48 of the Criminal Justice Act 2003 (c 44) (further provisions about trial without a jury), in subsection (6), for paragraphs (a) and (b) substitute 'the requirement under section 4A of the Criminal Procedure (Insanity) Act 1964 that any question, finding or verdict mentioned in that section be determined, made or returned by a jury'.

61   In section 50 of that Act (application of Part 7 to Northern Ireland), in subsection (13), for paragraphs (a) to (c) substitute—

'(a)   for 'section 4A of the Criminal Procedure (Insanity) Act 1964' substitute 'Article 49A of the Mental Health (Northern Ireland) Order 1986', and

(b)   for 'that section' substitute 'that Article'.'

62   In section 74 of that Act (interpretation of Part 9), after subsection (6) insert—

'(7)   In its application to a trial on indictment in respect of which an order under section 17(2) of the Domestic Violence, Crime and Victims Act 2004 has been made, this Part is to have effect with such modifications as the Secretary of State may by order specify.'

63   In section 151 of that Act (community order for persistent offender previously fined), in subsection (5), after 'compensation order' insert 'or a surcharge under section 161A'.

64   In section 305 of that Act (interpretation of Part 12), in subsection (1), insert at the appropriate place—

"compensation order' has the meaning given by section 130(1) of the Sentencing Act;'.

65   In Schedule 15 to that Act (specified offences for the purposes of Chapter 5 of Part 12 of that Act), in Part 1 (specified violent offences), after paragraph 63 insert—

'63A   An offence under section 5 of the Domestic Violence, Crime and Victims Act 2004 (causing or allowing the death of a child or vulnerable adult'

66   In Schedule 17 to that Act (Northern Ireland offences specified for the purposes of section 229(4)), in Part 1 (specified violent offences), after paragraph 60 insert—

'60A   An offence under section 5 of the Domestic Violence, Crime and Victims Act 2004 (causing or allowing the death of a child or vulnerable adult).'

SCHEDULE 11
REPEALS

Section 58(2)

Short title and chapter	*Extent of repeal*
Criminal Procedure (Insanity) Act 1964 (c 84)	Section 7. In section 8— (a) the proviso to subsection (3); (b) in subsection (4), the words from ', except' to 'courts-martial,'. Schedule 2.
Criminal Appeal Act 1968 (c 19)	Section 14A.
Courts-Martial (Appeals) Act 1968 (c 20)	In Schedule 3, paragraph 3(b).
Juries Act 1974 (c 23)	In section 11, paragraph (b) of subsection (5) and ' (b)' in subsection (6). In Schedule 1, paragraph 4(2).
Supreme Court Act 1981 (c 54)	In section 55(4)(a)(iii), the words 'of a jury'.
Mental Health Act 1983 (c 20)	In section 69(2)(a), the words 'or section 5(1) of the Criminal Procedure (Insanity) Act 1964'. Section 71(5) and (6). Section 79(1)(b).
Prosecution of Offences Act 1985 (c 23)	In section 16(4), the word 'or' preceding paragraph (c).
Coroners Act 1988 (c 13)	In section 16(1)(a), the word 'or' preceding sub-paragraph (iii). In section 17, in subsections (1) and (2) the word 'or' preceding paragraph (c).

Short title and chapter	Extent of repeal

Criminal Procedure (Insanity and Unfitness to Plead) Act 1991 (c 25)	Sections 3 and 5.
	
	In section 6
	
	    (a) the definition of 'local probation board' in subsection (1);
	
	    (b) subsection (2).
	
	Schedules 1 and 2.

Law Reform (Year and a Day Rule) Act 1996 (c 19)	In section 2(3), the word 'or' preceding paragraph (b).
Family Law Act 1996 (c 27)	Section 41. In section 42(5)(a), the words from 'or' to 'made'. Section 47(1). In section 49(4), the words 'or non-molestation order'.
Armed Forces Act 1996 (c 46)	Section 8. Schedule 2.
Protection from Harassment Act 1997 (c 40)	In section 5, the words 'under section 2 or 4' in subsection (1) and the word 'further' in subsection (2).

Crime (Sentences) Act 1997 (c 43)	In section 47
	
	    (a) in subsection (1), paragraph (d) and the word 'or' preceding it;
	
	    (b) in subsection (2), paragraph (c) and the word 'and' preceding it.

Protection from Harassment (Northern Ireland) Order 1997 (SI 1997/1180(NI9))	In Article 7, the words 'under Article 4 or 6' in paragraph (1) and the word 'further' in paragraph (2).
Crime and Disorder Act 1998 (c 37)	Section 32(7).
Access to Justice Act 1999 (c 22)	In Schedule 13, paragraph 163.
Powers of Criminal Courts (Sentencing) Act 2000 (c 6)	In Schedule 9, paragraph 133.
Care Standards Act 2000 (c 14)	In Schedule 4, paragraph 16.

Short title and chapter	Extent of repeal
Criminal Justice and Court Services Act 2000 (c 43)	Section 69. In Schedule 7, paragraphs 99 to 102.
Sexual Offences Act 2003 (c 42)	Section 135(4)(c).
Criminal Justice Act 2003 (c 44)	In section 246(6), in the definition of 'the required custodial days', the word 'or' preceding paragraph (b). In section 264(1), the word 'and' preceding paragraph (b).

SCHEDULE 12
TRANSITIONAL AND TRANSITORY PROVISIONS

Section 59

1 (1)   Section 1 and paragraphs 37 to 39 of Schedule 10 apply only in relation to conduct occurring on or after the commencement of that section.

(2)   In relation to an offence committed before the commencement of section 154(1) of the Criminal Justice Act 2003 (c 44), the reference to 12 months in subsection (5)(b) of section 42A of the Family Law Act 1996 (inserted by section 1 of this Act) is to be read as a reference to six months.

2   In section 5, the reference in subsection (1)(a) to an unlawful act does not include an act that (or so much of an act as) occurs before the commencement of that section.

3 (1)   This paragraph has effect, in relation to any time before the commencement of the repeal (by paragraph 51 of Schedule 3 to the Criminal Justice Act 2003) of section 6 of the Magistrates' Courts Act 1980 (c 43), where—
   (a) a magistrates' court is considering under subsection (1) of that section whether to commit a person ('the accused') for trial for an offence of murder or manslaughter, and
   (b) the accused is charged in the same proceedings with an offence under section 5 above in respect of the same death.

(2)   If there is sufficient evidence to put the accused on trial by jury for the offence under section 5, there is deemed to be sufficient evidence to put him on trial by jury for the offence of murder or manslaughter.

4   Section 10 applies only in relation to offences committed on or after the commencement of that section.

5 (1)   Section 12(1) and paragraphs 43(3) and 48 of Schedule 10 do not apply where the conviction occurs before the commencement of those provisions.

(2)   Section 12(2) applies only in relation to applications made on or after the commencement of that provision.

(3)   Section 12(4) and paragraphs 43(2) and 44 of Schedule 10 do not apply where the acquittal (or, where subsection (5) of the inserted section 5A applies, the allowing of the appeal) occurs before the commencement of those provisions.

6   (1)   Section 13(1) and paragraph 47(3) of Schedule 10 do not apply where the conviction occurs before the commencement of those provisions.

(2)   Section 13(2) applies only in relation to applications made on or after the commencement of that provision.

(3)   Section 13(4) and paragraph 47(2) of Schedule 10 do not apply where the acquittal (or, where paragraph (5) of the inserted Article 7A applies, the allowing of the appeal) occurs before the commencement of those provisions.

7   Section 14 applies only in relation to offences committed on or after the commencement of that section.

8   (1)   The provisions mentioned in sub-paragraph (2) do not apply—
   (a)   in relation to proceedings before the Crown Court or a court-martial, where the accused was arraigned before the commencement of those provisions;
   (b)   in relation to proceedings before the Court of Appeal or the Courts-Martial Appeal Court, where the hearing of the appeal began before that commencement.

(2)   The provisions are—
   (a)   sections 22 and 23;
   (b)   section 24 and Schedule 2;
   (c)   section 26 and Schedule 3;
   (d)   paragraphs 5, 6, 8, 17 to 21, 45, 60 and 61 of Schedule 10

9   The Schedule inserted by Schedule 2 has effect in relation to any time before the commencement of sections 8 and 37 of the Courts Act 2003 (c 39)—
   (a)   as if a reference to a local justice area were to a petty sessions area;
   (b)   as if a reference to a designated officer were to a justices' chief executive.

10   Each entry in Schedule 11 applies in the same way as the provision of this Act to which it corresponds.

Appendix Two

THE VICTIMS' CODE OF PRACTICE (INDICATIVE DRAFT)

1. INTRODUCTION

1.1 This code of practice governs the services to be provided in England and Wales by the organisations listed in section 3 below to victims of criminal conduct which occurred in England and Wales. It is issued by the Home Secretary under section 13 of the Domestic Violence, Crime and Victims Act 2004.

1.2 Where a person fails to comply with this code, that does not, of itself, make him liable to any legal proceedings. However, the code is admissible in evidence in both criminal and civil proceedings and the court may take failure to comply with the code into account in determining a question in any such proceedings.

1.3 Breaches of this code should be referred initially to the service provider(s) concerned. If the complainant remains dissatisfied, the complaint can be investigated and reported on by the Parliamentary Commissioner for Administration under the Parliamentary Commissioner Act 1967, as amended by Schedule 1 to the Domestic Violence, Crime and Victims Act 2004.

1.4 This code represents a minimum level of service in England and Wales. In some parts of England and Wales, organisations will be providing additional services in accordance with priorities agreed by Local Criminal Justice Boards (or equivalent groups). These additional services are not covered by this code.

2. DEFINITIONS

2.1 In this code –

'close relative' means a spouse, cohabitee, parent (including a step-parent) or guardian, sibling (including half-siblings and step-siblings) or a child;
'cohabitee' means a person who is living in the same household with another person as a husband, wife or same sex partner;

'criminal conduct' means conduct constituting a criminal offence;

'guardian', in relation to a person under the age of 17, means any person who, in the opinion of a service provider, has for the time being the care of that person; [see note on para 4.3]

'Local Victim Support Group' means a local group approved by Victim Support to provide services in the name of Victim Support;

'notifying a victim' means the posting of a letter, the making of a telephone call or a personal visit, or the sending of an e-mail or fax;

'relevant criminal conduct' means conduct in respect of which a victim is entitled to receive services under this code;

'service provider' means a person required to provide services under this code, as specified in section 3 below;

except where the context requires otherwise, 'victim' means a person entitled to receive services under this code as specified in section 4 below;

'Victim Support' means the National Association of Victim Support Schemes;

'working day' means a day other than a Saturday, a Sunday, Christmas Day, Good Friday or a day which is a bank holiday under the Banking and Financial Dealings Act 1971;

3. ORGANISATIONS REQUIRED TO PROVIDE SERVICES UNDER THE CODE

3.1 This code requires the following organisations to provide services to victims.

- The Court Service/Magistrates' Courts Committees (from April 2005 they will be one new courts agency)
- The Criminal Cases Review Commission
- The Criminal Injuries Compensation Authority
- The Criminal Injuries Compensation Appeals Panel
- The Crown Prosecution Service
- All police forces for police areas in England and Wales and the British Transport Police
- The Parole Board
- The Prison Service
- Local probation boards
- The National Association of Victim Support Schemes
- Youth offending teams

4. PERSONS ENTITLED TO RECEIVE SERVICES UNDER THE CODE

Which crimes?

This code requires services to be provided to any person who has made an allegation to a police officer or had an allegation made on his or her behalf that the person has been subjected to criminal conduct which:

(a) deprived the person of his or her property or damaged his or her property or was intended or likely to deprive the person of his or her property or damage his or her property;

(b) led, or was intended or likely to lead to the person's death or to cause physical or mental injury to the victim; or

(c) constituted a sexual offence against the person.

Which people?

4.1 The person who has made the allegation (or on whose behalf the allegation has been made) must be the **direct** victim of the criminal conduct. This code does not require services to be provided to third parties or indirect victims such as witnesses of violent crime.

4.2 Where a person has died as a result of criminal conduct, it is not necessary that an allegation to a police officer has been made. It is sufficient that a criminal investigation into the conduct causing the death has started.

4.3 Where a person entitled to receive services under this code is under the age of 17, then his or her parent or guardian is entitled to receive services under this code as well as the young person. However, the parent or guardian is not entitled to receive services under this code if he or she is under investigation, or has been charged, in respect of the criminal conduct of which the young person is a victim.

4.4 Where a person has died as a result of criminal conduct, the victim's family spokesperson is entitled to receive services under this code instead of the person who has died. A family spokesperson should be nominated by the close relatives of the person who has died. If the close relatives cannot nominate a family spokesperson, the senior investigating officer (SIO) working on the criminal investigation must nominate a family spokesperson. If the person who has died has no close relatives, the SIO may nominate someone who appears suitable to receive assistance under the code in respect of the death.

4.5 Only individuals or businesses with fewer than nine employees are entitled to receive services under this code. A business includes an organisation which does not carry on its activities for profit and could be constituted as a corporation, a partnership (including a limited liability partnership) or an unincorporated association. Employees include partners and directors who do not have a service contract but do not include volunteers or independent contractors.

Exceptions

4.6 This code does not require services to be provided to a person in circumstances where:

(a) the criminal conduct constituted a person driving a motor vehicle in a way which led or was likely to lead to physical injury to a person (except where a person has died as a result of the criminal conduct) or damage to property, except where the driver intended to cause physical injury or damage to

property (for example, where a driver deliberately ran over a victim); or
(b) the criminal conduct is the subject of an investigation by an inspector under section 20 of the Health and Safety at Work etc Act 1974 or prosecution by an inspector under section 39 of that Act (for example where an incident in the workplace is the subject of an investigation by the Health and Safety Executive).

Deciding whether a person is entitled to services under the code

4.7 In determining whether a person is entitled to receive services under this code, the service provider should only take into account the nature of the allegation of criminal conduct made by or on behalf of the person to a police officer. It is immaterial that:

(a) the service provider does not believe the allegation;
(b) no person has been charged with an offence in respect of the criminal conduct;
(c) a person has been charged with a different offence in respect of the criminal conduct (for example a person has been charged with handling stolen goods in circumstances where an allegation of theft was made);
(d) no person been convicted of an offence in respect of the criminal conduct (including where a person has been acquitted of an offence in respect of the conduct).

4.8 However, a person is only entitled to receive services under this code if an allegation of **criminal** conduct (ie conduct constituting a criminal offence) is made. If a service provider is satisfied an allegation of conduct which does not constitute a criminal offence has been made, the service provider is not required to provide services under this code.

4.9 If a service provider makes an incorrect assessment as to whether or not a person is entitled to receive services under this code, then this can be investigated and reported on by the Parliamentary Commissioner in the same way as any other breach of this code.

5. VULNERABLE VICTIMS

5.1 Some services under this code are only to be provided to vulnerable victims. A vulnerable victim is a person who is vulnerable by virtue of their personal circumstances or by the circumstances of the offence, including but not limited to a victim who:

(a) is under the age of 17;
(b) is suffering from mental disorder (within the meaning of the Mental Health Act 1983);
(c) has experienced domestic violence;
(d) has been the subject of recorded or reported incidents of harassment or bullying;
(e) has a history of self neglect or self harm;

(f) has made an allegation of criminal conduct which constitutes a sexual offence or which is racially aggravated, or aggravated on religious, homophobic or transphobic grounds;

(g) is the family spokesperson of a person who has died;

(h) is likely to be or who has been subjected to intimidation in respect of the allegation of criminal conduct which the person has made.

6. BREACHES OF THE CODE

6.1 Victims who believe that service providers have breached this code should first make a complaint through the internal complaints procedures of the service provider concerned. If a victim is not satisfied with the response of the service provider, the victim may raise the issue with a Member of Parliament, who can refer the case to the Parliamentary Commissioner for Administration.

OBLIGATIONS OF SERVICE PROVIDERS

7. THE POLICE

7.1 All police forces for police areas in England and Wales and the British Transport Police (the 'police') have the following obligations.

Identification of vulnerable victims

7.2 The police must take all reasonable steps to identify promptly vulnerable victims using the criteria given at section 5.

7.3 Where a vulnerable victim may be called as a witness in criminal proceedings and may be eligible for assistance by way of special measure under Chapter I of Part II of the Youth Justice and Criminal Evidence Act 1999, the police must explain to the victim the provision about special measures in that Act and record any views the victim expresses about applying for special measures.

Information about progress of investigation, arrest, caution, reprimand, warning, charge and release on bail

7.4 If a suspect is arrested or charged with an offence in respect of relevant criminal conduct, the police must notify the victim of these events and tell the victim whether or not the suspect has been released on police bail no later than one working day after the day of the event in the case of vulnerable victims and no later than three working days after the day of the event in the case of other victims.

(This obligation may be split between the police and the CPS if the current charging pilots are rolled out nationally. Arrangements on the ground should be clearer before the Home Secretary consults formally on the Code when the Domestic Violence, Crime and Victims Bill completes its Parliamentary passage.)

7.5 If a suspect is cautioned, reprimanded, or given a final warning in respect of relevant criminal conduct or the police make a decision to take no further action against a suspect in respect of relevant criminal conduct, the police must notify the victim of this event no later than one working day after the day of the event in the case of vulnerable victims and within three working days after the day of the event in the case of other victims.

[This obligation may be split between the police and the CPS if the current charging pilots are rolled out nationally.]

7.6 If no suspect is arrested, charged, cautioned, reprimanded or given a final warning in respect of relevant criminal conduct, the police must notify the victim, on a monthly basis, of progress in cases being actively investigated up until the point of the closure of the investigation.

7.7 The police must inform any vulnerable victim if the suspect in respect of relevant criminal conduct is given bail by the court in circumstances where the police requested that the suspect be remanded in custody or made an application to remand the suspect in custody. At the same time, the police must also inform the vulnerable victim of any conditions attached to the bail that relate to, involve or affect the victim, and what the vulnerable victim can do if conditions are broken. This information must be provided by the police no later than one working day after the day on which the police receive the information from the court, unless the vulnerable victim specifically requests not to be informed or there are good reasons why the information cannot be passed on (in which case a contemporary written record of the reasons should be kept).

Information about court proceedings

7.8 The police must inform victims of the date of all criminal court hearings in respect of relevant criminal conduct within one working day of receiving the date from the court in cases involving vulnerable victims and no later than four working days after the day on which the police receive the date from the court in other cases.

7.9 Where a criminal trial is held in respect of relevant criminal conduct, the police must inform any vulnerable victim of the outcome of all pre-trial hearings (excluding applications for special measures directions under section 19 of the Youth Justice and Criminal Evidence Act 1999) and the verdicts of the trial, including the sentence if the suspect is convicted, no later than one working day after the day of receipt of these decisions from the courts and must inform other victims of the sentence (or any not guilty verdict) no later than four working days after the day of receipt of the sentence or not guilty verdict from the courts.

7.10 If a person who has been convicted of an offence in respect of relevant criminal conduct appeals against their conviction or sentence, the police must inform any vulnerable victim and the probation service victim contact team of the appeal no later than two working days after the day the police are notified by the courts that the appeal has been lodged, and must inform any other victim no later than five working days after that day. When giving this information, the police must make both vulnerable victims and other victims aware of the Witness Service and explain that they will refer their details to the Witness Service unless they ask the police not to do so.

7.11 The police must inform any vulnerable victim and the probation service victim contact team of the result of an appeal in respect of relevant criminal conduct not later than one working day after the day the police are notified by the court of the result, and any other victim no later than five working days after that day.

Information about the Criminal Cases Review Commission

7.12 Paragraphs 7.13 to 7.15 below do not apply where the Criminal Cases Review Commission has decided to contact the victim directly under section 16 below.

7.13 If a conviction or sentence in respect of relevant criminal conduct is being reviewed by the Criminal Cases Review Commission and, taking all the circumstances of the case into account, it is likely that the review will come to the victim's attention, the police must contact the victim no later than ten working days after the day the police receive notification of the review.

7.14 If the Criminal Cases Review Commission decides not to refer a conviction or sentence in respect of relevant criminal conduct to the Court of Appeal or the Crown Court [and the victim has been informed of the review under paragraph 7.11 above], the police must inform the victim no later than ten working days after the day the police receive notification of the decision.

7.15 If the Criminal Cases Review Commission decide to refer a conviction or sentence in respect of relevant criminal conduct to the Court of Appeal or the Crown Court, the police must inform the victim no later than two working days after the day the police receive notification of the decision.

General information

7.16 Subject to the exceptions in paragraphs 7.17 and 7.18 below, the police must provide the appropriate Local Victim Support Group with the victim's contact details no later than two working days after the day an allegation of criminal conduct is made unless the victim asks the police not to do so.

7.17 In accordance with the victim referral agreement between the police and Victim Support, the police will not routinely pass over to a Local Victim Support Group the details of victims of the following criminal conduct unless there are aggravating factors:

(a) theft of a motor vehicle;
(b) theft from a motor vehicle;
(c) minor criminal damage; and
(d) tampering with motor vehicles.

7.18 The police will only pass Victim Support the details of victims of sexual offences or domestic violence or the details of the relatives of homicide victims if the victims or relatives have given their express consent.

7.19 When taking evidential statements from victims, the police must advise victims of their right to make a victim personal statement and its purpose, and provide the victim with a copy of the relevant information leaflet. When a victim personal statement is made, the police must take account of its contents when considering decisions, and record the outcome of this consideration.

7.20 The police must provide victims with a copy of the current Victims of Crime leaflet as soon as practically possible but no later than two working days after the day the allegation of criminal conduct is made.

7.21 Where a victim has died as result of criminal conduct or suspected criminal conduct, the police must assign a family liaison officer to the relatives which the police consider appropriate and make a record of the assignment. The police must also provide close relatives of the victim with the current Home Office packs 'Advice for bereaved families and friends following murder or manslaughter', or Advice for bereaved families and friends following death on the road. The police are not required to take these actions in respect of any relative whom they have not eliminated from suspicion in respect of relevant criminal conduct.

7.22 In cases where an offender is convicted of a sexual or violent offence (within the meaning in section 69 of the Criminal Justice and Court Services Act 2000) in respect of relevant criminal conduct and given a sentence of imprisonment or detention of twelve months or more, the police must provide the victim with a copy of the current 'Release of Prisoners: Information for Victims of Serious Sexual or Other Violent Offences' leaflet, and must refer the victim's details to the probation service no later than ten working days after the expiry of the period in which victims may opt out of the National Probation Contact Scheme. Both of these actions must be completed no later than twenty working days after the day the police is notified of the sentence by the court.

7.23 Where victims under the age of eighteen are to be called as witnesses in criminal proceedings in respect of relevant criminal conduct which involves sex, violence, or cruelty, the police must provide the victims and their parents or guardians with the current information pack 'Child Witness'.

7.24 In cases where the perpetrator of relevant criminal conduct is under the age of eighteen, the police must explain to the victim the role of the youth offending team (YOT) and pass the victim's contact details to the YOT (unless the victim asks the police not to) to enable victims to have access to reparation or other restorative justice type initiatives.

7.25 The police must provide victims who are to be called as witnesses in criminal proceedings in respect of relevant criminal conduct with a copy of the current 'Witness in Court' leaflet, or equivalent national information leaflet.

7.26 The police must respond to requests for information from the Criminal Injuries Compensation Authority or the Criminal Injuries Compensation Appeals Panel to enable a victim's claim for compensation to be assessed with the most accurate information available at that time, no later than 30 working days after the day on which the police receive the request.

8. THE CROWN PROSECUTION SERVICE

8.1 The Crown Prosecution Service (the 'CPS') has the following obligations.

8.2 The CPS must inform the victim if a decision is made to drop or substantially alter charges in respect of relevant criminal conduct and must provide an explanation for that decision unless in the particular circumstances of the case the prosecutor, in accordance with CPS guidance, decides that it is inappropriate or unnecessary to do so. Where it is not possible, for legal reasons, to provide an explanation beyond setting out the Code for Crown Prosecutors test which the prosecutor applied, the reasons for this should be recorded and the victim should be informed of this.

(May require amendment to take account of the CPS responsibilities in an increasing number of cases.)

8.3 Additionally, in cases involving a death allegedly caused by criminal conduct, such as murder, manslaughter, dangerous driving or careless driving; cases of child abuse, sexual offences, racially and religiously aggravated offences and offences with a homophobic or transphobic element, the CPS must offer to meet the victim to explain a decision to drop or substantially alter a charge in respect of relevant criminal conduct unless the prosecutor concludes that in all the circumstances a meeting ought not to take place. If the prosecutor decides that a meeting ought not to take place, he must record in writing the reason for that conclusion.

8.4 The CPS must have systems in place that help prosecutors to take account of victim personal statements and to record the outcome of this consideration.

8.5 Where a victim who is to be called as a witness in criminal proceedings in respect of relevant criminal conduct, has been identified as potentially vulnerable or intimidated, prosecutors must consider whether or not to make an application to the court for a special measures direction under Chapter I of Part II of the Youth Justice and Criminal Evidence Act 1999. The outcome of that consideration should be recorded.

8.6 The CPS must ensure that, where circumstances permit, prosecutors or, if prosecutors are unavailable, other representatives of the Crown Prosecution Service introduce themselves to victims at court. When meeting victims, prosecutors or their representatives should deal with any questions victims may have about court procedures and give an indication where possible of how long they will have to wait before giving evidence.

8.7 In the event of delays to criminal proceedings in respect of relevant criminal conduct, the CPS must, wherever possible, explain the reason for the delay and, wherever possible, tell the victim how long the wait is likely to be.

8.8 The CPS must pay expenses that the CPS has decided are due to the victim, in accordance with the Crown Prosecution Service (Witnesses' etc. Allowances) Regulations 1988) not later than ten working days after the day the CPS receives a correctly completed claim form.

9. VICTIM SUPPORT

9.1 Victim Support has contracted with the Home Office to provide certain services to victims. Nothing in this code requires Victim Support to provide services to victims which Victim Support has not contracted with the Home Office to provide.

9.2 This code does not require Victim Support to provide services to the family spokesperson of a person who has died as a result of another person driving a motor vehicle in a way which led or was likely to lead to physical injury or damage to property, except where the driver intended to cause physical injury or damage to property.

9.3 Subject to paragraphs 9.1 and 9.2, Victim Support has the following obligations.

Victims' Services

9.4 Victim Support must provide the Victim Supportline, a national telephone service that offers advice to victims and others affected by crime.

9.5 Victim Support must, wherever possible, ensure that the Local Victim Support Groups provide the services to victims specified in paragraphs 9.5.1 – 9.5.5. If it is not possible for a particular Local Victim Support Group to provide these services, then Victim Support must ensure, wherever possible, that the Local Victim Support Group concerned records the reasons for this in writing.

9.5.1 Local Victim Support Groups should offer assistance to victims of crime or to close relatives of victims who have died unless the victim or relative has indicated that they do not wish to receive their services.

9.5.2 Local Victim Support Groups should contact victims by phone, letter or personal visit, if the police have passed on details to their local branch or if victims have approached Victim Support for help, no later than two working days after the day the local scheme receives the referral from the police or is contacted by the victim.

9.5.3 Local Victim Support Groups should liaise with the Crown Court Witness Service and Magistrates' Court Witness Service to ensure a continuous service for victims if they are called as witnesses in criminal proceedings in respect of relevant criminal conduct, or decide to attend court to observe such proceedings.

9.5.4 Local Victim Support Groups should identify victims who may be eligible to apply for compensation under the Criminal Injuries Compensation Scheme and offer basic information and assistance in filling in the application form.

9.5.5 If the victim wishes, Local Victim Support Groups should refer the victim on to other local appropriate services.

The Witness Service

9.6 Victim Support must provide the Crown Court Witness Service and the Magistrates' Court Witness Service (the 'Witness Service') and ensure that, wherever possible, the Witness Service provides the services to victims specified in paragraphs 9.6.1 to 9.6.3. If it is not possible for the Witness Service in a particular area to provide these services, then either Victim Support or the person responsible for delivering the Witness Service in that area must record the reasons for this in writing. Although the Witness Service provides services to non-victim witnesses, this code only requires services to be provided to victims who are witnesses.

9.6.1 The Witness Service should provide information about their services to the police and to victims who have been referred to them as potential witnesses. When requested by a victim who is being called to give evidence at criminal proceedings in respect of relevant criminal conduct, the Witness Service should facilitate pre-trial court familiarisation visits before the court hearing. This may be done in conjunction with the court's own witness liaison officer and a police family liaison officer, where one has been appointed.

9.6.2 The Witness Service should provide appropriate support and practical information about court proceedings, as requested by victims who are called as witnesses in criminal proceedings in respect of relevant criminal conduct and, where appropriate, put them in contact with their Local Victim Support Group or other local services.

9.6.3 The Witness Service should, wherever possible, provide an enhanced level of support to victims in respect of whose evidence the court makes a special measures direction under section 19 of the Youth Justice and Criminal Evidence Act 1999. Where it is not possible to provide this enhanced level of support, Victim Support or the person responsible for delivering the Witness Service in the particular case should record the reasons for this in writing.

[These obligations may change in the light of the exploratory work, being led by the Home Office, to devolve the funding and accountability of witness services to Local Criminal Justice Boards (paragraphs 6.5–6.8 of the National Strategy for Victims and Witnesses refer).]

10. THE COURTS (INCLUDES COURT SERVICE AND MAGISTRATES' COURTS COMMITTEES)

10.1 The Court Service and Magistrates' Courts Committees (the 'court staff') have the following obligations.

10.2 The court staff must ensure that they liaise effectively with the police and the Crown Prosecution Service so that information about court decisions in criminal proceedings in respect of relevant criminal conduct is passed to victims promptly. The court staff should ensure that, in cases which the court staff have been notified involve vulnerable victims, decisions reach the police no later than one working day after the day the decision is made and, in cases involving other victims, no later than three working days after the day the decision is made. If this is not possible in a particular case, a record should be made of why the decision did not reach the police within the appropriate time-limit.

10.3 The court staff must ensure that, where possible, at criminal proceedings in respect of relevant criminal conduct victims have a separate waiting area and a seat in the courtroom away from the defendant's family or friends.

10.4 Where the court hearing criminal proceedings in respect of relevant criminal conduct makes a special measures direction under Part II of the Youth Justice and Criminal Evidence Act 1999, the court staff must ensure the availability of those special measures so far as is possible, to help improve the quality of the evidence given by the victim.

10.5 The court staff must ensure, as far as is reasonably within their control, that victims who are witnesses do not have to wait more than two hours before giving evidence in criminal proceedings in respect of relevant criminal conduct in the Crown Court or magistrates' courts.

10.6 Where victims are witnesses in criminal proceedings in respect of relevant criminal conduct, the court staff must, if appropriate, take contact telephone numbers for the victims so that the victims are able to leave the court precincts and be contacted when they are needed.

10.7 The court staff must, whenever possible, provide an information point where all victims who are witnesses in criminal proceedings in respect of relevant criminal conduct, can find out where to go and what is happening in their case.

10.8 The court staff must inform the police of the date of all court hearings in respect of relevant criminal conduct no later than one working day after the day the date is set in cases involving vulnerable victims and, no later than three working days after the day the date is set in other cases.

10.9 The court staff must inform the police and probation service victim contact teams if a person who has been convicted of an offence in respect of relevant criminal conduct appeals against their conviction or their sentence no later than two working days after the day the appeal is lodged and must inform the police and probation service victim contact teams of the result of the appeal no later than one working day after the day of the result.

11. PROBATION OBLIGATIONS

[Through a clause in the Bill, the responsibilities of local probation boards under section 69 of the Criminal Justice and Court Services Act will be made subject to the oversight of the Parliamentary Commissioner for Administration.]

12. THE CRIMINAL INJURIES COMPENSATION AUTHORITY

12.1 The Criminal Injuries Compensation Authority ('CICA') has the following obligations.

12.2 CICA must process efficiently, fairly and sensitively all applications for compensation made under the Criminal Injuries Compensation Scheme ('the Scheme'), in accordance with the rules of the Scheme.

12.3 CICA must make available clear information on eligibility for compensation under the Scheme.

12.4 CICA must respond to all correspondence regarding applications for compensation under the Scheme which requires a reply, no later than 20 working days after the day the correspondence was received by CICA.

12.5 In the event of a claim for compensation under the Scheme being refused or reduced, CICA must ensure it gives explanations for its decisions to the applicant.

12.6 If CICA is unable to send a decision letter to an applicant for compensation under the Scheme within 12 months of receipt of the application, it must inform the applicant of the status of their claim after 12 months of receipt of the application.

12.7 When issuing its decision, CICA must inform applicants of their right to a review of the decision, and provide information on the procedure and the time limit for applying for review

12.8 Where an applicant requests a review, CICA must process the review efficiently, fairly, and entirely afresh on the basis of all available information.

12.9 CICA must provide explanations of the review decision to the applicant, and must inform them of the process of applying for an independent appeal by the Criminal Injuries Compensation Appeal Panel.

12.10 Where an appeal is lodged, CICA must provide the applicant and the Criminal Injuries Compensation Appeals Panel with copies of all papers required for the appeal, as soon as is reasonably practicable. The applicant should be given sufficient time to deal with any new issues raised in the papers.

13. CRIMINAL INJURIES COMPENSATION APPEAL PANEL

13.1 The administrative staff of the Criminal Injuries Compensation Appeal Panel ('CICAP') have the following obligations at all stages of the process of an appeal under the Scheme, including at oral hearings.

13.2 CICAP staff must make available to claimants relevant information regarding the procedure for appeals by producing and keeping up to date guidance materials.

13.3 CICAP staff must respond to all correspondence relating to appeal cases under the Scheme which needs a reply, no later than 20 working days after the day the correspondence was received by CICAP.

13.4 CICAP staff must ensure explanations for appeal decisions under the Scheme are available to applicants.

14. THE PRISON SERVICE

14.1 The Prison Service has the following obligations.

14.2 The Prison Service must maintain their telephone helpline to ensure that victims have a number to ring if they:

(a) receive unwanted contact from a prisoner who has been convicted or remanded in custody in respect of relevant criminal conduct;
(b) have any concerns about the prisoner's temporary release or final discharge.

14.3 When issuing release licences for prisoners who have been convicted in respect of relevant criminal conduct in circumstances in which the Secretary of State is entitled to specify conditions in the licence, the Prison Service must consider whether to impose additional conditions requested by the Probation Service or recommended by the Parole Board as a result of information offered by the victim. Where such a licence condition has been requested or recommended but the Prison Service do not propose that the condition be included in the licence, the Prison Service must give reasons to the body which requested or recommended its inclusion and provide that body with a way to have the decision reviewed.

14.4 In addition the Prison Service must ensure that this information is passed to the Probation Service so that it can inform the victim and explain how the decision can be reviewed.

14.5 The Prison Service must ensure that information which, if disclosed would compromise the confidentiality of the victim or the victim's family, will be kept securely and will not be made available to prisoners who have been convicted or remanded in custody in respect of relevant criminal conduct. Under no circumstances will a victim's views be made available to a prisoner unless the victim is aware that the information may be disclosed.

15. PAROLE BOARD OBLIGATIONS

(section still under consideration)

16. THE CRIMINAL CASES REVIEW COMMISSION

16.1 The Criminal Cases Review Commission (the 'Commission') has the following obligations.

16.2 The Commission must consider the extent of contact to be made with a victim where, during the course of a review of a conviction or sentence in respect of relevant conduct, the Commission considers there is a likelihood of the case coming to the victim's attention. The Commission must record the reasons for its decisions as to the extent of contact with a victim.

16.3 If the Commission decides, under paragraph 16.2, to contact the victim during the course of the review the Commission must inform the victim that an application has been received and that the case is under review. If, following the review, the Commission decides not to refer the conviction or sentence to the Court of Appeal or the Crown Court, the Commission must inform the victim of that decision.

16.4 If the Commission refers a conviction or sentence in respect of relevant criminal conduct to the Court of Appeal or Crown Court, the Commission must inform the victim of its decision, unless the victim has made it clear that they do not wish to be informed, or the case includes no identifiable victim. In doing so the Commission must, so far as possible, ensure that arrangements are in place to ensure that the victim is notified of the decision to refer at the same time as the person whose conviction or sentence has been referred. The Commission must not issue a press statement when a case has been referred until arrangements have been made for notifying the victim.

16.5 If the Commission contacts a victim, under paragraph 16.2 or 16.4, this may be done either directly by the Commission or with the assistance of the police. In either case the victim must be provided with information about Victim Support and the Witness Service.

17. YOUTH OFFENDING TEAMS

17.1 Youth offending teams ('YOTs') have the following obligations.

17.2 On receipt of a victim's details from the police, the YOT must decide if it would be appropriate to invite the victim to become involved in a restorative justice intervention relating to relevant criminal conduct.

17.3 The YOT must keep victims' personal details securely and separate from details kept on offenders. Information on victims should be destroyed when the restorative justice intervention in a case is at an end, apart from information that would be relevant for future research and evaluation.

17.4 If it decides to make contact with victims, the YOT must explain its role fully and clearly and allow victims to make informed choices about whether they want any involvement and if so, the nature of that involvement. The involvement of victims must always be voluntary; victims must not be asked to do anything which is primarily for the benefit of the offender.

17.5 YOTs must ensure that all staff working with victims have had appropriate training

17.6 If the victim agrees to be involved, either directly or indirectly in a restorative justice intervention in respect of relevant criminal conduct, the YOT must, if the victim requests this, keep the victim informed about the progress of the case and inform the victim when the intervention has concluded.

17.7 The YOT must give victims who ask for additional support before, during or after a restorative justice intervention in respect of relevant criminal conduct access to information about appropriate services.

INDEX

Please note that references to the right-hand side of the column are to Chapter (in bold) and paragraph numbers